JA Mylor

27 June 1993

THE GALLEON

The

Great Ships

THE GALLEON

of the

Armada

Era

PETER KIRSCH

First English language edition published
in Great Britain in 1990 by
Conway Maritime Press Ltd,
24 Bride Lane, Fleet Street,
London EC4Y 8DR

© Conway Maritime Press Ltd 1990

First published in 1988 under the title
Die Galleonen
© Bernard & Graefe Verlag, Koblenz, 1988

British Library Cataloguing in Publication Data
Kirsch, Peter
    The Galleon.
    1. Warships. Sailing ships, history
    I. Title
    623.8′225

    ISBN 0 85177 566 2

Translated by Rachel Magowan
Designed by by John Mitchell
Typeset by Inforum Typesetting, Portsmouth
Printed and bound in Great Britain by Butler & Tanner Ltd, Frome

Contents

Introduction

THE term galleon is frequently employed in literary works, in romantic seafarer's tales and in dramatic portrayals of battles at sea. We are all familiar with the word, having perhaps absorbed it from our childhood reading, but none of us can say exactly what a galleon is. This book will not be able to give an unequivocal answer either. We will discover that the term galleon does not refer to a specific type of vessel which sailed the seven seas, but rather to a trend in the development of naval architecture.

Dictionaries generally tell us that the term galleon refers to a Portuguese or Spanish warship or trading vessel, which was in use from the sixteenth to early eighteenth centuries and was distinguished by having a high superstructure and poor sailing qualities. That is, of course, correct, but it is only part of the story. Galleons were much more than that. Even the Spanish or Portuguese origin is not certain: they were also found in other countries early in the sixteenth century. The origins cannot be precisely defined, and the name itself is the subject of speculation. Is it derived from the relationship with rowing galleys and powerful galleasses, or from the ram-style projection on the front stem, which was a feature of some galleons?

The word galion is old. It existed in medieval Latin. Over the centuries it was applied to various different types of vessel.[1] For example, in thirteenth-century French, galion meant 'small light ship', but by the fourteenth century it had come to mean heavy warship. In the sixteenth century the term was applied to the large sailing ships which are the subject of this monograph.[2]

Galleons were the most important type of large sailing ship at the turn of the seventeenth century. To discover more about them, however, we must bear in mind the fact that galleons were built in many places – in the Mediterranean, on the Atlantic, in Asia and America – by many seafaring nations. Detailed plans are generally not to be found. There were galleons in Ragusa and Genoa; in Spain and Portugal and their colonies; in France and the Netherlands, but no records of their construction have survived. Venetian sources shed some light on this darkness, but even these raise more questions than they answer.

The term galleon was applied to very different types of vessel. Initially they had only one thing in common: their proportions, which distinguished them from their predecessors, the carracks. To begin with, this difference would only have been slight. We can infer that much from the shipwrights' traditional, and understandable, habit of sticking to designs that had been tried and tested. We can assume that, at first, only the main proportions of conventional carracks or round ships were changed – the lines became more graceful and the superstructure lower. This assumption applies, at least, to Venetian and Portuguese galleons. The situation seems to have been quite different in England, where, among the multifarious ship styles of Henry VIII's fleet, we find vessels which could be considered prototypes for later English galleons. These forerunners had nothing in common with carracks.

England's rich archives fortunately harbour some information about shipbuilders' working techniques from around 1600. Alongside the notes and drawings of Matthew Baker, Master Shipwright (1530–1613), which are our earliest source for the lines of large sailing ships of the period (but which have yet to be published in their entirety), we find, amongst other things, the *Treatise on Shipbuilding* (c.1620), by an anonymous author, who seems to have been an interested layman. The *Treatise* is a detailed description of the method of construction most commonly used by the master shipbuilders of the time: the old method of whole-moulding, and is of great techno-historical importance. It shows how the ribs and hull were constructed from a series of different arcs. This technique differed susbstantially from the method of construction used in later centuries, when ships were planned and presented in draught form. Nevertheless, whole-moulding was the technique used in the early development of a type of sailing ship which survived until the introduction of the iron hull.

I have attempted to bring together all the available material about the galleon, and to examine the impact of whole-moulding on the appearance of the galleon. I well remember the impression made on me by the large model of a four-masted galleon, when I first saw it hanging in Stockholm Cathedral. And I also remember how little I knew about this type of ship, although I had been concerned with the history of shipbuilding for many years. This is, in itself, significant; literature on the subject of galleons is rare, only to be found piecemeal, and often full of errors. The model galleon is both a copy and a reconstruction. The original is on display in the Statens Sjöhistoriska Museum in Stockholm. There I found the terse description: 'West European galleon, c.1600'. From this we can conclude that the Swedes have no records which prove that a ship of this type was ever built on their shores. Nor can I proffer a more precise description for this model, despite the research needed to write this book.

The side elevation of the topsides of the original model (Fig 40) gives the impression that it was constructed according to scale. If we deduce the position and the number of decks from the arrangement of the gunports and wales on the ship's side, we get measurements for their length, position and height in the hull which are completely in keeping with the old shipbuilders' rules. In spite of its missing parts and imperfections, we can therefore consider this model to be a rare record in shipbuilding history. Its rich, renaissance decoration hints at the ornamentation on larger, more impressive ships. Previously only the meagre adornment of the English Elizabethan galleons was known in northern Europe.

I have not been able to resist the temptation to try a reconstruction of the Stockholm galleon, with insights from my reading of the literature. Perhaps it will provide a fresh stimulus to experienced ship modelbuilders. This reconstruction is, however, not intended as a precise modelbuilding primer; too many details are missing for that, particularly with regard to the rigging. These details have already been covered by other authors. References cited in Chapter 8 should enable anyone interested to obtain the necessary information.

I have deliberately refrained from portraying the sundry historical events in which galleon-type ships played a role. What I have done is to define the somewhat nebulous term galleon more clearly, and to present hitherto unpublished material from a variety of sources. As for the people, without whom these ship buildings or water palaces (as the engineer and artist Josef Furttenbach, 1591-1667, called them) would have been nothing, I have sifted sources for information about the use to which these ships were put, about life on board and about the men who sailed on them. Many sources give only brief descriptions of the armaments on ships of this type, so I have devoted one chapter to naval weapons from the galleon era.

Heartfelt thanks are due to Herr Dr Ing. J Wiegand, Karlsruhe, and Herr Oberstudienrat A Strobel, Heidelberg, for reviewing parts of the manuscript; to Herr Dr M Kästner, Heidelberg, for stylistic points and to Herr Dr F Möhren, Heidelberg, for etymological hints on the subject. My especial thanks are due to W Jaeger, Duisburg, shipbuilding engineer, who critically reviewed parts of the manuscript and gave me some worthwhile tips, before his unfortunate death in 1986. His scepticism about the reconstruction of something so complex as a ship almost 400 years old made me proceed very carefully with my work and adhere to the sources as closely as possible. Last but not least, I would like to thank my dear wife, whose patience and help with proofreading were instrumental in the production of this book.

PETER KIRSCH
Autumn 1987

CHAPTER 1

The development of the galleon

THE term galleon brings to mind a large, unwieldy, high-sided ship: Spanish treasure ships, perhaps, and their undiscovered wrecks, still being sought out in the Caribbean today. What sort of ships were they, those huge sea-castles with their yawning tiers of guns that we know from narrative poetry and fanciful illustrations? They may seem podgy and clumsy to our eyes, in comparison with the flush-decked warships of the eighteenth and nineteenth centuries. To sailors of the sixteenth century (when galleons were widespread in Europe), however, they represented something else: a step forward in manoeuvrability and seaworthiness. They allowed a new method of carrying heavy guns at sea (Fig 1). When the first gunports were cut into the sides of ships at the beginning of the sixteenth century, many maritime powers soon owned monster ships – huge, unwieldy vessels, armed with a quantity of the most varied guns. Thus in 1514 the English had the *Harry Grace à Dieu* with 186 guns; the French had the *Grand François*; the Portuguese the *Sao João*, which allegedly carried not less than 366 guns. Even the Swedish *Elefanten* of (probably) 1532 had 71 guns, 24 of which were made of bronze.[1]

These large floating fortresses had developed from carracks, and despite the difficulties in using them effectively, they incorporated worthwhile improvements in ship construction. The stability and load-bearing capacity of the hull and the decks had been increased, for the heavy guns placed greater demands on the inner structure than on the carracks of the fifteenth century. At that time, guns were only carried on the upper decks (Fig 2). Fashion and the rulers' needs to keep up with each other made the powerful, floating fortresses inevitable. After the peak of this development was reached, shipbuilders and their sovereigns acknowledged that it was in their interests to install as much artillery as possible on ships which were as manoeuvrable and seaworthy as possible. This led to the development of slimmer and more graceful galleons, vessels which were seen not only as warships, but also as armed trading ships. We can date this development to around 1550.[2]

Venice

We first find the term galleon in Venetian sources from around the beginning of the fifteenth century, where a high-sided, oared riverboat, which served as support for military operations on land, bears this classification.[3] The description of the vessel implies a hybrid, one element of whose composition stemmed from the oared longships, the galleys. However, later, the Venetians also used the term for a vessel built for the open sea. We can thus infer that this new vessel combined the principles of construction of the oared riverboat (and consequently of galleys) with the proportions of the traditional sailing roundship, the barze.

We know the name of one of the shipbuilders' foremen in the Arsenal at Venice: Leonardo Bressan, who built barze, which were sailing ships for trading. Matteo, another member of the Bressan family, built this first galleon for the city's Signoria, between 1526 and 1530. It soon proved to be a satisfactory warship, owing its development to the need for a convoy ship with heavy guns, for use against agile pirates. Matteo's galleon was declared unseaworthy in 1547, and broken up. Its age, seventeen years, was not bad for a time when hulls only lasted, on average, ten years. The Senate

Fig 1: Spanish carracks and galleons after Pieter Breughel (1525/30-69) in De Nederlandsche Scheepsbouwkonst *(Cornelis van Yk, 1697). P Breughel probably prepared the drawings for these ships during a trip to Italy in 1551–5. The massive construction of the carracks in the left-hand side of the picture contrasts with the vessel on the right. The light stern and the low forecastle, clearly separated from the beakhead, are characteristic features of the galleon. The vessel second from the right has a carrack-like stern; the forecastle, however, is sharply reduced, and is reminiscent of Spanish caravels. The low beakhead is typical of a galley, so it is conceivable that contemporary sources were already referring to ships such as this as a galleon. We should bear in mind that these ship portrayals could come from the 1550s – the early period of galleons.*

decreed that the galleon's measurements should be taken before it was broken up, so that they could be used for future construction work.

Interestingly, the next galleon to be built in Venice was a constructional failure. It capsized on sailing out of the harbour of Malamocco (in the Venetian lagoon) in 1558. The ship is supposed to have been too narrow in the floor and in its maximum breadth. It was therefore unable to carry its heavy guns.[4] That could indicate that the Venetian shipbuilders had, in their inexperience, overstepped the mark in one aspect of the construction of this second galleon: that they had reduced the breadth of the hull too severely in proportion to the straight keel. We can infer from this that the task of incorporating the character of the galley hull into the lines of the traditional sailing roundships was a matter of concern to the architect of the first galleon. The oared longships, or galleys, had a large keel length in proportion to their breadth, a tiny freeboard and a row of identical rib sections amidships.

Fig 2: Large Portuguese carrack from a painting by C Anthoniszoon (1521) from the National Maritime Museum, Greenwich. It is probably the Santa Caterina do Monte Sinai. *The ship is an example of the floating fortresses of the sixteenth century, whose poor seaworthiness and sailing qualities made desirable the development of the more nimble galleons. The lower part of the hull still has no gunports; the high, heavily equipped stern and forecastle look like a fortress which could be defended even after the enemy had boarded.* (Drawing by Pino G Dell'Orco from *The International Journal of Nautical Archaeology and Underwater Exploration,* vol 10, no 1, 1981)

The next galleon was not launched in Venice until 1570. As people were afraid that it, too, might capsize, it was only used on rare occasions. The development process had already gone further in other countries; many seafaring European nations now had galleon-type vessels, but we must beware of thinking that the galleon was a standard, clearly-defined type of ship. There was, in fact, a variety of designs and hybrid shapes (Fig 3). We can, however, identify the following common features: a sailing warship or merchant vessel, which carried guns in broadsides; which sometimes used oars as auxiliaries; and which had slimmer lines than the traditional roundships and carracks. The ratio of the greatest breadth to keel length was 2½–3:1. The draught had been decreased. The ship's silhouette (without rigging) was relatively low, as the superstructure, particularly the forecastle, was reduced, and its behaviour under sail improved. The association with Spanish ships which the word galleon brings to mind can no longer be sustained when we consider their typological distribution. As we will see, Spain was certainly not in the forefront of galleon building. The influence of the Mediterranean tradition of galley building on its Atlantic and Mediterranean coasts was more of a hindrance than a stimulus to the development of a new type of sailing ship. It was in the north European states that the new ship type acquired its distinctive shape.

Spain

Spanish sources on ship construction in the sixteenth century are few and far between. So we have to look at information which originates not from the Spaniards themselves, but from their erstwhile adversaries, the English. The

Fig 3: A four-masted ship, which could be a galleon, portrayed on a chart (dated 1555) by Le Testu, the Huguenot freebooter and hydrographer. It still has a high forecastle. In the waist area we can see a border of railings or netting for protection against enemies coming on board. It is interesting that the foremast is inclined forwards and the main, mizzen and bonaventure masts are well to the aft. (From Howard, Sailing Ships of War, 1979)

Fig 4: The Spanish admiral, Alvaro de Bazán, the first Marquis of Santa Cruz (1526–88), commanded a part of the allied fleet at Lepanto (1571). He was the first commander-in-chief of the Spanish Armada, and died shortly before its departure for England. Bazán's abilities were not only military: he also designed galleons for the Spanish treasure fleets. (From a painting by an unknown master in E M Tenison, *Elizabethan England*, vol 2)

naval conflict with Hapsburg Spain is well worked ground for English historians. We thus have source material on Spanish naval affairs which is quite unlike the material available on other naval powers. Contemporary English reports of Spanish fleets are bound to include tendentious and disparaging elements. Nevertheless, some objective information wins through.

Spanish galleons were already being mentioned in sources by 1540. At that time, Admiral Alvaro de Bazán, Marquis of Santa Cruz (1526–88) volunteered to the Spanish Crown to undertake convoy duty in the Mediterranean, with two of his galleasses and two galleons.[5] Spanish entrepreneurial admirals, of whom Alvaro de Bazán (Fig 4) was typical, owned whole fleets of galleons and galleasses. They would hire them out to the Crown at an agreed rate, which varied with the length of time and the size of the ship. Any economy in equipment or crew would therefore be a financial profit to the contractor. In 1550 Bazán received a ten-year monopoly in the construction of large galleons, which he had himself designed for service in the 'Armada de la guardia de la carrera de las indias' (convoy fleet for the route to the Indies). We know very little about the appearance of these galleons. They were private warships which escorted the treasure fleets from the 'indias' (West Indies). There was, therefore, a group of standardised ships of this sort in Spain from the middle of the sixteenth century.

Admiral Pedro Menéndez Avilés was another such entrepreneur, who likewise designed new types of warships. He owned galleons, along with other ships. Although royal control and supervision of naval forces was stronger in Spain than in England, the king at first owned only a few galleons. He had to rely on the private enterprise of his admirals, and on his merchants' fleets. During the reign of Philip II (1556–98), a royal Spanish fleet grew up, consisting of an increasing number of warships, including some galleons. They were also intended as protection for the treasure fleets. A decree in the year 1565 laid down that the capitanas, the leading galleons, were to be at least 300 tons in size. The crew should not amount to less than two hundred men. The minimum armaments were also specified. The ships were not allowed to carry any freight, so that their defence capability would not be hampered.[7] According to English reports, the construction of these galleons made them less suitable for a contemporary naval battle than those of their opponents. Moreover, there was an insufficient number of royal Spanish warships after the Armada catastrophe (1588). In 1601 the Duke of Medina Sidonia, the former commander-in-chief of the Armada, wrote that the king should get the necessary ships built himself, instead of hiring them from private individuals. The latter were often ruined in consequence: the Crown used to force merchants to build ships larger than they needed, in order to have them available in an emergency (Figs 5, 6).[8]

Spanish galleons, with their high superstructure looming out of the water, seemed large and powerful in comparison with English galleons. This method of construction had been abandoned by the English before the Armada, as it was synonymous with poor manoeuvrability. The Spanish were interested in their opponents' successful ship designs, and

Fig 5: Smaller, three-masted Spanish galleon from a painting depicting a battle of the Armada (1588) in the National Maritime Museum, Greenwich. The ship has a forecastle with a front bulkhead, on which stands the foremast. The knee of the head, between the stem and the beakhead, is still missing. Aft we can see a halfdeck and a cabin. The guns on the waist and on the halfdeck have land carriages.

there are indications in contemporary English and Spanish sources that English-style ships were built for King Philip II. A William (or John) Lambert from Liverpool was a shipbuilder in Philip's service for a year, and certainly designed some ships for him. In general, though, fear of the Inquisition in the host country meant that the Spanish could only recruit a few specialists from the north. Besides, the Spanish desire for ships in the English style was initially small. The English method prevailed neither with the government nor amongst private individuals. However, we do find that when Philip II attempted to rebuild his fleet after the Armada catastrophe, foreign methods of constructing galleons were experimented with. In 1589 Julian de Isati signed a contract to build twelve English-style galleons in the province of Biscay; these ships were later known as the Twelve Apostles. A further nine galleons were laid down in the Portuguese style for the Spanish in Lisbon. In 1591 an English spy reported that eight new galleons, four of which were 1000 tons, had been built in Santander. The others were from 700–800 tons. In 1592 an English agent reported that forty galleons, most of which were being built in the English or French style, were under construction in Spanish harbours, under the supervision of English people in Spanish service.[10] We can take this as an indication that developments in ship construction methods did not move outwards from Spain to the north European countries.

Fig 6: Four-masted Spanish galleon from a contemporaneous painting depicting a battle of the Armada. The forecastle, with its two decks, is still quite high, in contrast with classical English galleons. Aft we can see two open galleries. The ship has a halfdeck and a quarter-deck, but no poop. The diagonal, wickerwork-like grating, is only occasionally found on ship illustrations of the period, so may be considered a rarer form of grating construction.

Portugal

We know a little more about Portuguese galleons (Fig 7). By 1520 ships were being referred to as galleons in some sources, but it is not clear how typical they were. They later became distinguishable from large carracks by tiny changes in their proportions. Carracks (Naus or Naós da Carreira da India, as the Portuguese called them), were the warships and merchant ships which sailed to India. It is possible that the term galleon developed in Portugal along a different route from that in Venice and England, where it denoted a hybrid between galleys and round ships. The Portuguese galleon, designed as a warship, could have undertaken functions which had hitherto been the preserve of the classical warships, the galleys.[11] The name may thus have arisen through the use to which the ship was put.

Galleons in Portugal also represented an improvement over carracks. Contemporary experts who had to undergo a voyage on a carrack had reason to complain; as, for example, the pilot Gaspar Ferreira Reimao: 'May God forgive the man who built it, and who constructed such top-heavy works on so small a keel, that when there is little wind she loses way and lies a-hull, which makes my blood curdle, finding myself in such a ship.'[12] If we compare the dimensions of a

Fig 7: In their description of the 'Civitates Orbis Terrarum', 1576, Braun and Hogenberg depicted a large Portuguese galleon in the harbour of Lisbon. The beakhead of this ship sits low, giving the large bow-chaser a clear field of fire. The construction of the beakhead is still reminiscent of the ram of a galley, and is possibly responsible for the naming of this ship type. The superstructures are lower and shorter than those of a carrack, and on the lower deck the ship's side is pierced with gunports. The lower masts of the foremasts and mainmasts are evidently portrayed too high. The lower yards are furled, which suggests that the topmasts could not yet be brought down.

Portuguese galleon with those of a carrack of the same tonnage, we find that the length of the keel itself was greater; however the distance between the perpendiculars was smaller. That meant that the galleon stem had less of a rake (Fig 8). Both types of ship had the same height of stem. The superstructure of the galleon was rather lower, the armament heavier. So the differences between galleons and carracks were not very marked.

Around 1550 the main ribs of galleons of this type were virtually circular, with a narrow floor. By 1600 they were egg-shaped with only a slight tumble-home. That left a wide deck. The main rib on one side was constructed from only two arcs. Both carracks and galleons had a keel length to breadth ratio of about 2:1.[13] So it is hardly surprising that many Portuguese people, and most foreigners, could not tell such ships apart without some further distinction. The Portuguese galleons were, however, extremely manoeuvrable. Many were renowned amongst contemporaries for their craftsmanship. The largest and most durable galleons were built in India, from teak. This wood was considered preferable even to best European oak, which was becoming increasingly difficult to obtain. A ship made of teak could easily last twice as long as one made in Europe.

Although every seaman knew that smaller ships of about 500 tons or under were more seaworthy and manoeuvrable, gigantic galleons of 1000 tons and over sailed to India. The explanation for this lies in the fact that higher profits could be made from voyages using large ships: people put up with the poor safety conditions. It was, of course, also clear to Portuguese seamen that galleons, as contrasted with carracks, had the same advantages as small ships over large ones. There is also a good reason why the construction of carracks was not suspended in favour of galleons, as some experts recommended: human greed. A carrack had a rather higher freight capacity than a galleon of the same size. As well as the official cargo, every crew member had the right to bring back one or more free chests (caixas de liberdade). Goods which would otherwise have fallen under the Crown's trading monopoly could thus be exchanged privately. Spices, objets d'art and other commodities could be transported duty-free in this way, which often meant that the decks of a ship were so full that it was only possible to get from one end to the other by crawling. A ship overloaded in this way was scarcely in a position to defend itself in an emergency; no-one could get to the guns, so some of the cargo had to be thrown overboard. The personal profit promised by a couple of extra chests prolonged the useful life of the unwieldy carracks of the Carreira da India.

One of these large galleons was the famous *Bom Jesus*, which was laid down in Indian Goa in 1630. Six years later, in 1636, the English traveller Peter Mundy reported:

> Att our beeing here was launched a New Galleon off 14 Foote by the Keele as they say [Perhaps Mundy means 114 ft?], 'beeing First blessed, Christned, and named *El Buen Jesus* by the Archbishoppe thatt came over in the Carracke as aforementioned. Shee was launched in a Device wherin shee was built, called a Cradle, which is a world of tymber Made uppe and fastned on either side to keepe her uprightt, and soe with Cables, Capstanes and a Multitude of people, they Forced her into the Water, the way beeing first very well tymbred and tallowed.[14]

Mundy also visited the carrack in which the Archbishop had sailed to Goa. Ships like this had not been seen in England since the time of Henry VIII, and Mundy was surprised:

> I went aboard the Carracke . . . Shee is said to bee of 1600 tonnes, of a straunge Forme, her beakehead in such a manner and soe capacious thatt would measure Near 20 tonnes, and the biggest longboat in our Fleete would easily ly in her forechaines; 12 mayne shrowdes of a side; steered below with takles fastned to her tiller: all Monstrous strange, meethought.[14]

Three years later, the galleon *Bom Jesus* impressed another traveller: the German Johann Albrecht von Mandelslo, who recorded in his journal (in his idiosyncratic style):

> When we got to the Portuguese galleons in the Roda district, we went to the General on board, who was on the principal galleon *Bon Iesus*. He received us honourably, with many heavy guns. He led us to his room in the stern,

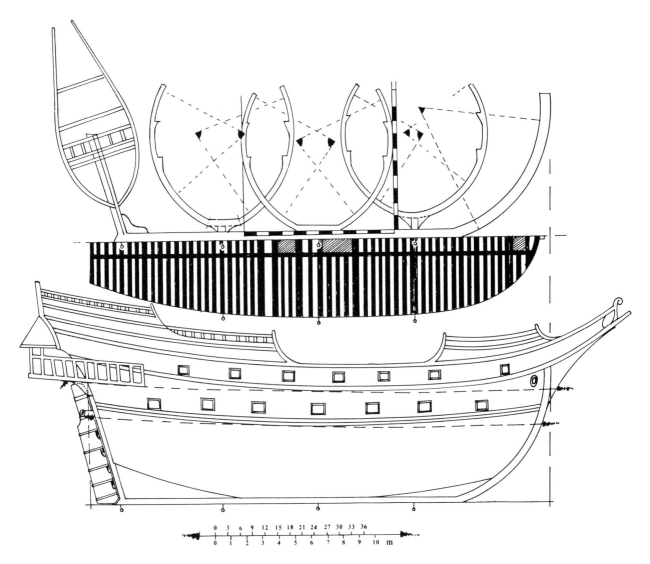

Fig 8: Timbers, orlop deck and sideview of a small Portuguese galleon of 300 tons, after Manuel Fernades, Livro de Traças de Carpintaria, *1616. We can see the keel with both the stem and the sternpost. On it are the three timbers and the deadwood of the stern. The stem and the futtocks are designed from arcs. The ship has two through decks, a forecastle, a halfdeck and a quarter-deck. The ratio of the keel length to maximum breadth is 2.8:1. Venetian galleons of 1550 had a keel length to breadth ratio of 2.5:1. The classical English galleon of c.1600 could have a ratio of up to 3:1. The unit of measurement on the drawing is the palma de goa (pg), which is (approximately) 0.25m. The measurements of this galleon are therefore: keel length c.20.9m, maximum breadth c.9.2m, length c.38m.*

very large and with a large, wide gallery on both sides. Under this was another such room, with a similar sort of gallery. The General began by presenting us with a drink of wine (as is their custom), with confectionery and preserves. Then he showed us round the ship. She has four decks, or floors, carries 64–70 metal guns: whole and half cannon. The smallest of these are quarter pieces. She has two extraordinarily long cannons right at the front of the bow. There were about 600 men on this galleon, all very nicely accommodated with little hanging beds. This ship is only called a Galleon, but she exceeds many carracks in size. Is very strong and well-built, as are the other 5 galleons, which are not much smaller. The Vice-admiral was newly built in the English style, a very fine ship. None of these galleons carried less than 50 guns. The galleon *Bom Jesus* had performed a lot of service with the Dutch last year, at

Scharmützel. At that time she carried 700 men. Afterwards we took our leave from the General, who accompanied us to the door where you go in and out of the ship. (This method of entering a ship through doors is more luxurious, and more comfortable, than the Dutch and English method of climbing a ladder right up the side of the ship).[15]

In the middle of the seventeenth century, Pater Vincentio Maria, the Italian Carmelite missionary who travelled to India in 1655, wrote:

The Portuguese galleons are noteworthy because of their size and numerous comforts. Each one looks like a fortress, and carries 80 or more bronze guns. The deck is so spacious that the crew often play ball. There are so many large, high rooms that the galleons are more like comfortable houses than ships. The ropework is mainly moved with the help of capstans. The planking is thick enough to withstand cannon balls. In short, these ships would be excellent if they did not move so sluggishly, and if they were better manned.[16]

Perhaps Pater Vincentio had confused a galleon with a nao. The roominess of the ship was more than offset by the overloading of the decks.

In the 1630s and 1640s Portuguese carracks and galleons looked so similar that often they could not be told apart. In some documents the terms nao and galleon are used to describe the same ships. The term galleon remained current in Portugal for a long time. In 1680 the *São Pedro da Ribeira*, which was sailing to India, was described as a galleon in the source documents.[17]

But let us return to the year 1550. At that time the galleon style was firmly established in many European countries. Even French and English shipbuilders were constructing vessels of this type. Galleons were not just warships, but also good cargo ships. On the one hand, they were expensive to operate, because of the size of the crew and their costly weapons; on the other, they could be defended extremely well. They were therefore assigned to dangerous trade routes, and carried goods of a value high enough to justify the costs. The most dangerous pirates were in the Mediterranean. There a merchant ship had to contend not only with Algerian corsairs but also with north Europeans and Turks, who seized every opportunity to plunder.[18] In the second half of the sixteenth century, galleys were still playing a dominant role as warships, as they had done since the Middle Ages. Off the north European coast, however, they did not perform well in comparison with the sailing warships. One of the galley's weaknesses was that its guns could only fire forward, and, on occasion, aft. The shipbuilders hoped to compensate for this drawback with the galleass, a high-sided heavy oared ship with inadequate sails (Fig 9). Galleasses also carried weapons on their broadsides. But, as often happens when one tries to combine advantages, the disadvantages mount up. After the naval battle of Lepanto (1571), the galleass appeared to be the warship of the future. But after the defeat of the Spanish Armada (1588) in the English Channel, it forfeited its reputation as an invincible fortress.[19]

The rugged Atlantic climate and new strategic requirements favoured another type of vessel: the heavily armed sailing ship. Its mobility might be somewhat restricted, but it had many advantages; for example, excellent seaworthiness, and the ability to carry sufficient provisions and war materials with low labour costs. Increased independence from replenishments meant that a fleet could stay at sea longer, which was a prime strategic consideration. A port or coastline could only be properly blockaded by sailing ships, not galleys. Galleons benefited further from another factor: the guns which were being cast in sixteenth century Europe were getting larger and larger. Fortresses and besieging armies were already well equipped with them. Increasingly heavy artillery had to be installed on ships as well. People in countries which maintained fleets became more and more aware of the importance of the armaments on the ships and of the value of their operation.

*Fig 9: A Venetian war galleass from the middle of the sixteenth century. In designs of this type the shipbuilders were attempting to combine the advantages of a gun-carrying sailing ship with those of an oared long ship. (*From a tomb in the Basilica of St Anthony, Padua*)*

England

In England, the development of the galleon began during the reign of Henry VIII (1509–47). To begin with, the King's warfare belonged to the medieval tradition. For his first war against the French (1511–15), his fleet consisted of carracks and other types of old sailing ships. Henry's shipbuilders were still experimenting with galley-type ships. These vessels were already more seaworthy, and consequently heavier and less manoeuvrable, than the archetypal galleys. The artillery officer, Anthony Anthony, shows us what these hybrids looked like in his famous Ships List of 1545. The *Anthony List* is one of the most important sources for the English fleet under construction, and shows that old, proven types of ships were in service at the same time as new, experimental models. Like the famous 1586 manuscript *Fragments of Ancient English Shipwrightry*, which is ascribed to the shipbuilder Matthew Baker, the *Anthony List* is to be found in the Samuel Pepys Library: Pepys having been first secretary of the admiralty under King Charles II before becoming renowned for his diary. It is conceivable that Anthony Anthony was the anglicised name of Anthonis Anthonisz, and that he was a brother of Cornelis Anthonisz (c.1500–55), an eminent painter and cartographer from Amsterdam. Perhaps Cornelis even painted the beautiful ship paintings in the *Anthony List* for his brother, who is, after all, known to have been an artilleryman, not an artist.[20]

The *Anthony List* shows vessels which, for the first time in England, were called great galleons. They are the *Grand Mistress* (Fig 10) and the *Anne Gallant*, both built in 1545. They were also called galleasses in the sources, perhaps because similar oared vessels existed at the time.

Ships like the *Grand Mistress* and the *Anne Gallant* were prototypes for the later English galleons of renown. As we will see, they drew less on the carrack than the galleass, which was in the process of reverting to a simple sailing ship. The *Grand Mistress*, for which a tonnage of 450 is cited, seems to have been a simple, four-masted sailing ship. We can already make out the low silhouette of the later galleons. Only the diagonal, clinker-built planking of the forecastle reminds us of earlier times. And we recognise the bow chaser projecting out to the front of the beakhead from the days of the galleys. The bow chaser and the gunbarrels on the broadside were cast. The guns projecting aft were of the older type, made of pieces of metal forged together. Unfortunately the proto-galleon's rigging is only shown schematically. The two front masts were probably square-rigged, while the two rear masts would have had lateen sails.[21] With the ships portrayed in the *Anthony List*, Henry VIII created the first workable English fleet, which he needed to protect his kingdom from the Continental states. In view of the overwhelming power of Spain, there were no adventurous voyages of discovery or piracy during his reign, as there were during the reign of Elizabeth I. He is, however, credited with having founded the Royal Navy, which played such an important part in his country's later maritime successes. One respect of the encouragement and expansion of the fleet was the establishment of the Royal Dockyards at Woolwich and Deptford.[22]

Henry's personal achievement lay in his feeling for the direction in which shipbuilding and naval defence would develop. He also appreciated the weaknesses in his country's artillery, which still featured many old, cast guns. The only foundry for bronze was in the Tower. Much of the income arising from the dissolution of the monasteries in England went towards the construction of the fleet and artillery. Unlike the King of Spain, however, Henry VIII did not have a constant stream of money flowing in. So English gun founders began experimenting with cheaper cast iron at an early stage. English shipbuilding capacity was insufficient for the needs of the royal fleet, so Henry purchased ships abroad: the *Jesus von Lübeck* from the Hanseatic League (Fig 14), and other ships from Italy and even Spain, despite the fact that Spaniards faced severe penalties for selling ships.[23] The decisive influences in the development of English galleons seem to have come from Italy, in particular from Venice. The Venetians had been operating the Flanders

Fig 10: In 1545 the artillery officer, Anthony Anthony, described and drew (?) the fleet of his King, Henry VIII. The Grand Mistress *can, at 450 tons, be considered a prototype for future galleons. (*The British Library, London*)*

convoy since the fourteenth century. A fleet of merchant ships put into Southampton as well as Bruges and Antwerp. The type of ships used for this purpose were the Galeazze di Mercanzia, large merchant galleasses, which, during their visit to England, impressed even the native shipbuilders (Fig 11). The galleasses were so large and heavy that by 1480 complaints were reported to the Venetian Senate: they could barely be manoeuvred in the Arsenal canal, and should really be called ships, not galleys.[24] Coronelli (quoted by Corbett), described these vessels in his *Atlante Veneto* of 1691:

> . . . generally upon the lines of a war-galleasse, but with a length of over three and three-fifths its beam . . . In order to enable them to work in and out of confined waters and rivers, but as an auxiliary means of movement only, they were furnished with oars. But instead of thirty aside, like the war-galleasses, they carried but seventeen, and these were rowed between the fuocone or cooking place amidships and the forecastle . . . They were rigged with three masts, the foremast carrying square sails, the main and mizzen lateens.[25]

We should not assume that these Galeazze di Mercanzia were the direct forerunners of the English galleons. But some prototypes did develop from their influence. Initially these were described as galleys, galleasses and, eventually, also as

Fig 11: The Venetian trading galleass in which Bernhard von Breydenbach, the Canon of Mainz, travelled to the Holy Land in 1483. It resembles the galleazze di mercanzia which were still sailing between Antwerp and Southampton in the first half of the sixteenth century, and which, conceivably, inspired English shipbuilders to experiment with galleasses or oared galleons. (Woodcut by E Reuwich in Breydenbach's Peregrinatio in Terram Sanctam, 1486)

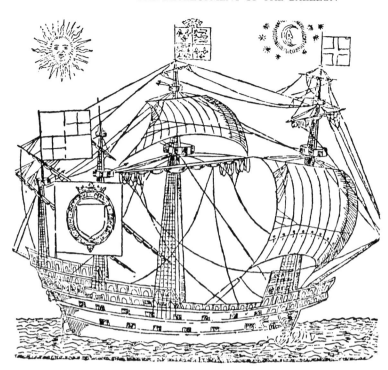

Fig 12: This early English galleon is depicted on the title page of the navigational book A Regiment for the Sea, *by William Bourne, 1577. The short, but high, forecastle is striking. The ship seems to have had two continuous battery decks, a rarity for the time.* (*From* Mariners Mirror, *Vol 3, 1913*)

galleons. Ships which the English shipbuilders called bastard galleasses had a keel length three-and-a-half times their greatest breadth. At the same time the pure sailing galleon developed. As well as its low-lying silhouette, its distinguishing feature was its dimensions: it had a keel length of up to three times the greatest breadth.

Over the years, Henry VIII increasingly preferred pure sailing ships for his fleet. As late as 1541 he had invited galley builders from Italy to England: then sailing ships became the important 'capital ships' in his fleet. The course was set for the galleon and thence to the ship-of-the-line of later centuries. At the same time, shipbuilders in the Mediterranean were still trying to solve the problem of sails and oars in favour of a more freely movable oared ship. A sailing ship was not considered a worthwhile warship.[26] When Elizabeth I became Queen in 1558, she had Henry's ships and weapons at her disposal. She did not increase the size of the fleet she had inherited, but maintained it at the strength reached by her father.[27] The growth of trade facilitated Elizabeth's successes in naval battles with the Spanish, and also the success of English colonisation. The English and Dutch learned, rather sooner than the Spanish would have liked, how to trade with the newly discovered parts of the world. The absence of commercial initiative amongst the Spanish left a gap in the market which the English sought to fill, although this was forbidden by the Spanish Crown. The English had been trying to find a market for their cloth, by every possible means, since the beginning of the fifteenth century. They fought at sea and on land to hold the newly discovered markets in Africa, Asia and America. At this time, England's shipbuilding industry, and also her navy, were in fine fettle. The population of England was smaller than that of France or Spain, but it included a large number of sailors with experience of the Atlantic crossing.[28]

We hardly know anything about the first galleons built in Elizabeth's reign. They were probably still being built in the older, bulky style, and not yet in the 3:1 keel length to breadth proportion of the later ships (Fig 12). The early galleons were between 400 and 600 tons in size. They were manoeuvrable and seaworthy vessels, which sailors preferred to the large, conventional ships.[29] In 1567 and 1568 John Hawkins, the English captain (and later admiral), undertook one of the voyages which were a common feature of the period (Fig 13). It served the purposes of trade in slaves and other 'goods'. Hawkins sailed first to Guinea, on the West African coast, and from there to the Spanish West Indies. The *Jesus von Lübeck*, the large, 600-ton carrack which Henry VIII had purchased from the Hanseatic League in 1544, was the flagship of his six ships. Queen Elizabeth, who supported commercial and marauding action of this

Fig 13: The English Admiral Sir John Hawkins (1532–95). He was the first Englishman to compete with the Spanish and Portuguese as a slave-trader. His battle in the harbour of the Mexican town San Juan de Ulúa (1586) was the start of England's conflicts with Spain. As treasurer of the navy he was heavily involved in the design of English galleons. (From Henry Holland, Herwologia Anglica, Arnhem 1620. National Maritime Museum, Greenwich)

sort, entrusted the ship to him. It had been built in the style of the old floating fortresses, and was no longer in good condition. The carrack was top-heavy, and a poor sailer. Hawkins reported that the *Jesus* pitched so much during a storm off the coast of Florida that the upper part of the superstructure had to be dismantled (Fig 14). It was during the course of this voyage that the celebrated battle took place between Hawkins and the Spanish in the harbour of the Mexican town of San Juan de Ulúa. Hawkins let himself be duped, and the battle ended when the English ships withdrew. Before doing so, however, they managed to sink one or two of the large, advancing Spanish ships, by gunfire alone. Another was shot down in flames. The *Jesus* had to be abandoned after serving for some time as a defence against Spanish artillery.[30]

Hawkins learned an important lesson from the destructive effect of the English broadsides, and from his bad experiences with high-sided ships of the old style. He was to rise to the position of treasurer of the navy in 1577, and thenceforth to exert a decisive influence on the construction of modern English galleons. Like certain gentlemen of the Elizabethan period, John Hawkins led an adventurous life. His family had previously carried on trade with the West African coast. John expanded this trade, inasmuch as he became the first Englishman to sell black slaves to the Spanish colonists in the Caribbean. He reached his position in naval administration through family connections. In addition to being the treasurer, he became the comptroller of the navy in 1589. Hawkins belonged to the Navy Board. One of his tasks was to design and supervise the construction of new ships to replace the old models of Henry VIII's time. He can thus be described as the architect of the Elizabethan fleet. He was convinced that, sooner or later, there would be a test of naval strength between England and Spain. With foresight, he systematically promoted the construction of classical Elizabethan galleons. Through their design and armaments, these ships were to counter the Spanish fighting methods in a particular manner. The Spanish practice was to board an enemy ship after a short, sharp burst of artillery at close range. Force and the fighting strength of the Spanish soldiers often settled the issue. With their new galleons, the

Fig 14: The carrack Jesus von Lübeck, *as it appears in the* Anthony List. *It is a 600-ton ship with the characteristic high fore and aft superstructures and the enclosed beakhead of the large sailing ships of the sixteenth century. The* Jesus *only seems to have one continuous battery deck, the lower deck. The upper deck apparently only carries guns aft of the mainmast. The guns on the vessel, which Henry VIII had purchased from the Hanseatic League in 1544, consisted of two bronze cannons, two bronze culverins, and two bronze sakers. As well as the forged-iron breech loaders, there were also on board: four portpieces, ten serpentines, four fowlers, twelve bases, two top guns (for the tops), and twenty each of revolving case-shot and hand guns. It is remarkable that there are no gunport lids on this ship – perhaps they could be closed from the inside. The four-masted rigging is portrayed schematically: we may assume that both the aft masts were rigged with lateen sails. In 1567 this carrack served as flagship for John Hawkins (later the co-creator of the Elizabethan galleon) on his expedition to the Spanish West Indies. (By permission of the Master and Fellows, Magdalene College, Cambridge)*

English intended to conduct an artillery duel of attrition from a distance, so as not to give the fearsome Spanish soldiers a chance.

Hawkins commanded the galleon *Victory* during the Spanish Armada campaign. His queen made him a knight during the course of the campaign. Later, in the year 1595, he and Drake shared the command of an expedition to the West Indies, but the trials and tribulations of a voyage of this nature were too much for the 63-year-old man. He became ill with dysentry, a common seaman's illness in the age of sail, and died. The galleons which Hawkins favoured were the sort which we know from the manuscript mentioned earlier, *Fragments of Ancient English Shipwrightry* (Fig 15). That important document probably had more than one author. The oldest part is ascribed to Matthew Baker, one of Queen Elizabeth I's master shipbuilders. It can be dated c.1586. We cannot be certain whether the drawings portray ships of the Crown, or, indeed, whether these vessels were ever actually built. Either way, the earliest surviving details of north European ship lines are to be found in this manuscript.

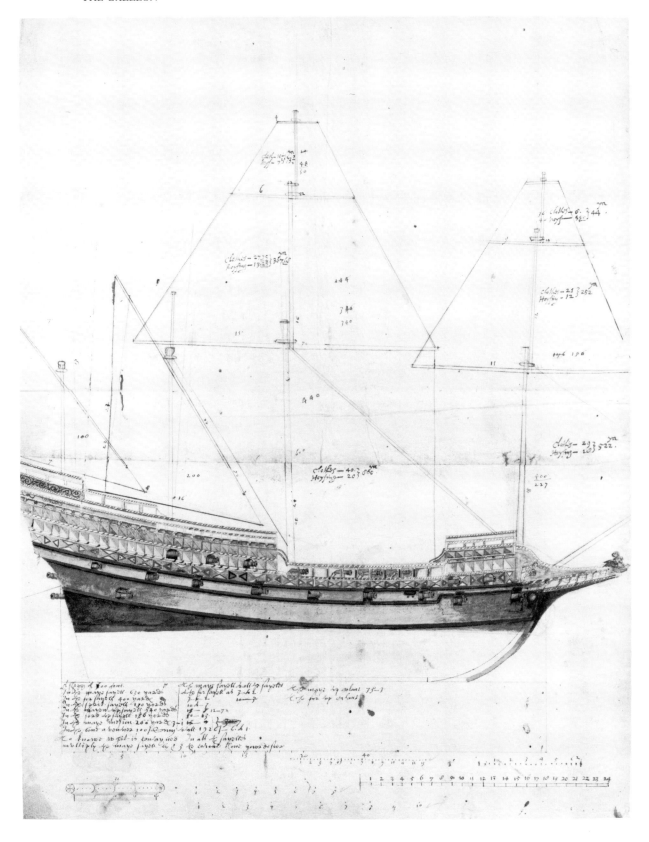

The typical Elizabethan galleon had a keel length to maximum breadth ratio of 2½–3:1. The mackerel sketched in on the underwater hull of a galleon in Fig 16 shows what contemporary experts considered to be the ideal shape for a ship gliding through the water. The main beam (and consequently, the maximum breadth) of a ship like this was, roughly speaking, aft of the front third of the keel. In large galleons, the lowest deck was a short, often unplanked row of deck beams amidships, below the waterline. It was called the false orlop deck. The galley was situated there (see the longitudinal section of the reconstruction, nos 22 and 24. The numbers in the following description of the galleon refer to this section). Then came the lower battery deck (no 17). It lay amidships, 2–3ft above the waterline, and ran from the middle of the ship to the stem. It thus followed the run of the wales. The lower deck drops down aft of the mizzenmast (no 13). It continues at a deeper level, and forms the base of the gunroom with its broadsides and stern chasers. Some shipbuilders even raised the forward end of the lower deck. This might be the case in the vessel shown in Fig 17.

The next highest deck, the main or upper deck, ran from the stern straight over the waist through to the forecastle (no 44). Its height (measured from plank to plank) was approximately 6ft (1.82m) above the lower deck. Above it ran the halfdeck, at a height of approximately 6ft (no 67). It started aft of the mainmast and ran to the stern. The forecastle deck (no 80) was at the same height as the halfdeck. In large galleons, a quarterdeck ran aft above the halfdeck (no 95); and, above that, the floor of a cabin (no 96). The bulkheads of the forecastle and the halfdeck (nos 71 and 75), going towards the waist, were massive and equipped with gunports. The middle part of the upper deck could still be raked with gunfire, if the enemy had already occupied it. Many galleons had a firing position, which was reached from the upper deck (no 58). Large ships sometimes had a second gallery, reached from the halfdeck (Figs 18–22).

The beakhead which projected from the front bulkhead of the forecastle (no 82) was a weak point in the construction of contemporary ships. Rather than breaking the sea, it served to protect the rigging and to make it easier to work on. The running rigging of the bowsprit and the foremast were led in and belayed there. The height and length of the beakhead varied according to fashion.

The *Rainbow*, whose measurements and other details are given below, was a typical medium-sized English galleon. The ship was built by Peter Pett, Master Shipwright, in Deptford Dockyard in 1586. The figures given are approximate values, as these vary slightly in the different source documents.[31]

Keel length	100ft (30.5m)	Anchors	6
Beam	32ft (9.7m)	Anchor cables	6
Depth of hold	12ft (3.65m)	Weight of anchors	9000lb
Rake forward	33.6 (10.21m)	Weight of ordnance	35 tons (35.8 metric tons)
Rake aft	6ft (1.83m)	Crew in harbour	12
Freight Capacity (Burden)	384 tons	Crew at sea	250
		Crew breakdown:	150 mariners
Tonnage	480 tons		30 gunners
Weight of masts and yards	12 tons 11 cwt		70 soldiers
	(12.4 metric tons)	Monthly cost at sea of	£379 3s 4d
Weight of rigging and tackle	10,500lb (4.75 metric tons)	wages and victuals	
Bolts of sailcloth (28 yards x 3/4 yard)	67 (67 x 0.68m x 25.2m = 1161.78m^2)		

Fig 15: A galleon from the manuscript Fragments of Ancient English Shipwrightry, *by Matthew Baker, c.1586. This elegant ship has a low forecastle, a halfdeck, and a poop. The lower deck is set back aft and in the forecastle area, resulting in a break in the wale. This structural weakness was abandoned in later ships. The cathead shown here does not appear in many other drawings of the time. It is questionable whether the rigging scheme shown belonged originally to this hull sketch. (*By permission of the Master and Fellows, Magdalene College, Cambridge*)

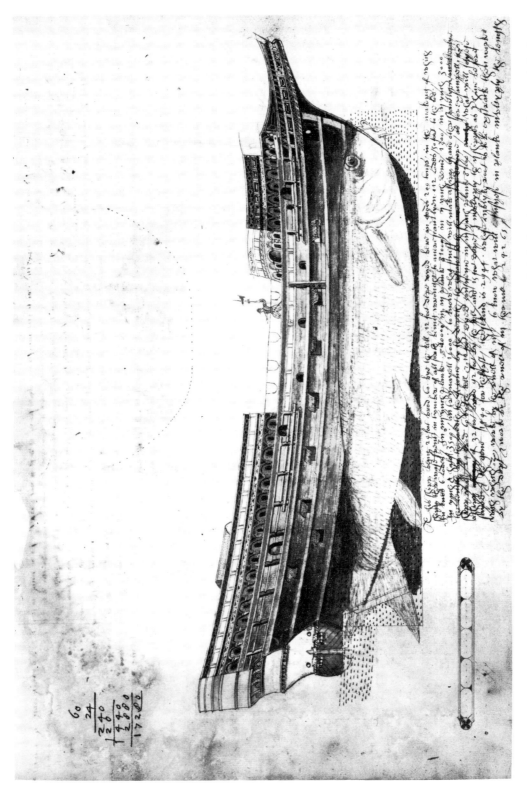

Fig 16: Drawing of a three-masted galleon from Matthew Baker's manuscript c.1586. The ship has two through decks, but there is no quarter-deck or poop deck above the halfdeck. Nor is there a stern gallery. The structure projecting over the rail in the centre of the halfdeck may be a roof under which stood the helmsman at the whipstaff. The fish sketched in the underwater part of the hull, with its stumpy head and long, tapering tail symbolises the ideal shape of hull gliding through the water. The decoration on the ship's side is, like that of the Stockholm galleon, reminiscent of elements of land-based architecture. The large rails running through to the stern, and supported with vertical struts, are an interesting detail. The 'chain rails', an additional parallel structure to which fixed parts of the standing and running rigging were secured, can be seen above the wales. (By permission of the Master and Fellows, Magdalene College, Cambridge)

Fig 17: Sketch of the forecastle and beakhead of a galleon from Matthew Baker's manuscript, c.1586. Here we can see important elements of the galleon style: a beakhead, open on the top surface, projecting forwards; the forecastle with forward bulkhead severely reduced in size. Many (but not yet all) galleons had beakhead figures. Dragons, lions, unicorns and tigers are mentioned in the literature. The beakhead figure portrayed here is reminiscent of the winged lion of St Mark. Perhaps the ship was destined for a Venetian client? The guns projecting forwards in the forecastle area stood on the chase on the upper deck; they were chasers – generally long culverins. A carriage-mounted gun can be seen on the rail of the waist. (By permission of the Master and Fellows, Magdalene College, Cambridge)

In 1592 the English captured the Portuguese carrack *Madre de Dios*, and with it a substantial booty. The ship was considered one of the largest of its time. It was brought to England and plundered. Then it became a sight-seeing attraction in Dartmouth harbour. Visitors marvelled at the four flush-decks in the huge hull, and at the three additional decks in the forecastle and in the aft superstructure. Then people lost interest, and the ship fell into decay, but not before it had first been measured; its main dimensions compared favourably with those of an English galleon, for example, the *Rainbow*. Both ships had a keel length of 100ft. The maximum breadth of the *Madre de Dios* was 46ft 10in (14.28m), while the *Rainbow* was only 32ft wide (9.76m). The maximum length of the carrack was 165ft (50.3m); the galleon measured only 136ft 6in (42.54m).[32] If we then allow for the high fore and aft superstructures on the carrack, we can begin to understand the difference in character of the two vessels.

In the course of time, the lines of large ships began to vary, depending on the use for which they were intended. At first there was no great difference between armed merchant ships and war galleons, apart from the fact that the warships had stronger fastenings and decks. Orders (rules of proportion) for different types of ships are laid down in a document originating from William Borough (1536–99), who was comptroller of the navy from 1589 to 1598 (cf Fig 71):

1 For merchant ships, 'for most profit', the length of the keel should be 'double the breadth amidships and the depth in hold half that breadth'.

2 For merchant ships which may be used for other (military) purposes, the length of the keel should be 'two or two and a quarter that of beam. Depth of hold eleven-twenty-fourths that of beam'.

3 For 'galleons or ships for the wars, made for the most advantage of sailing' the length of the keel should be 'three times the beam. Depth of hold two-fifths of beam'.[33]

The term keel length implies the straight part of the keel, and the greatest breadth means the width of the main beam. We can obtain the depth of the hold by measuring the distance between the main beam and the upper edge of the keel. Sometimes, however, the measurement was taken from the lower edge of the orlop deck beam to the keel; there were as yet no standard terms of measurement.

Fig 18: A stern view of the English galleon Griffin *c.1588, by the Dutch engraver and printer Claes Jansz Visscher (1580–1660), who depicted many ships of the Elizabethan period. The ship has two gun-bearing decks in the lower part of the stern. The lower one is the gunroom; the upper, which is half the distance below the upper deck, was known as the upper gunroom. We can see one typical galleon feature: the high stern, in contrast with the low forecastle. (*National Maritime Museum, Greenwich*)*

Details of the tonnage of a ship from the period before 1580 also vary widely in different documents. We can assume that tonnage figures are based on comparable estimates. In 1582 an English document appeared, which, for the first time, gave examples for the calculation of tonnage. It is attributed to the master shipwright Matthew Baker.[34] The freight capacity of a merchant ship (burden of merchant goods) is measured in pipes of oil (527 litres) or casks of Bordeaux wine. The claret trade was the oldest branch of English maritime trading, and had been the most important for two centuries. The 'wine ton' unit of measurement consisted of two casks with a combined capacity of approximately 225 gallons (1144.08 litres). To calculate the tonnage ('ton and tonnage') of a ship – that is, the weight of the displaced water – you added one-third of the freight capacity to itself. This tonnage was important for calculating harbour fees and in estimating material requirements and building costs.

For 'Mr Bakers old way', as the Elizabethan measuring system later came to be known, the primary measurement was the keel length, excluding the stempost and sternpost. The second measurement was the breadth at the main beam, inside the planking. The third was the depth, measured from the lower edge of the main beam to the upper edge of the keel. The product of these three figures (in English feet) was divided by 100, and gave the ship's freight capacity ('tons burden'). To obtain the tonnage, you added one-third of the freight capacity to this.[35] Sometimes the divisor used was 97, or even 94. This seems to indicate that ships with a wider floor had a different shape of hull, and consequently a different displacement. The formula was:

$$\frac{\text{Keel Length x Greatest Breadth x Depth}}{100 \ (97 \ \text{or} \ 94)} \text{ x } (1 + \tfrac{1}{3}) = \text{Tonnage}$$

Tonnage calculated in this way has, of course, very little in common with the freight capacity of a ship as calculated today. It was simply a measurement by which different vessels could be compared.

Rules for measuring ships varied from country to country. In 1590 a Spanish Reform Commission put forward the following formula:

$$\frac{\text{Half Breadth x Depth x Deck Length}}{8} \text{ x } 19/20$$

Breadth meant the greatest width, including the planking; depth the clearance between the orlop deck beam and the floor of the hold. The length of the orlop deck was the distance between the inner edges of the stempost and the sternpost. The unit of measurement was the Castillian ell (codo) which was 0.574m. The formula gave the ship's freight capacity (tonelos machos); to calculate the tonnage (toneladas) you added one-fifth of the freight capacity to this.[36] The

Fig 19: This classical English galleon of the Elizabethan period is shown in the centre of an anonymous contemporary painting of the Battle of the Armada in the English Channel (1588), in the National Maritime Museum, Greenwich. The stern of this four-masted ship, with its open gallery, is lower than that of contemporary carracks. The height of the forecastle is also sharply reduced. The rigging details cannot be seen, but the dimensions portrayed are realistic. The topmasts and yards are short, and suited for weather conditions in the North Sea and North Atlantic.

difference between the Spanish and English formulae shows how much care is required in comparing tonnage figures for ships from different countries. Spanish tonnage merely gives a code number, from which freight and charter rates could be calculated, so their figures were often higher than the English equivalents.

With regard to the later part of Queen Elizabeth I's reign, and the reign of her successor King James I, we have reports and drawings from an English seaman who was an eye-witness at many maritime events of his time. William Monson (1568–1643) summarised his experiences in his *Naval Tracts*; these six books, which he wrote towards the end of his life, range from the time when he went to sea as a boy 'led therunto by the wildness of my youth', through his command of a privateer, participating in the battles of the Armada, to his time as a galley slave in Spanish captivity. He commanded the English galleon *Rainbow* in the English expedition to Cadiz (1596), and was vice-admiral in the battle of Sesimbra Bay (1602) (see p 63). Monson succeeded in becoming admiral of the English fleet,[37] and his writings will be quoted frequently in this monograph. He is the source of the following list of the ships comprising the Royal Navy at the time of Elizabeth I's death in 1603:

2 galleons of 1000 tons	2 of 700 tons
3 of 900 tons	4 of 600 tons
3 of 800 tons	2 of 400 tons

and 21 additional ships of 350 tons or less.[38]

Every fleet had only a few large war galleons, in contrast with a profusion of medium-sized and smaller vessels. Realistic portrayals of contemporaneous naval engagements show only a few capital ships, looming large in a sea of smaller vessels.

The last two galleons built under Elizabeth I were the *Warspight* and the *Repulse*. The latter had a keel length of three times the breadth, and was therefore a 'true' galleon. The *Warspight*, however, had a keel length of only two-and-a-half times the breadth. That shows that shipbuilders were still not in agreement over the ideal proportions for the hull. Ships with features from both the past and the future were being built at the same time.[39]

Another issue of the time was whether preference should be given to high-built ships or low-built ships. Monson's opinion on the subject came from his wealth of experience as a soldier, not as a seaman. He showed how ship construction could be influenced by considerations of defence and tactics in naval battles:

There are two manner of built ships: the one with a flush deck, fore and aft, snug and low by water; the other lofty and high charged, with a half deck, forecastle, and cobridge heads. The ship with a flush deck I hold good to fight in, if she be a fast ship by the wind and keep herself from boarding. She is roomsome for her men, and yare to run to and again in her; but she is not a ship to board, unless it be a merchant, or another ship that is inferior to her in strength and number of people. For if it happen that she be boarded, and put to her defence, she lieth open to her enemy; for gaining her upper deck you win her, having neither forecastle nor other close-fight to retire unto; and in that case half the defensive part of the ship is the strength of the forecastle. When her deck shall be gained, and her people beaten down into the second deck, the only help is to use stratagems by fire in making trains of divers fashions to blow up the upper deck and men upon it.[40]

Monson then cites an anecdote from his own experiences. The account shows the strong impression which the event made on the 17-year-old boy. It was his baptism in fire:

. . . and this did the Biscainer I have formerly spoken of in my First Book, in the voyage I first went to sea and the first fight I did ever see, in 1585. This ship had a flush deck fore and aft, which in boarding we won upon her, and her men being beaten into her other deck spent the most part of their powder in making trains to blow us up; which, by fortune, we prevented, and with our firepikes fired them before they could be brought to perfection. And thus after twelve hours' fight in the night, we being upon a flush deck, and commanding their scuttles aloft that they

Fig 20

Fig 21

*Fig 22 Figs 20–22: English galleons from a painting of the Armada Campaign, 1588. (*National Maritime Museum, Greenwich*)*

could not come up to us, and they commanding the scuttles below that we could not go to them, what with wearisomeness, want of powder, and the death of their people they yielded as I have before described.[40]

Monson continues with his evaluation of the respective advantages of high-sided and low-sided vessels:

A high built ship is the better for these reasons – majesty and terror to the enemy, more commodious for the harbouring of men. She will be able to carry more artillery, of greater strength, within board and make the better defence. She will overtop a lower and snug ship; her men cannot be so well discerned, for that the waist-cloths will take away the view and sight of them.

A high-sided English galleon of this sort is shown in Fig 23. It is interesting to note what William Monson, as a champion of the classical method of English galleon construction, thought of the next development in warships, the three-decker, for example, the English *Prince* of 1610:

And lastly, to speak of a ship with three decks, thus it is: – she is very inconvenient, dangerous and unserviceable; the number and weight of the ordnance wrings her sides and weakens her. It is seldom seen that you have a calm so many hours together as to keep out her lower tier, and when they are out, and forced to haul them in again, it is with great labour, travail and trouble to the gunners when they should be fighting. She casts so great a smoke within board that people must use their arms like blind men, not knowing how to go about their work nor have a sight of the ship with whom they encounter.[41]

Three-deckers of this sort cannot really be classified as galleons. They were a decisive step in the direction of the later sailing ships-of-the-line. For people like Monson, who had fought in the classical Elizabethan galleons, these new, large, poor-sailing artillery platforms, with all their adverse qualities, were to be mistrusted. Countless obstacles were placed in the path of Phineas Pett, the shipwright who built the *Prince* (see Chapter 7, p 128). The hull construction of these early three-deckers, as with galleons, still contains all the elements of whole-moulding. This did not provide hulls with sufficient load-bearing capacity for heavy guns. Whole-moulding, which is covered in detail in Chapter 7, consisted of achieving the shape at the main beam of a ship through several contiguous arcs. The arcs of the main beam then served for the construction of the remaining timbers of the hull. The English manner of applying this method partly resulted in barely rounded, flat areas of the ship below water with minimal buoyancy.

Galleons were frequently overloaded with guns. Heavy armament can be traced back to the ideas of Henry VIII. Some ships, well-equipped for the outward voyage, laid some of the heavy guns in ballast on their homeward voyage. Sailors feared the heavy weight of the guns, as it reduced the seaworthiness of their ships.[42] Sir Walter Raleigh, seafarer and writer (1552–1628), was also of this opinion; he was opposed to ships that were too large, believing that a medium-sized 600-ton galleon could carry guns as successfully as a 1200-ton ship, and fire her broadside twice before a large ship could fire once. He wrote:

> The high charging of ships it is that brings them all ill qualities, makes them extreme leeward, makes them sink deep in the water, makes them labour and makes them overset. Men may not expect the ease of many cabins and safety at once in sea-service. Two decks and a half is sufficient to yield shelter and lodging for men and mariners and no more charging at all higher, but only one low cabin for the master.[43]

In 1618 a navy commission was set up in England and made recommendations for the construction of new ships. From this we can find out something about the dimensions and equipment of the late galleons: the keel length was now to be three times the breadth, 'but not to draw above sixteen feet' (4.87m) 'because deeper ships are seldom good sailors'. The new galleons were to be seaworthy: 'they must be somewhat snug-built, without double galleries and too lofty upperworks, which overcharge many ships'. In the experts' opinion, that sort of thing made ships 'loom fair but not work well at sea'. Persuading master shipwrights to construct lower vessels was, however, no easy matter: experiences of the disadvantages in battle (as, for example, William Monson's), weighed heavily. The dimensions given by the navy commission were arrived at from the recommendations of the most respected master shipwrights. But that did not prevent ships from having to be 'girdled' after completion; they were covered with thick planks below the water-line, as they lay too deep in the water. The recommendations also stated:

> For strengthening the ship we subscribe to the new manner of building – 1st, making three orlops, whereof the lowest being placed two feet under water, strengtheneth the ship though her sides be shot through; 2nd to carry this orlop end to end; 3rd, the second or main deck to be sufficiently high to work guns in all weathers.[44]

We see here a transformation in the nomenclature of the decks. Hitherto, a short deck which lay below the waterline had been called the false orlop deck, and the first deck lying above the waterline the true orlop deck. The guns on the newly-named main deck (the lower ports) were to be at least 4½ft (1.47m) above the water-line. The orlop (lowest) deck was to carry the bread and other store rooms, the cables and officers' cabins, 'besides a certain number of the crew who were also to be berthed upon it'.

The galleon *Lyon*, which was evidently built to a proven design, served as an example for the measurements recommended by the commission. It had been rebuilt in 1609; countless old pieces of wood from an earlier hull were assembled anew. The ship was 650 tons, had 38 guns, a maximum breadth of 35.2ft (10.73m); a keel length of 91ft

Fig 23: Four-masted English galleon, c.1600, by an unknown master. The ship has a low forecastle in contrast with the high-stern structure. It is interesting to see the arming cloths, made from decoratively painted canvas, as these are only rarely shown elsewhere. There was, as yet, no standard colour scheme for ships. Red, green and white were the favourite colours for superstructures. Only small parts of the decoration (for example, coats-of-arms) were gilded. (Rijksmuseum, Amsterdam)

(27.7m); and a depth in hold of 16ft (4.87m). Amongst the many other measurements laid down, was one which specified that the main (second) deck of the new ships should be 5½ or 6ft above the orlop (lowest) deck. There should be nine ports a side, and four chase ports fore and aft of the lower gundeck (second deck), and they should be at least 2ft 3in (0.66m) square.[44]

The English fleet was less in demand amongst the rulers who followed Queen Elizabeth I (James I 1603–25; Charles I 1625–49); and no great progress was made in the development of ship construction. In the middle of Charles I's reign, however, galleons were built with keel lengths which were three times that of the breadth. It is not clear whether this resulted from theoretical calculations, or observation of ships of foreign origin. In the case of new ships launched between 1646 and 1647, the master shipwrights occasionally even achieved a keel length of three-and-a-half times the breadth. Pepys thought that the master shipwright Pett had taken these proportions from a French ship anchored in the Thames. There was no systematic scientific examination of ship dimensions. Specialists complained that shipbuilders were no longer able to build identical ships according to a proven design. Many vessels whose size and proportions had been specified by the king turned out, on completion, to be substantially different.[45] We can, perhaps, understand the shipbulders' reluctance to alter the main proportions of a ship, if we consider the implications of doing so; a large ship was an enormous capital investment, and a total loss could not be ruled out.

Netherlands

At the time when galleons were being developed by other seafaring peoples, shipbuilding in the Netherlands seems to have been restricted to merchant ships. A regular shipbuilding industry existed, based on numerous wind-powered sawmills. Ships were constructed according to tried and tested designs, using planks and beams sawn at these mills. They were built to contract, and to the buyer's specification. The ships were solid and durable, and were sold all over Europe. At first warships existed in the Netherlands only in the shape of merchant ships which had been converted for convoy service. Specialised warships began being built around the middle of the sixteenth century.[46] They were, however, smaller vessels, probably pinnaces, as they were known from about 1600. In building their ships, the Dutch always had to take into account the shallow navigable waters of their harbours and coastline.

A particularly large Dutch war/merchant ship is portrayed in the engraving by C I Visscher (after Barentsoen), dated 1594 (Fig 24). It is a typical galleon. In size, and in many details, it resembles the vessel on which the Stockholm galleon model (see Chapter 6) would have been based. Perhaps it is the *Neptunus*, which was built in 1594, and lost by 1597. It is portrayed as the *Fortunas*. Even the large 'Aspect of Amsterdam from the year 1606', attributed to J P Saenredam, shows only one large four-masted galleon (Fig 25), in spite of the plethora of ships. It has been identified as the *Hollandsche Tuyn* by the historian G C E Crone.[47] This galleon, together with the *Löwen* from Rotterdam, was one of the three large Dutch war/merchant ships of the time. In terms of construction and proportion there is really very little difference between these large ships and the smaller three-masted vessels. Even the term galleon was not commonly used by the Dutch for ships of this sort. Nevertheless, they do correspond to the type being discussed in this monograph.

The *Hollandsche Tuyn* was measured at 500 lasts. In relation to the size of the ship, a last meant a carrying capacity of 4000lb.[48] It is hardly credible that this huge galleon, so clearly depicted in Amsterdam harbour, had really made the dangerous passage up the Zuider Zee. First it would have to negotiate the Pampus, a shallow where ships often had to lie waiting for weeks on end for a spring tide.[49] From 1690 onwards a camel was used; this was a floating dry dock, which lifted deep-drawing ships. Vessels of more than 4.5m draught went to the roadsteads of Texel, Vlieland or Terschelling to be unloaded. Contemporaneous sources confirm that the passage through the Zuider Zee was as dangerous as a voyage to Spain. Consequently, large galleons were chiefly used for journeys in deeper waters, perhaps round the Iberian peninsula to the Mediterranean, or on voyages to Asia or America. In the end, the Admiralty of the States General had to sell the unmanoeuvrable *Hollandsche Tuyn*. The Dutch could not even compensate for the

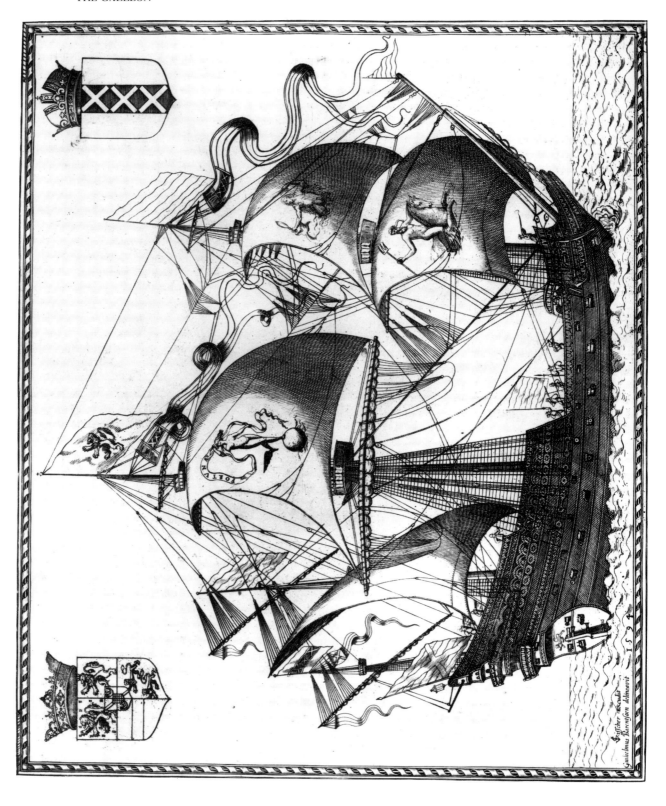

draught of big ships with the characteristic shape of their main beam – broad floor, with steep box-like futtocks. So virtually no heavy, deep-drawing ships were built in the Netherlands.

There is no trace of a differentiated system of proportions in hull construction comparable with that found in England. In the Netherlands Witsen (1671) and Van Yk (1697) certainly gave hints on the construction of the midship frame, and a contrived system of rules of thumb undoubtedly existed, but they were never recorded. They are lost and forgotten, as a result of the trade secrecy which the Shipbuilders Corporation felt would fend off competition.

Scandinavia

By the beginning of the seventeenth century, the large ships of Denmark and Sweden were by no means technically inferior to those built in England and the Netherlands. There had already been a technology transfer in the north European countries; Dutch carpenters worked in Danish and Swedish shipyards; the Dutchman Henrik Hybertsson built the *Wasa*, which sank in Stockholm in 1628; the Sheldons, the famous English shipbuilding family, worked in Sweden; Scottish shipbuilders worked in Denmark, for example, David Balfour and Daniel Sinclair, who built the *Norske Löwe* for King Christian IV.[50]

English shipbuilders were also in evidence in southern Europe: in Spain, as we have already seen. However both sail-travel and ship construction began to go into a decline there in the early decades of the seventeenth century. Contemporaneous comparisons of Spanish and Dutch ships indicated why the Spanish vessels were inferior. The government attempted to improve the qualities of its galleons by standardising the main proportions.[51]

France

French shipbuilding was also inferior to Dutch and English shipbuilding at the beginning of the seventeenth century. When Cardinal Richelieu ordered the construction of the French navy in the 1620s, its first ships were built in Rotterdam.[52]

The classification of ships

The term galleon began to disappear even before the middle of the seventeenth century. The great ship meta-morphosed into the warship, and into the ship-of-the-line of the war fleets. In their heyday, galleons were always seen as armed merchant ships which could defend themselves well, and, of course, serve well under attack. When ships which carried only guns, and no longer any merchandise, began to develop out of the military components of the vessels called galleons, the term galleon had lost its meaning.

The appearance of the great ships also changed. The old method of whole-moulding was no longer used as the means of construction in the second half of the seventeenth century. The master shipwrights developed new methods of constructing the midship frame and the other shapes of the timbers of the ship's hull. Construction with the help of water lines came to the fore; the midship frame became more rounded; ships were built fuller in the bow and stern. This method resulted in hulls with sufficient load-bearing capacity for the ever-increasing weight of the guns. The

Fig 24: This Dutch galleon, which Barentsoen portrayed as the Fortunas, *resembles the Stockholm galleon model in many details. The engraving is dated 1594. The ship is probably one of the few large Dutch war/merchant ships of the time, possibly the* Neptunus, *which was built in 1594 and had sunk by 1597. Because of their draught, the use of such ships in Dutch waters was severely limited, so large four-masters soon vanished from the fleet. The richly appointed rigging is considerably more than was necessary, reflecting the riggers' and sailors' needs for decoration. (Prins Hendrik Maritime Museum, Rotterdam)*

Fig 25: This Dutch galleon was depicted by Saenredam in his 'View of Amsterdam' (1606). The large four-master is considered to be the Hollandsche Tuyn, *which was of 500 lasts. The artist has left out some of the details of the rigging, as other ships appear in the background in the engraving and the tangle of lines would otherwise be too great.*

superstructures thus appeared broader and heavier. The old shape of galleon – with a narrow stern, high and slender aft superstructures, a narrow forecastle and a wide and flat projecting beakhead – had ceased to exist (Fig 75).

The classification of large sailing ships always varied among the seafaring nations. Often it was simply a matter of the place of origin of a document containing the names of different types of ships. The Portuguese, for example, hardly ever used the term carrack for their ships sailing to India, preferring naos. The Dutch and English, on the other hand, always called these ships carracks in their reports (see Fig 1). Dutch, English and Spanish usages of this term for Portuguese ships sailing to India can be found up to the last quarter of the seventeenth century. At this late date the term no longer applies to the famous gigantic ships from the end of the sixteenth century, but to vessels which rather more resembled galleons. In contrast to their practice regarding carracks, the Portuguese always termed their galleons as such. The English were different: they generally called a galleon a ship, as the word galleon was never really indigenous to normal maritime language. However, everyone knew what was meant by a galleon: a sailing ship with finer lines than a normal merchant ship.

The word had not been clearly established at the time of Henry VIII, when there were new types of ships with auxiliary oars, so these were known simultaneously as galleon, galley or galleot. The term did not yet have a standard technical definition, apart from the rules of proportion for length and breadth. So people still called ships, with keel lengths of more than three times the breadth, galleasses, although they were no longer rowed. A bastard galleass was halfway between a galleon and a galleass. Here we can see old names being carried over to new designs.

Initially the term galleon must have had to compete with other words designating a particular group of vessels. Although the galleon ship type developed more and more distinctly, it was called a ship much more frequently than a galleon in England. Galleon was more of a technical term, used by shipwrights.

There was no system of ship classification (rates) in England during the Elizabethan period – as there was later on – but rather a grouping of ships into larger, medium-sized and smaller types. First came the galleons, as ships; then barks, (smaller, pure merchant ships); then the oared pinnaces. Barks were from between 50 and 150 tons, and resembled the *Mayflower*, as we know it from the reconstruction. In 1586 Queen Elizabeth I's ships were classified by the naval authorities as ships, barks, pinnaces, brigantines and frigates. The three last-named were oared vessels. At the same time, shipwrights classified their products as galleons, barks and pinnaces.[53]

The term galleon was still in use as late as the nineteenth century; the Manila galleon was the name given to vessels of the famous year-round link which the Spanish maintained between Manila in the Philippines across the Pacific to Acapulco in Mexico. The cargo of these galleons was very valuable. The Spanish brought the silver from Peru via Manila to China and Southeast Asia. There they traded it for luxury goods like silk, porcelain, spices, musk and pearls. These riches were brought to Central America by the Manila galleons. Then they were transported back to Spain across the Atlantic. Initially the Manila galleons would have been true galleons, built in the Philippines. Their voyage from Manila to Acapulco took from six to eight months without a break; they often made the return journey in less than three months. The design of these vessels varied, naturally, over the centuries. But they had one thing in common: they were built from the same durable, worm-resistant wood from the Philippines. By the time of Napoleon, the Spanish were in a position to exercise their time-honoured trading monopoly. When the last Manila galleon arrived in Acapulco in 1815, there was no longer any market for her merchandise.[54]

CHAPTER 2

Rigging

T HE galleon era not only ushered in progress in the lines of ship's hulls, but also changes and improvements in rigging. Some arrangements of round timbers, sails and ropework in old pictures seem bizarre to us today. But the general technical trend of the time was towards a sharper differentiation and subdivision of sails on large ships, better suited to wind and weather; and to a decrease in the number of people needed to control the huge areas of canvas.

At the beginning of the seventeenth century, the rigging of a square-rigged ship, both bow and stern, was its weakest point. It was the most fragile part, which was most subject to wear and tear. Incomplete rigging was the reason why ships like galleons sailed poorly across the wind. This impotence was not caused by the shape of their hulls.[1] A detailed description of ships' rigging c.1600 does not come within the scope of this book. At that time the sailors' and riggers' art had reached a bewildering level of differentiation, particularly in the case of large imposing ships. I have tried to do justice to this aspect, without going into too much detail, in the reconstruction of the rigging of the Stockholm galleon. But I would prefer to cover the general trends in development, and present views which were considered important at the time, and which differ in part from our modern understanding of mast and sail. For modelbuilders and other interested persons, searching in vain for some detail about rigging, the excellent books by Anderson,[2] Lees,[3] Howard,[4] Hoeckel[5] and Mondfeld,[6] amongst others, should suffice. They cover the rigging of large ships at the beginning of the seventeenth century.

Masts

In many portrayals of galleons from the second half of the sixteenth century and the early decades of the seventeenth century, we find four masts and a strong, simple bowsprit. Smaller galleons and many merchant ships had three masts. The typical north European galleon was just as likely to be used as a warship as a well-armed merchant ship for long voyages, so it was generally medium-sized (500 tons or over) rather than small. With larger vessels, as most galleons with appropriate keel lengths were, sailors initially considered it inevitable that the sails which the ship needed aft would be carried on two masts behind the mainmasts: the mizzenmast and the bonaventure mast. They were both rigged with Mediterranean triangular lateen sails. The two forward masts on large ships were square-rigged (Fig 26). The three-masted rig and square-rig were fully developed in northern Europe by the fifteenth century. But the earliest example of a four-master in England comes from the year 1487: the 1000-ton *Regent*, which was one of the largest ships in Henry VII's (1485–1500) navy. This ship, which was a carrack, already had topmasts on the fore and mainmasts, which were, however, fastened permanently and could not be struck down on deck. A square spritsailyard was readily available, and could be taken inboard in bad weather. The mizzenmast and the fourth mast (aft of it) on the *Regent* were rigged with lateen sails.[7]

This fourth mast, which later became a characteristic feature of large galleons, was already known as the bonaventure mast in Henry VII's time (no 2 in the rigging plan of the reconstruction. The reference letters and numbers which

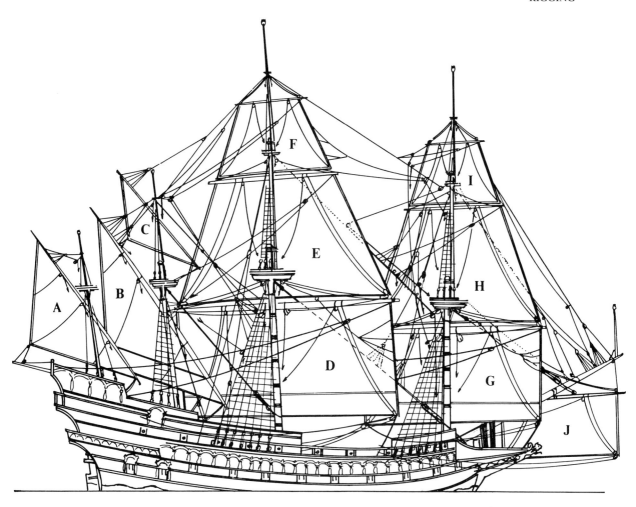

Fig 26: Sketch after the reconstruction drawing for the rigging of the Stockholm galleon, which Sam Svensson prepared in 1952 for the construction of a replica of the model. In comparison with the reconstruction presented in this monograph, the masts and upper yards of this drawing are longer, and the sails larger. The whole appearance of the rigging is more modern. The sails which a large, four-masted galleon of around 1600 carried were:

A Bonaventure sail	*C Mizzen topsail*	*E Main topsail*	*G Foresail with bonnet*	*I Fore topgallant sail*
B Mizzensail with bonnet	*D Mainsail with bonnet*	*F Main top gallant*	*H Fore topsail*	*J Spritsail*

follow refer to this drawing). The name comes from the Italian, and means good luck. This expression seems to imply that it would indeed be a fortunate thing if such a small, exposed mast could defy the winds. But it is also conceivable that the English first saw a fourth mast on a ship from, say, Italy, which bore the name *Bonaventura*. It was not an unusual name for ships at the time.[8] The bonaventure mast, which stood very far back, let the aft clew of its triangular sail hang out over the stern of the ship. So it became necessary to have an outlicker, which was another spar projecting aft.

The term galleon is not defined by the ship's sails, but by the distinguishing features of the hull. Galleons therefore did not have a particular rig, but followed the general trend in square-rig. Bonaventure masts were frequently used during the heyday of the galleon. In the Elizabethan era, ten of the largest galleons in the English fleet, which fought against the Spanish Armada in 1588, were four-masters. But the large carracks of this period were also four-masters. Use of the fourth mast became so widespread during the reign of Queen Elizabeth's successor James I (1603–25), that approximately half of all warships were four-masters by 1618.[9] Ships at that time were already carrying square-rigged sails above the lateen sails on the mizzenmast. Sailors soon realised that the area of sailcloth required aft was better obtained by increasing the size of the mizzenmast than by using a fourth mast. So the bonaventure mast, which had been a characteristic feature of early galleons, fell into disuse. Only two large ships in the English fleet of 1623 (including the three-decker *Prince*) were rigged with four masts. By 1640 the bonaventure mast had completely disappeared from the English fleet.[10]

Progress was made in other areas of ships' rigging and fittings around the year 1600. We are indebted to Sir Walter Raleigh for a summary of these achievements. Raleigh, an expert in maritime matters, was an adventurer, an explorer, and (for a while), Queen Elizabeth's favourite. In 1596 he led the English fleet in the successful expedition to Cadiz. His star began to fade, however, after Elizabeth's death. Raleigh was executed in the Tower in 1618, one of the sacrifices in James I's policy of appeasement with Spain. Raleigh had this to say about the development of English ships of his time:

> Whosoever were the inventors, we find that every age hath added somewhat to ships, and to all things else. and in mine own time the shape of our English ships hath been greatly bettered. It is not long since the striking of the topmast (a wonderful ease to great ships, both at sea and in harbour) hath been devised, together with the chain pump, which takes up twice as much water as the ordinary did. We have lately added the Bonnet and the Drabler [Reconstruction rigging plan: B,D,G]. To the courses we have devised studding sails, topgallant-masts [nos 17, 26], spritsails [J], topsails. The weighing of anchors by the capstone is also new. We have fallen into consideration of the lengths of cable, and by it we resist the malice of the greatest winds that can blow.[11]

At the beginning of Queen Elizabeth's reign, tops (nos 14, 23) on ships' foremasts and mainmasts were still firmly attached to the lower masts. Large, imposing ships already had topgallant masts, which were also firmly attached. For example, the *Harry Grace à Dieu*, a carrack in Henry VIII's fleet, which was built in 1514, carried these round timbers. This unusual ship already had a triangular mizzen topsail (Fig 26 and rigging plan C), as could be seen approximately fifty years later on the large galleon *Ark Royal* (1588) and on the Dutch galleon depicted by W Barentsoen (Fig 24). This fair weather sail is furled. We do not know the exact details of its rigging and usage. The lateen mizzen topsail was not officially dispensed with in the Royal Navy until 1618, when it was replaced by a squaresail, the crossjack.

We have an example of the rigging equipment of a large galleon from this period, the *Bear* or *White Bear* (Fig 27). The specification of the lengths of the old and new round timbers of the galleon *Bear* in yards, feet and inches (and metres) is interesting in view of the later developments in rigging:[12]

	Old				New					Old				New			
	yd	ft	in	metres	yd	ft	in	metres		yd	ft	in	metres	yd	ft	in	metres
Mainmast	30	0	0	27.4	30	0	0	27.4	Sprit topmast	--	--	--	----	7	0	0	6.3
Mainsail	31	2	8	29.1	28	2	8	26.3	Spritsail topsail yard	--	--	--	----	7	1	5	6.7
Main topmast	16	1	0	14.9	15	0	0	13.7									
Main topsail	13	0	1	11.8	12	1	1	11.2	Mizzenmast	22	1	0	20.4	22	0	0	20.1
Main topgallant	--	--	--	----	6	1	6	5.8	Mizzen topmast	(not given)				10	0	0	9.1
Main topgallant sail	--	--	--	----	5	1	0	4.8	Mizzenyard	33	1	0	30.4	23	0	2	21.0
									Crossjack yard	--	--	--	----	17	0	9	15.7
Foremast	28	0	6	25.6	28	0	0	25.5	Mizzen topsail yard	--	--	--	----	7	1	5	6.7
Foresail	24	2	8	22.7	23	0	2	21.6									
Fore topmast	14	0	0	12.7	14	0	0	12.7	Bonaventure mast	19	1	0	17.6	19	0	0	17.3
Fore top sail	10	1	1	10.2	9	0	3	8.2	Bonaventure topmast	(not given)				8	0	0	7.3
Fore topgallant	--	--	--	----	7	0	0	6.3	Bonaventure yard	(not given)				17	0	9	15.7
Fore topgallant sail	--	--	--	----	4	0	10	3.8	Crossjack yard	--	--	--	----	13	0	0	11.8
Bowsprit	28	0	0	25.5	28	0	0	25.5	Bonaventure topsail yard	--	--	--	----	5	1	8	5.0
Spritsail yard	17	0	3	15.5	17	0	0	15.5									

Fig 27: This impression of the English galleon White Bear, *which was built in 1563, is by C J Visscher (1580–1660). Here we see it with the pre-1618 rigging. Later it carried a main topgallant and a fore topgallant sail, an upper spritsail on the spritmast, and a square mizzen topsail on the mizzenmast. There are iron hooks on the fore and main yard arms, for grappling with an enemy's rigging. The ship had two open firing galleries. The belfry with a ship's bell at the halfdeck rail is an unusual feature for this period. (*National Maritime Museum, Greenwich*)*

According to a list from 1602, the *Bear*, which had been built in 1563, was a very large ship with the following dimensions:[13]

Keel length	110ft (33.5m)
Beam	37ft (11.2m)
Depth of hold	18ft (4.5m)
Rake forward	36ft (10.9m)
Rake aft	6.6ft (2.0m)
Burden (Freight Capacity)	732 tons (743.7 metric tons)
Tonnage	915 tons (929.6 metric tons)
Weight of masts and yards	24 tons (24.3 metric tons)
Weight of rigging and tackle	17,000lb (7.7 metric tons)
Bolts of canvas (28yd x ¾yd)	88 bolts (1525.9 sq m)
Anchors	7 x 15,300lbs (6.9 metric tons)
Anchor cables	7 x 30,000lbs (13.6 metric tons)
Weight of ordnance	63 tons (64 metric tons)
Crew	500 men

The *Bear*'s rigging equipment shows that this large four-master had a bonaventure mast: both this and the mizzenmast carried a squaresail above their lateen sails – the mizzen topsail with its topsail yard and crossjack yard. On the recommendation of a naval commission, a mast on the top of the bowsprit (the spritsail topmast) with the spritsail topsail yard was officially introduced at the same time. But we know from pictures that masts and sails like this had appeared on some ships around 1600. These novelties (top gallant sail, square mizzen topsail and spritsail topsail) were characteristic features of large ships in the late seventeenth century. But we can no longer ascribe them to galleons. From the dimensions of the round timbers of the *Bear*, it seems that topmasts and yards were still short at the beginning of the seventeenth century, becoming longer towards the middle of the century. So these round timbers seem to be too long on some of the models and reconstructions of ships from this period.

Topgallant sails were carried only on a few large ships at this time; they are hardly ever found on medium-sized and small ships. Although the *Bear* was a large ship, her old rigging did not have a topgallant sail and the appropriate spars. Even the largest ships carried these sails only in the summer. For winter use, they left their topgallant masts, mizzen topmasts and sprit topmast at home (compare Fig 27).[14]

The sixteenth and seventeenth centuries were not a time of standardisation and rigid, binding rules. So there are no precise instructions for, amongst other things, the location of the masts of a ship. The sources merely mention that the heel of the mainmast should be on the middle of the straight keel, or slightly forward.[15] That was probably the case if the mast had a steep rake aft. The other masts seem to have been placed according to personal discretion and experience. There is an exposition of this problem in an interesting English document, the anonymous *Treatise on Rigging*, c.1620:

Somme ships have 2 missons ether in regard of ther length or qualeties, when in regard of length it is for handsomnes because to much distance betewene masts is unseemly. In regard of ther qualety is when a ship will not keepe the winde and that her head falles of, which is incident to all ships hie built or which have those sails which flatts of the head of the ship (which are those of her ffore masts and spritsayles) stronger than those of her Mayne mast and Misson, which ar the sayles which keepes the heade of a ship to the winde. Sometymes we geve a ship 2 Missons to keepe her head to the winde when she hulles to the ende that she may ride easely on the waves, and not lie tumbling in the trough of the sea betweene two billowes.[16]

Sir Henry Mainwaring (1587–1653), who made the transition from pirate to vice-admiral, gave the gentleman captains of his time an introduction to mast position in his *Seaman's Dictionary*, c.1620:

We say a ship doth gripe when she is apt (contrary to the helm) to run her head or nose into the wind more than she should. There are commonly two causes of this: the one, when a ship may be too deep ahead that her head is not apt, by reason of the weight which presses her down, to fall away from the wind; the other may be the staying of her masts, for if she be a short ship and draw much water, if her masts be stayed too much aftward on, it will cause her head still to run into the wind. The Flemings, being generally long floaty ships, do stay all their masts aftward on very much, else their ships would never keep a wind: for it is apparent to sense that all sails from the mainmast aftward on, the farther aft they stand, the more they keep the ship to the wind; as the head sails, the more forward they stand, the more they have power to flat the ship about from the wind.[17]

The mizzensail was not only important for keeping the bow of the ship to the wind, but was also used by sailors to support a ship at anchor aft, and to prevent the anchor cables becoming entangled when the tide changed.[18]

We also have only general instructions for the rake of masts aft. There were two reasons for the rake of the mainmast: firstly, it diminished the pressure of the sail on the bow; secondly, it shifted the thrust of the expanses of sailcloth aft and countered the ship's tendency to luff. Mainwaring wrote:

Generally, the more aft the masts hang, the more a ship will keep in the wind; and the forwarder, the less. The Flemings stay their masts much aft, because else their ships, being long floaty ships, would never keep a wind; but short and deep ships rather covet upright masts.[19]

By the last-mentioned short and deep ships, Mainwaring almost certainly means vessels built according to English methods. Unfortunately, contemporaneous sources such as this give no directions as to the size of the angle between the masts and the keel. There probably never were any hard and fast rules. We have to look at contemporaneous illustrations for further details: in general, the foremast is vertical and the mizzenmasts are parallel to the rake of the main mast, or at an even sharper rake. The trim, which affects the steering balance of a ship in the water, was always the thing to watch. By trim, Mainwaring and his contemporaries meant not just the more or less horizontal position of the keel, but also the tension of the stays and shrouds, and the play of the mast in its partners.[20] These details had to be found out by trial and error for each ship.

The extent to which a square-rigged ship of this time could sail into the wind is interesting: not more than six compass points.[21] Angles for courses steered, wind direction, one's own position in relation to other ships and to land were expressed by sailors of old through the 32-point divisions of the compass rose. So a quadrant had 8 points, each comprising 11¼°. A square-rigged ship could not sail more than 22½° against the direction of the wind.

A series of rules of thumb have survived regarding the dimensions of masts and yards – all to some degree different from each other. Shorter, stouter round timbers were essentially preferred on safety grounds for ships which had to go on long journeys far from all base points.[22] High lower masts with correspondingly large sails carried shorter tops and yards, to reduce the sail pressure above. People were wary of letting the shrouds and stays put too much pressure on a ship's sides.

In English sources there is a basic unit of measurement for the proportions of the masts and spars: the length of the main (lower) mast. On this was based the length of the other masts and their topmasts. The length of the mainmast could, however, be calculated in different ways: as a fraction of the ship's keel length; as a multiple of the maximum breadth; or according to a formula which contained both the keel length and the breadth. Mainwaring, for example, expressed these rules thus:

. . . the rule and way whereby we give the true proportion for the length of any mast is to take ⅕ of the breadth of the ship, and that multiplied by 3 shall give the just number of feet that the mainmast shall be in length; the bigness to be one inch to a yd in length, but more if it be a made mast.[23]

The following typical dimensions of the masts and spars of large square-rigged ships at the beginning of the seventeenth century can be distilled from a simplification of these rules of thumb:[24]

Mast lengths

Mainmast (as a multiple of the breadth)	2.38–2.7
Foremast and bowsprit (as a fraction of the mainmast)	0.90–0.93
Mizzenmast (as a fraction of the mainmast)	0.73–0.76
Bonaventure mast (as a fraction of the mainmast)	0.58
Main topmast (as a fraction of the mainmast)	0.067

We must bear in mind that the length of the foremast only adheres to this scheme if the mast is based on the straight keel. This rule cannot be applied if the mast heel is located on the curved stem. The length of the mizzenmast and the bonaventure mast also depends on the location of the mast heel. And the height of the mast heel itself is an additional uncertain factor.

Mast diameters

Mainmast (at the partners)	$\frac{1}{36}$ of its length
Foremast and bowsprit	$\frac{15}{16}$ of the mainmast
Mizzenmast	$\frac{1}{36}$ of its length

The masts tapered to flat arc shapes above and below the partners (the framework round the hole in the deck). If, for example, the mast diameter at the partners was 1, then it would be ¾ below the hounds, or position of the cross-trees, and ⅔ at the head and heel. That the mast diameter should be $\frac{1}{36}$ of its length was not a binding rule, and evidently only applied to medium-length masts. Shorter masts, of around 36ft, could have a length-to-diameter ratio of 1:56. Long masts of 96ft could even have a 1:35 ratio, according to a late sixteenth-century manuscript.[25] It is not clear whether these instructions apply to natural or made masts. The thickness of a made mast, which did not consist of a single tree trunk, depended on the available materials and the method by which it was assembled. Made masts were thicker than natural ones. High, natural masts were a luxury in England around 1600. Often only one tree out of thousands would be suitable for use as a mast.[26]

Topmast lengths
The lengths of the topmasts (Rigging plan nos 8, 14, 23)[27] are expressed as fractions of the length of the mainmast:

Fore topmast	0.38–0.44
Main topmast	0.45–0.25
Mizzen topmast	0.28
Bonaventure topmast	0.21–0.24

Topmast diameters
As a fraction of the diameter of the mainmast at the partners:

Fore topmast	0.45
Main topmast	0.50–0.60
Mizzen topmast	0.30–0.36

Topgallant mast lengths (nos. 17, 26)
As a fraction of the length of their topmasts:

Fore topgallant	0.50–0.67
Main topgallant	0.25

The keel length and the greatest breadth of a ship were also used in rules of thumb for the calculation of the yard lengths. Here there are also considerable discrepancies between the various rules. We can sympathise with Captain John Smith (1580-1631), the explorer and founder of the first lasting English settlement in North America, writing in the 1620s:

But to give a true Arithmeticall and Geometricall proportion for the building of all sorts of Ships, were they all built after one mould – as also their Masts, Yards, Cables, Cordage and Sailes – were all the stuffe of like goodnesse, a methodicall rule, as you see, might bee projected; but their lengths, bredths, depths, rakes and burthens are so variable and different, that nothing but experiences can possibly teach it.[28]

Rigging

That also applies, in large measure, to rigging dimensions. We find the following instructions for the length of the mainyard (no 12): half keel length plus breadth of ship, or ⅚ of keel length (Mainwaring), or, simply, the keel length (Harriot). For the foreyard (no 21) we find: ⅘ of the mast length (Mainwaring), or, ¾ of the keel length (Harriot), or, ⅘ of the mainyard (Smith). The top yards (nos 15, 24) were 3⁄7 of the length of the lower yards (Mainwaring), or ⅓ of the lower yards (Harriot), or half of the lower yards (Smith). The topgallant yards (nos 18, 27) could be half the length of the topsail yards (Smith). The sprit yard (no 30) and the mizzen topsail yard could be ¾ of the length of the keel (Harriot), which produces a very long yard. The outlicker was about 2–3yds long (1yd = 0.914m). Unfortunately contemporary sources do not have any details about the dimensions of the tops, which would certainly also have differed enormously.

With standing rigging we come across the feature of elasticity: the leaning of the masts on all sides. At that time it had more meaning than it does today, when stays and shrouds consist of steel ropes. The materials available for constructing the rigging of a sailing ship were wood, hemp and sailcloth – all of varying quality. New hemp hawsers stretched, wood bent – yielding to, rather than resisting, forces like wind pressure and the movement of the hull. Sailors thus distributed the pulling and pushing forces over many points of the hull, which was, in any case, pliant. This resulted in, firstly, adaptability to sudden, heavy stresses; and, secondly, relief of the load on parts in heavy use, thereby lengthening their useful life. The standing rigging of the masts could be slack or taut. This was considered an important factor in the sailing qualities of a ship. Even the play of the mast in its partners was not forgotten, but seen as a possible, if dangerous, means of improving the sailing qualities or trim.[29]

For lateral support of the foremast and mainmast, the rigger first laid the eyes of the tackle pendants over the tops of the lower masts (nos 13, 22) and the trestletrees of the tops. There were thus two pendants, each two to three fathoms (c.3.5–4.5m) long on either side of the mast side. Double or fiddle blocks, through which passed the appropriate tackle, were attached to it. The standing part consisted of a single block, which was secured to a ring on the rails (upper deck no 62) by a hook. Side rigging like this allowed a quick additional pull on the masts, which was not possible through the shrouds alone. This tackle was, of course, also used for moving heavy loads.

After the side tackle came the burton pendants (no 55) on the head of the mast, used for lifting heavy loads over the hatches. After that, the eyes of the shrouds (no 31) were laid above the mast tops, on each side in turn, so that there was always a pair of shrouds leading to the rails on a ship's side, where it was made fast with deadeyes and lanyards. A further pull on the mast could be made through the aft pair of shrouds. These were called swifters, and functioned as forestays and were sometimes also stiffened with tackle. There was one further variable in this highly elastic system: it could be tautened by the catharpins (Fig 28, no 15). This arrangement of ropes ran through small blocks from the shrouds on one side of a ship to the other. In this way sailors could make the shrouds closer to the mast, which was also useful in bracing the yards. This quality of elasticity explains, for example, why there were three further pieces of tackle and their pulleys on the mainmast swifters: the front stay of the mizzen topmast (no 34); the braces of the main topyard (no 43), which were previously on the mizzenmast shrouds; and the tack of the mizzenyard (no 49). Even more pieces of tackle were attached to this swifter later in the seventeenth century.

The number of shrouds on masts of comparable lengths decreased steadily from the sixteenth to the eighteenth centuries. This may possibly have been due to improvements in the quality of the hemp rope. There is no firm rule on this: the number of lower shrouds on the Stockholm galleon model, which appears to be based on a medium-sized ship of about 570 tons (see Chapter 8), can be calculated from the nails used to secure the chain plates. The foremast and mainmast each had seven shrouds (Plan 1, p 86); the odd number is due to the single swifters. The mizzenmast had four shrouds, which were secured without rails. No remnants of the lateral supports for the bonaventure mast have survived on the model. We can assume that there were three shrouds on either side, secured by deadeyes or by tackle, in the same way as galley shrouds. We do know the number of shrouds on the aforementioned large galleon *Bear* of 1563:[30]

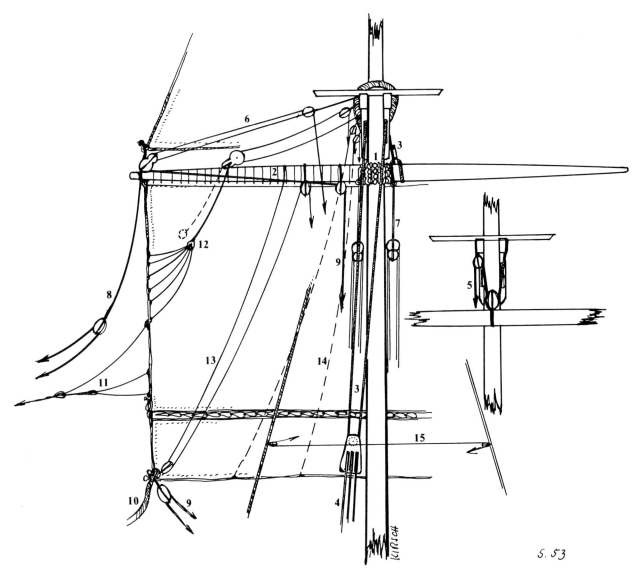

Fig 28: Rigging for a mainyard, c.1610; for clarity, no sails are shown. The various elements, which are not drawn to scale, are numbered in the list on page 45.

1 Parrel	4 Halyard	7 Downhaul	10 Tack	13 Clewline
2 Robbands	5 Jeer	8 Brace	11 Bowline	14 Buntline
3 Tie	6 Lift	9 Sheet	12 Martnets	15 Catharpins

Mainmast	10	Mizzen mast	5
Main topmast	6	Mizzen topmast	3
Main topgallant mast	4	Bonaventure mast	4
Foremast	8	Bonaventure topmast	3
Fore topmast	5	Spritsail topmast (after 1618)	3
Fore topgallant mast	3		

The large eye of the mainstay, one of the thickest ropes in the ship's rigging (no 35), was placed on the mast top, above the shrouds, for the important front support of the mast. It was typical of this period that even the mainstays served as a fixed point for many other parts in the highly elastic rigging. Thus the riggers avoided having to attach their blocks for the running rigging on to firm structures, like spars and trees, if there was a possibility of using the next part of the standing rigging. So the blocks for martnets (no 51), clewline (no 52) and lift (no 38 and Fig 28) are fixed on the eyes of the mainstay. Sailors of the time may have considered that the elasticity was increased further by the profusion of crows' feet (for example, no 36). As the science of rigging later taught, too much importance was attached to them. Specialists knew at the time that crows' feet were follies; Mainwaring tersely remarked: 'They are of no necessity, but only set up by the boatswains to make the ship show full of small rigging.' The decoration on some ships shows that galleons were no longer mere functional constructions, but powerful symbols. So it is hardly surprising that riggers also wanted to contribute something to the splendid appearance and tried to impress the laity, at least, by a maze of rigging. The size of a galleon and its plethora of guns meant that it had a crew of sufficient size to maintain tackle of this sort.

In reading old records, we are often reminded how astonishingly quickly and totally a crew could be weakened and decimated by illness and death. This explains the many labour-saving tackles: a crew reduced after a long voyage was no longer able to move the heavy mechanical appliances which controlled the enormous sails of the time. An anonymous English manuscript from the beginning of the seventeenth century [31] describes the running rigging of a main yard or fore yard. The numbers of the following elements of tackle correspond with those in Fig 28:

1 The Parrell fastens the yeard to the mast.
2 The Robins fasten the saile to the yeard.
3 The Tyes carry the yeard.
4 The Halliers hoyse the yeard.
5 The Gere serves to ease the Tyes and slinge the yeard.
6 The Liftes serve to top the yeard 2.
7 The Trusse serves to heave downe the yeard.
8 The Braces serve to steddy the yeard and set the mayne Topsaile fitly 2.
9 The Shetes serve to round aft the saile and fitt it to every winde 2.
10 The Tackes hale forward the saile and steddyes it downe by a winde 2.
11 The Bowlings serve to keepe the sayle from shaking in the winde.
12 The Martnets hale the outer Litch of the sayle with the shetes and Tackes close up to the yeard.
13 The Clewgarnets hale up the Clew of the sayle close to the yeard.
14 The Buntlines hale up the Bunt of the sayle close to the yeard.
15 The Catharpins serve to set the shroudes stiffe thei belong properly to the rigging of the mast.

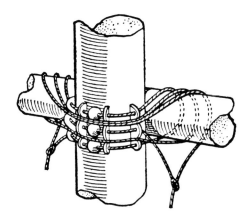

Fig 29: A parrel, c.1600. This is one of various possible interpretations of the hazy written and pictorial sources. We must imagine that there were even more ribs and trucks on the parrel of a ship's mainmast, which have been omitted here for clarity. One downhaul is missing. (From C N Millward, Modelling the Revenge)

It is difficult to reconstruct the precise arrangement of the parrels (no 41 in the rigging plan) from contemporary instructions. Fig 29 shows one interpretation. We must, however, imagine many more beads and ribs on a parrel for a mainmast or foremast. They have been omitted in the interests of clarity. The ends leading downwards went to a tackle, the truss (no 7 in Fig 28). It is difficult to understand from the example in Fig 29 how they could come clear with the leech of the hoisted sail. They probably led over an eye on the yard. The reference to jeers (no 5 in Fig 28) in the aforementioned inventory of the running rigging of a lower yard is interesting: we have to imagine that these were additional to the ties and halyard system (nos 3 and 4 in Fig 28) in large ships. They were sometimes confused with these and are often not shown on reconstructions. They were fitted either singly or in pairs: the halyard was secured to a trestletree on one mast side, led through one block on the yard to another block on the trestletree on the other mast side then to a block on the upper deck, and from there to the jeer capstan in the waist (no 73 in the longitudinal section).

Old sources do not have much to say about sails. Their aerodynamic function was not appreciated in 1600, and Mainwaring wrote, 'We give a bunt to all sails to the intent they may receive much wind, which is the *anima sensitiva* of a ship.' Opinion on the cut of the sail was evidently divided, as contemporary pictures show a diverse range of bunts. From English sources we can infer that sails were sewn together from strips ¾yd (0.68m) wide. They did not yet have any reep bands. For striking they were furled loosely to the yard and secured there. The yard was taken down in this process. Sailors of the galleon era practised the striking of yards, even the main yard, more frequently than those of later times. Footropes were not yet in general use. To secure the sail, the crew would lie on the yard on their stomachs. Mainwaring does, however, mention horses on the sprit yard (no 30). The reason for this was that this yard could not be struck for furling sails. If the area of the large lower sail had to be reduced, the bonnets (detachable strips of sail) were taken down; they measured about one third of the size of the sail to which they belonged.

The mizzen and bonaventure yards were on the lee side during sailing. They were brought round to the other side of the mast if the parrel and the halyard had so much play that the yard could be brought behind the mast in a vertical position. The foot would then be placed on the appropriate side of the mast – surely a difficult job. The dimensions of blocks and rigging is the Cinderella of source material from around 1600. The first lists of rigging dimensions on English warships come from the middle of the seventeenth century. Many other details of the rigging are discussed in Chapter 8.

Alan John Villiers (1902–82), the British sailor and maritime author, made a special voyage in 1956. To celebrate the famous journey made by the Pilgrim Fathers migrating from England to North America in the *Mayflower* in 1620, a replica vessel was launched, to sail from Plymouth, England, to Plymouth, USA. The original *Mayflower* was a typical, small, three-masted merchant ship from the early decades of the seventeenth century. It was a bark of about 180 tons. Sticking as closely as possible to contemporaneous sources,[32] William A Baker, the American shipbuilder, designed a reconstruction of this ship. For power, the ship had, of course, no engine; only its three-masted rig, which followed its 300-year-old predecessor as closely as possible in design and materials. As commander of the ship, Captain Villiers had the unique opportunity of observing the behaviour of such a vessel under realistic conditions on the Atlantic. He could even compare the new *Mayflower* with the large, steel square-riggers he had previously sailed.[33]

At the outset of the voyage, no-one knew how the high-sterned ship would behave under sail. No-one knew how to trim a spritsail whose tacks projected into the open; and no-one knew how to handle the mizzensail and its yard when manoeuvring the sails. Once at sea, the wind rose and the going became rough. The first thing that Villiers, who had hitherto only come across steel stays on steel square-rigged ships, noticed was the amount of movement of the wooden masts, which were stayed with hemp ropes. The specialists had adhered to the old rules of thumb for the thickness of the round timbers, but now all the spars seemed to be too thin. The new *Mayflower*'s masts and bowsprit were hard at work. Villiers saw that the top of the mainmast moved about a foot (0.305m) to the side every time the ship heeled. Of particular concern were the movements of the unstayed bowsprit. It jerked about and bent sharply when pressure was put on it via the spritsail. The spritsail could not be reefed, but had to be furled if the wind became too strong. In practice it had to remain set at any hint of wind, as the counterforce for the high aft superstructure came from it. When the twentieth-century sailors saw, to their amazement, the spars – in particular the bowsprit – bending like fishing rods, they comforted themselves with the thought that, over the centuries, hundreds of thousands of sailors had coped with this problem on thousands of ships. But working on the steeply projecting bowsprit to reach the reeling spritsail yard remained a dangerous matter. The *Mayflower* rolled and lurched badly. Even without any sails, the masts tended towards the sides as the wind increased. The topsails could only be set with difficulty, as the wind pressure made the running rigging billow. The shrouds would be as stiff as a board one moment, then suddenly, so it would seem, have too much play, even when the catharpins had been well tightened. The yards could, in any case, be more sharply braced up by this process than in modern square-rigged ships.

In the course of the voyage Villiers learned how to trim the spritsail. As the bowsprit had no standing rigging, the sprit yard could be canted and brought into a vertical position. The spritsail then functioned as a quadrilateral jib, and pulled well. The ship responded reliably and quickly to this sail – better, Villiers found, than would have been possible with a jib of later centuries. Even the lateen sail on the mizzenmast performed well when the ship had to sail close to the wind. Hampered by the standing rigging of the mast, it was useless in a following wind, but in other respects proved to be a good balancing sail. The mizzen yard always stood in the lee of the mast. It was not difficult to move it from one side to the other when tacking, and it was raised up by the lift. The tackles at the lower end were let loose and the spar behind the mast levered round. This meant that the sail was furled during the operation, as otherwise it would flap about. The *Mayflower*'s heavy rolling caused many parts of the rigging to wear out. So in the early days of the voyage, the crew's main priority was to put mats and fenders everywhere. The foot of the topsail rubbed against the tops; ropework and sailcloth everywhere chafed on wood or on the shrouds. Despite all this care and attention the top and mizzen sails were badly worn.

As old sources stated, the ship could sail at six points into the wind. In ideal conditions the *Mayflower* covered 6½ knots. Its full bow and the drag on its flat stern meant that it could not go any faster. A mile-long wake trailed behind it. Pressure of time and the fixed length of the voyage prevented Villiers from experimenting as much as he would have liked with the hull and the rigging. But on one occasion he was able to scud and thus attempt an important manoeuvre performed by sailors of old: when the wind became so strong that a ship could no longer carry even the smallest sail, they would let it run before the wind. The high aft superstructure held the bow against the sea. The test result was convincing: the *Mayflower* stayed safe and dry. Villiers, the twentieth-century seaman, summed up his experiences with the ancient vessel by saying that he had underestimated Elizabethan sailors. He remembered how, when he first went to sea, old mariners would say that wooden ships with wooden spars and hemp ropework 'came alive' at sea, and moved in a way which iron ships were unable to do.

CHAPTER 3

Ordnance

Trying to picture the ordnance carried on warships in the decades before and after 1600 can be very confusing. There was no standard naming convention for the guns, the dimensions of which sometimes varied from decade to decade; furthermore, there was a plethora of gun types and sub-types. Some types of guns were cast to the same model over a long period of time; others were developed further; yet others were discontinued. Their names, however, might, survive on other models. Some were combinations of various types of guns. They varied in appearance, depending on whether they had been cast (from bronze or iron), or whether they had been forged. Further discrepancies between the different types of guns arose because gun-founders, like shipwrights, worked in non-standard ways. Different countries had different names for similar types of guns. People had different ideas as to what constituted the correct armaments for a ship. And, last but not least, the armaments carried on a ship depended on what was available in the arsenals at the time.

Over the years, and in the course of service, the guns on a ship would be changed, and there were ongoing discrepancies between the (theoretically) ideal equipment of a vessel, and its actual equipment for a particular engagement. In contrast to the eighteenth-century standardised ship's armaments, guns at the time of the galleons were a result of the above-mentioned factors. It all depends at which point in time we home in on the ever-changing process of their development. For this reason, it is not possible to give a precise description of a ship's armaments, in the way that the Stockholm galleon served as a prototype for ship design. We can only try to delineate what was typical of ships' armaments around 1600. Even a contemporaneous specialist would have been unable to give a definitive description of a ship's guns other than those it was carrying at a specific time on a specific voyage.

In England, historians like Julian S Corbett, M Oppenheim and Michael Lewis have covered the development of ships' artillery in the age of the galleon thoroughly. The origins of this development are tied up with Henry VIII, who supplied the impulse for quantum leaps in the development of shipbuilding and gun-founding. At the beginning of his reign, the English were still learning the art of gunnery from the Dutch and the Flemish; along with the Italians, French and Spanish, they had not yet reached the peak of technical progress. That, however, changed with the outbreak of the Anglo-Spanish War (1585–1603).[1] Henry VIII had heavy field and siege weaponry placed on board his ships. There they augmented the small breech-loaders, whose missiles were unable to pierce or split ships' sides.[2]

The various types of guns found on board the carrack, *Mary Rose*, are an example from this period of transition. This capital warship from Henry VIII's fleet sank during a fight with a French fleet on 19 July, 1545. On it were found antiquated forged iron guns on block mounts, next to modern cast bronze guns on wheeled carriages, similar to those in use hundreds of years later.[3] Henry's opportunities for acquiring guns were, at this time, still limited. The only gun foundries in England were in the Tower of London and at Houndsditch, in East London. So he had to purchase most of his guns abroad. Money was scarce, and copper (the main component of the gun-bronze), was expensive. The 'Right to Bells', which allowed an artillery officer to demand the local bells when a fortress capitulated was a partial solution. In addition, many bells in England were confiscated during the Dissolution of the Monasteries, to serve as material for gun-casting.[4]

Later, towards the end of Queen Elizabeth I's reign, the Sussex foundries had developed the casting of iron guns to

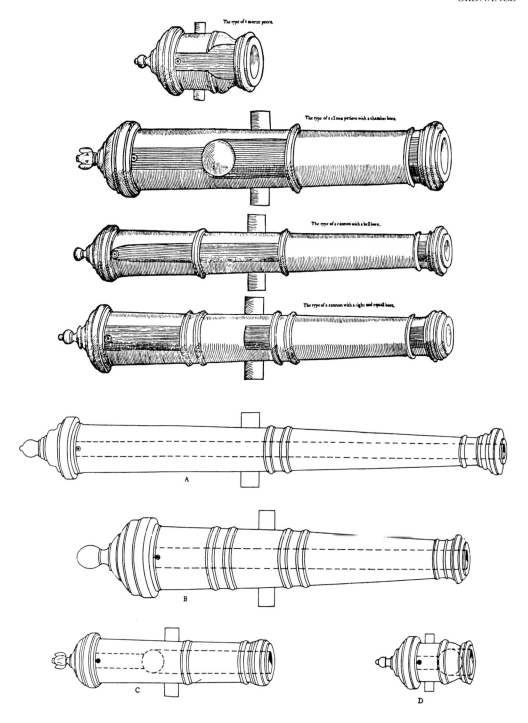

The type of a morter peece.

The type of a canon petriero with a chamber bore.

The type of a cannon with a bell bore.

The type of a cannon with a right and equall bore.

Fig 30: Elizabethan gun-types from Lucar's Three Bookes of Colloquies concerning the arte of Shooting, *1588. As the barrels are not shown to scale, Michael Lewis has redrawn them according to Lucar's measurements.*

Barrel A is a full culverin; a 17-pounder with a bore of 5¼ inches, and a length of 32 calibre. Full culverins were generally positioned on ships' bows and galleries as chasers.

Barrel B is a full cannon; a 42-pounder with a bore of 7in and a length of 18 calibre. Heavy guns like this were rarely seen on ships: the heaviest guns on board were usually demi-cannons.

Barrel C is a perier, a gun with a chambered barrel for 24lb stone shot. (From M Lewis, 'Armada Guns', in Mariners Mirror, Vol 28, 1942)

such a degree that guns and knowledge of the methods of their production were counted among the most valuable assets of the English Crown. Iron guns may well have been heavier and had thicker sides than bronze guns, but they were also cheaper, and therefore suited to mass production.[5] Other European countries soon attempted to acquire such guns. By 1575 the Spanish Governor in the Netherlands was urgently seeking to acquire iron guns from England. By 1613 the Council of Hamburg had the same request, and was asking King James I of England to export, tax-free, 20 'tormenta bellica majora, ponderis gravioris, ex isto genere quod ex ferro funditur' (heavy iron guns) for the use of the town.[6]

How were the guns arranged on a galleon? We get a glimpse of the armaments list for an English galleon from a contract drawn up for a particular voyage:

This Indenture made the seventeenth of July 1585, in the seven and twentieth year of the reign of our sovereign lady Queen Elizabeth, between the right honourable Ambrose, Earl of Warwick, Master of her Majesty's Ordnance General, of the one part, and the right worshipful Sir Francis Drake, knight, on the other part.[7]

The *Elisabeth Bonaventure*, a medium-sized ship which was rebuilt in 1581, was one galleon equipped with guns. Its statistics were:[8]

Keel Length	80ft (24.4m)	Crew	250 men, of whom there were:
Maximum Breadth	35ft (10.6m)		150 sailors
Depth in hold	16ft (4.8m)		30 gunners
Tonnage	560 tons		70 soldiers
Weight of Ordnance	40 tons		

To arm this ship, Drake required:

4 brass demi-cannons	6 brass sakers
4 brass cannon-periers	1 brass minion
8 brass culverins	3 falcons
12 brass demi-culverins	

These guns were all carriage-mounted. The following were also to be supplied for the *Elisabeth Bonaventure*: barrels and chambers for smaller breech-loaders like fowlers and portpieces, which were mounted on blocks and brackets; spare block mounts, and the appropriate wheels, axles and linchpins; various loading devices, munitions and pieces of ropework. The ship's remaining military equipment consisted of coarse and fine powder, lighting fuse, smaller muskets, bows and arrows, halberds, partisans and spears, together with long and short pikes.

This list gives us a good overview of the armaments and other fighting equipment that a warship of about 400 years ago carried on board. It ranged from demi-cannons (then the heaviest guns carried on ships) to bows and arrows, which were a relic from the medieval English longbow tradition. The bow was not officially discarded as a war weapon in England until 1595.[9] In sixteenth and seventeenth century books on gunnery, some authors attempted to classify the proliferation of gun types. Sometimes they ranged the guns according to the ratio of barrel length to calibre (diameter of the bore); sometimes according to the ratio of 'metal to weight of shot'. The second method was, however, a rather theoretical one.[10] In his important work, *Armada Guns*, Michael Lewis divides the guns into four classes (Fig 30):[11] cannons, culverins, periers, and mortars. Only the first three types are larger guns, for use as ship killers, but we will retain this classification for the ensuing exposition.

Cannons were originally called land-guns, for destroying the walls of fortresses. They were bronze muzzle-loaders, which at first fired stone shot; then later, iron cannon-balls. Their bore (they were, properly speaking, cast round a core) was relatively short. Their calibre ranged from 18 to 24 – that is, 18 to 24 cannon-balls laid side by side reached the length of the bore. The latter was smooth; there was no special chamber for loading powder. The sides of cannons

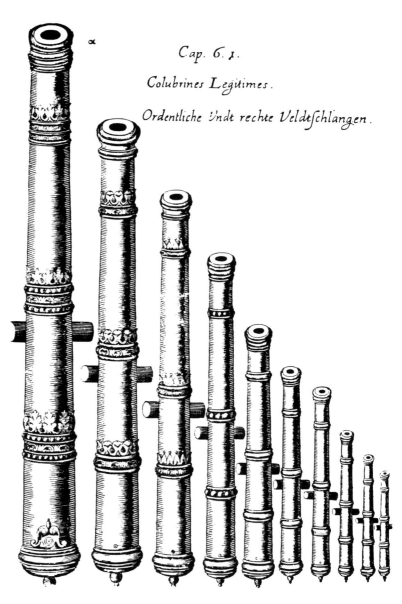

Fig 31: This organ-pipe-like family line-up of culverins apparently belies the difficulties encountered in their naming and classification. The main artillery of armed ships around 1600 consisted of weapons like these, and their shortened versions. (From Norton, The Gunner Shewing the Whole Practise of Artillerie, *London, 1628)*

were weaker than those of other types of guns. Even the required powder load was lighter. Cannons could, however, fire a relatively heavy missile into the middle distance. Lucar, a sixteenth-century author, cites the following proportions for cannon wall strength to calibre in 1588:[12]

Touch-hole	Trunnion	Muzzle
9/8	5/8	3/8

Large cannons, which were known as cannons royal or whole cannons, were not, in practice, taken on board ships. They were too heavy for that. Monson writes that the heaviest ship-guns were demi-cannons, but even this reduced version was only carried in small numbers. In any event, the Spanish plumped more heavily for ship-killer guns of this sort on their Armada ships (1588) than did their adversaries, the English. The latter had opted for more manoueverability and lightness of ships. An average demi-cannon of around 1600 had the following statistics:[13]

Bronze muzzle-loader, iron shot:

Calibre:	6¼–7 in	Weight of gun:	5000–6000lb
Diameter of shot:	¼in less than calibre	Length of mount:	5ft (1.5m)
Weight of shot:	26–38lb (English)	Range (Point-blank):	c.340ft
Length of gun:	10–12ft (3.0–3.3m)		

These guns resembled the later 32-pounders.

Culverins (Fig 31) and the group of smaller guns leading down from them, right down to hand-held weapons like the harquebus, were the most commonly used guns, at least on English ships, around 1600. The name is derived from the Latin, colubrinus (snake-like). They were long guns with high muzzle velocity, a range of widths and high impact. Lucar cites the following metal to calibre ratios:[14]

Touch-hole	Trunnion	Muzzle
9/8	63/64	3/8

Culverins had smooth, unchambered bores, with a length of 25–32 times their calibre. Their differing lengths can be explained by the fact that they generally had to be cast shorter for ships, so as to save on space and weight. The only culverins which retained their original length were those placed on the bow and stern as long-range chasers. An 'average' culverin of around 1600 had the following statistics:[15]

Bronze muzzle-loader, iron shot:

Calibre:	5–5½in	Length of gun	
Diameter of shot	¼inch less than calibre	(normal):	12–13ft (3.6–3.9m)
Weight of shot:	15–17½lb	(shortened):	8½–9ft (2.5–2.7m)
		Weight of gun:	4000–4500lb
		Range (point-blank):	c.400ft

These guns resembled the later 16-pounders.

The demi-culverin, which was the gun most commonly found on English warships of this time, was a smaller version of the culverin. An 'average' demi-culverin of around 1600 had the following statistics:[16]

Bronze muzzle-loader, iron shot:

Calibre:	4½–4¾in	Length of gun	
Diameter of shot:	¼inch less than calibre	(normal):	12ft (3.6m
Weight of shot:	9–9½lb	(shortened):	8½–9ft (2.5–2.7m)
		Weight of gun:	3000–3400lb
		Range (point-blank):	c.400ft

These guns resembled the later 9-pounders.

The next smallest gun of the culverin type was the saker, on which we find the following statistics:[17]

Bronze muzzle-loader, iron shot:

Calibre:	3½–4in	Length of gun:	8-10ft (2.4–3.0m)
Diameter of shot:	¼in less than calibre	Weight of gun	1300–1800lb
Weight of shot:	5–7lb		

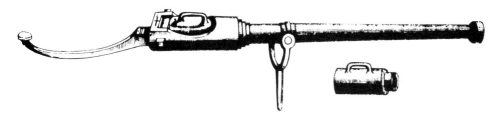

Fig 32: This Kammerstück or Drehbasse roughly corresponds to the English sling or base. It had a removable chamber for the powder which was secured in a housing behind the barrel by a wedge. The length of the barrel was approximately 1.2m; that of the chamber 0.22m. Breech-loaders like this were used against enemy crews. (From A Essenwein, Quellen zur Geschichte der Feuerwaffen, *Leipzig 1877)*

These guns resembled the later 6-pounders.

The minion was an even lighter culverin, with the following statistics:

Bronze muzzle-loader, iron shot:

Calibre:	3–3¼in	Length of gun:	7½–8ft (2.2–2.4m)
Diameter of shot:	¼in less than calibre	Weight of gun:	1200lb
Weight of shot:	3–4lb		

There are even lighter guns in the English nomenclature: falcons, falconets and bases. The base was a breech-loader with a calibre of approximately 1¼ in; a barrel length of 4ft (1.2m) and a chamber of 9in.[18]

Periers were a group of guns which, (particularly the small, light models) were carried on board ship as breech-loaders. Drake, however, specified four of the heavy bronze cannon-periers in his equipment list for the galleon *Elisabeth Bonaventure*. These soon became obsolete on English ships. The name perier comes from the Italian petriero; that is, stone-firing gun. They were short, light guns, which somewhat resembled the later howitzers and carronades. They had a barrel length of 8 calibre or less. The early models still fired stone shot and so had a chambered barrel, as these missiles had to be fired with a small load of powder only, or they would break up. Periers could also fire firework-like munition, to spark off fires and create confusion on enemy ships.[19] The periers' thickness to calibre ratio was as follows (continued on page 54):

Fig 33: A forged breech-loading gun with a replaceable chamber in its block mount, which sank in 1545 with the carrack Mary Rose, *a capital ship in Henry VIII's fleet. The gun was salvaged in 1840. A number of the iron rings on the barrel and the bedding, joining the two parts with ropes, have rusted away. English portpieces and fowlers, still part of the equipment of armed ships towards the end of the sixteenth century, would have looked like this.*

Touch-hole	Trunnion	Muzzle
1/2	1/4	1/6

Heavy perier models were hardly ever found on English or Dutch ships of around 1600. Only the Portuguese continued to use them.[21] The large cannon-periers had the following statistics:

Muzzle-loader; stone, later iron, shot:

Calibre:	6in		Weight of gun:	3000lb
Weight of shot:	24lb			

Smaller stone-firing models were known as portpieces, fowlers and slings (Fig 32). They were all breech-loaders with several interchangeable chambers of smaller diameter than the barrel. The chambers contained the powder load and, in contrast to muzzle-loaders, allowed a quick succession of fire. A portpiece was a gun with an internal barrel diameter of 5½in, and a chamber of 3½in. The stone shot were 5¼in in diameter and weighed 9lb. The barrel of guns like these was known as the hall, after the main room in houses of the Tudor period; and in contrast to the small, interchangeable chamber. The hall of a portpiece was about 8 calibre long, that is, less than 4ft (1.2m). The chamber was 16in long.[22] Portpieces and fowlers were mounted on blocks (Fig 33):

> Instead of trunnions the chase of the piece had on either side two square tenons which were morticed into the block or carriage, so that the piece was held fast in it.[23]

The block sometimes had two short legs at the front. The tail was supported by an upright post with locking holes for wedges or pins. This meant that the gun could be lifted up. In its firing position on board ship, the gun muzzle lay on the lower edge of the gun port and was secured by a rope. It could not recoil.

Slings and bases were rather smaller breech-loaders than portpieces. The breech mechanism seems to have been very similar in all these guns:

> Welded upon the 'hall' by means of cheek-pieces and enfolding it from trunnion ring to breech, was a kind of stout iron stirrup with a cradle on the under side. Into this, the 'chamber' was placed, and its chamfered fore end then wedged home into the breech by means of discs of wood and lead or leather driven in between the butt of the chamber and the base of the stirrup. This frame or stirrup was known as the 'tail'. To prevent the chamber jumping when the piece was discharged, it was locked in its place by a wedge and forelock, slots being cut for this purpose on either side of the stirrup.[24]

This method of securing the chamber was not without danger. Lucar wrote:

> When a gunner will give fire to a chamber-piece he ought not to stand upon that side of the piece where the wedge of iron is placed to lock the chamber in the piece, because the said wedge may through the discharge of the piece fly out and kill the gunner.[24]

The mortars on board ships of this time were smaller, large calibre, short-barrelled guns. They were used to repel boarders. They were loaded with uncompacted ammunition and fired at people: small wonder then that they were known as murderers.

It is not easy to say how guns were arranged on ships' decks at this time. We do have a list, from 1595, of the guns for a new English ship, probably the *Warspite*. The ship had the following statistics:[25]

Fig 34: This rigging-less ship shows different types of fireworks used to set fire to an enemy ship. Furttenbach listed the fire weapons in use. They range from 'guns loaded with small-shot and chains' and 'chambered guns standing on iron brackets' which were loaded with wildfire to 'hand guns' and 'grenades or storm-shot'. They served to create 'not just a great row, but also considerable confusion amongst the people'. (From J Furttenbach, Architectura Navalis, 1629)

Keel length (excluding stempost and sternpost)	90ft (30.1m)
Maximum breadth	36ft (10.9m)
Depth in hold	16ft (4.8m)
Freight capacity	518 tons
Tonnage	648 tons
Weight of masts and yards	17 tons
Weight of other rigging	14,400lb
Anchors and anchor ropes	7
Weight of ordnance	40 tons
Crew at sea	300 men, of whom there were: 190 sailors 30 gunners 80 soldiers

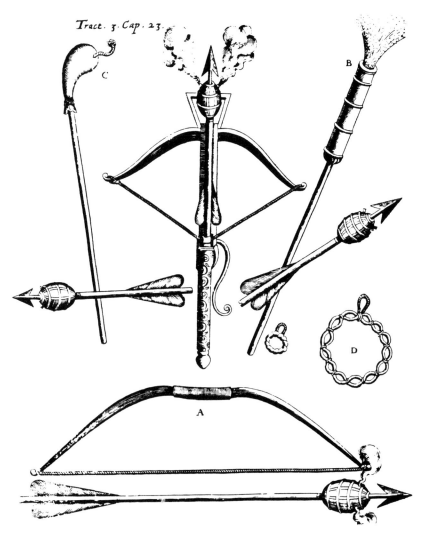

Tract. 3. Cap. 23.

Fig 35: *Firework-type weapons like these were used to set fire to an enemy ship. Fire arrows could be fired from a bow or a crossbow. The staves with powder loaded at the point were used to repel enemy boarders. The rings were powder-filled tubes, for throwing at an enemy ship. Perhaps the real skill in using weapons like these lay in not setting fire to one's own ship.* (From Norton, The Gunner Shewing the Whole Practise of Artillerie, *London 1628*)

The *Warspite* carried the following guns:

Lower deck, side	12	culverins
Lower deck, stern and bow	4	culverins
Upper deck, broadside	8	demi-culverins
Upper deck, stern and bow	4	demi-culverins
Waist, fore and aft,	6	sakers
Half-deck	2	sakers

If we multiply the number of guns on the *Warspite* by the weight of artillery given in the foregoing description of gun types, we arrive at a minimum of 47 English tons: considerably more than the galleon's quoted artillery weight. We should attribute this partly to differences in the measurements of individual authors; partly to the possibility that the ship was carrying a different combination of guns when the statistics were compiled. This is only one example of the difficulties we encounter when we try to establish the artillery carried on a warship of this time.

The culverins and demi-culverins listed separately for the *Warspite*'s bow and stern are regular, long chasers. We can

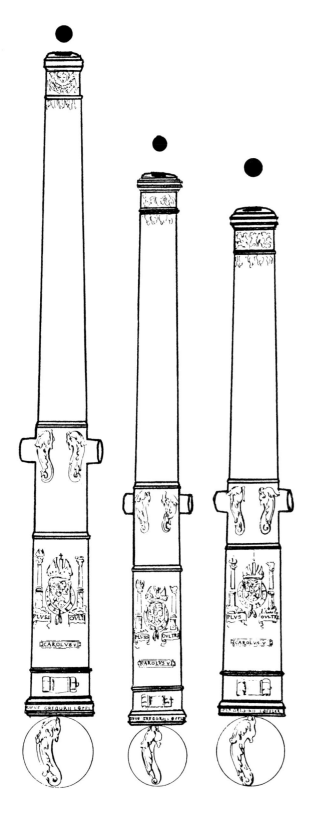

*Fig 36: From Emperor Charles V's artillery book (1542). These long-barrelled guns, a long Schlange, next to a half Schlange and a shortened Schlange, corresponded to English culverins. (*From A Essenwein, *Quellen zur Geschichte der Feuerwaffen*, Leipzig 1877*)*

assume that the remaining guns on the broadside were of the type shortened for use on board ship. The *Warspite*'s guns listed above belonged to the main armament, which could inflict damage on an adversary. The secondary armament, which was employed against individual people, is not specified. It consisted of breech-loading guns placed on rails, galleries, mast tops and bulkheads. The ship could still be defended with these guns even after the enemy had taken part of the deck. Only breech-loading guns could be used for defence from behind bulkheads, as, of course, these could not be reloaded from the front. Furttenbach wrote (1629): '[At the bulkheads there are] small secured chambers, or hail-shot guns on iron brackets, which can be loaded very quickly from the rear, and can rake and enfilade the whole upper floor (upper deck).'[26] From the *Warspite*'s list, we know that the heaviest guns on a medium-sized galleon of around 1595 were culverins. Ten years earlier, Drake had had his rather smaller *Elisabeth Bonaventure* equipped with four heavy demi-cannons and four cannon-periers. The trend in heavy arms on galleons (a relic from Henry VIII's time) was receding. Sir Richard Hawkins (see p 17), the most advanced naval expert of the day, listed the advantages of lighter guns:[27] they could be loaded more easily, and they could be moved from one side of the ship to the other more easily; they weighed the ship down less, and it was simpler to place them on their mounts. Apart from that, Hawkins did not think much of long-range guns at sea, with their inaccurate firing. Short guns and close combat with artillery were his preference.

Elizabethan galleons had a small weight of artillery, in comparison with ships of the same size in later centuries. This was due to the lines of the hulls: ships which were constructed by the whole-moulding method did not have the carrying capacity later achieved when the rib futtocks were rounded out. Opinion at the time was divided on the correct length of a gun barrel. Monson was afraid that long guns held the pressure of the powder gases longer, and consequently there was a higher risk of explosion on board ship. Bursting guns could cause appalling injuries, and sometimes cost more lives than enemy action. On the other hand, powder burned better and more economically in a long barrel: short guns wasted a lot of powder. Like Hawkins, and many contemporary experts, Monson considered long-range firing at sea with long-barrelled guns to be a futile exercise: 'for he that shooteth far off at a ship had as good not shoot at all.'[28]

From the point of view of the metal-founder, the length of a gun barrel helped to compensate for the deficiencies in contemporary metallurgy. Guns were cast standing upright, with the muzzle upwards. The mould contained a central core (later to become the bore) around which the metal was poured. This casting technique meant increased stability of the barrel in the powder chamber area. The metal in the muzzle region was more brittle and less resistant. To compensate for this, the metal-founders made a thicker ring round the barrel muzzle. This became a characteristic feature of European guns.[29] Long guns required more bronze in relation to the weight of the cannon-balls fired, and were consequently more expensive. Shortened 9ft culverins were generally introduced into the English fleet through the Navy Programme of 1588. However, the weight of the barrels gradually increased over the decades, as the sides became stronger to match the more powerful powder.[30]

Non-rusting bronze remained the best material for guns at sea until well into the seventeenth century. It was, however, expensive, so people soon began to experiment with cast-iron guns. These often exploded during testing; if they had safe walls of sufficient thickness, they would be too heavy for use on board ship.[31] But experiments continued, as bronze artillery cost from three to four times as much as iron. Not until 1626 did an English Naval Commission announce that it had finally succeeded in casting iron guns which were equal to, or even superior to, bronze guns. The English were now leaders in the field of iron-gun casting, and the specialists from other countries learned the art of iron-casting from the English, just as they had previously used Dutch, Italian or French expertise for their bronze-cast guns. Iron guns gradually replaced bronze ones on smaller European ships during the course of the seventeenth century. Large, first-rate ships retained their bronze artillery rather longer.[32]

In the first half of the seventeenth century the motley composition of ships' broadsides began to be replaced with uniform batteries. This simplified the procedures for loading and storing missiles and powder. The formerly prized culverins were gradually replaced by cannons, as progress was made in the casting of iron guns and the quality of the powder improved. The destructive power of a heavy cannon-ball now counted for more than its speed through the muzzle and, consequently, its range. Culverins became shorter; their calibre and barrel length approaching those of cannons. Small wonder, then, that the word cannon came to be used as the general term for all weapons larger than muskets.[33] At the beginning of the eighteenth century the terms cutt and butt (shortened culverins and sakers) disappeared completely from English usage; just as they had disappeared somewhat earlier from the vocabulary of continental gunners.

Were heavy guns on ships of around 1600 discharged with recoil, or not? Recoil could not be taken for granted, in the way that it could in Nelson's time. Contemporaneous reports describe how guns should be tied fast in battle and loaded in the outboard state. The deck breadth alone of smaller ships would not have sufficed for the recoil of a long culverin. As we will see later, this is borne out by the tactics used by galleons in attack. Even in the middle of the seventeenth century, the recoil and loading of guns behind closed gunports was no routine matter, even on large ships. On 17 February 1658 three Dutch warships, lying in the harbour at Goa in India, attacked three Portuguese galleons at sea. The German mercenary soldier Johann Jakob Saar was on board one of the Dutch ships, and wrote:

> They had to load their guns from outside: we, in contrast had gunports which we could let down as soon as a shot was fired, and then pull up when the gun had been cooled off with vinegar and reloaded. They had large, heavy ships: ours, being lighter, meant we could fire two broadsides before they could fire once. They had many fatalities and had to retire to their harbour.[34]

The chain wales on the foremast and mainmast of the Stockholm galleon model are very wide (see view on the upper deck of the reconstruction, no 62 and the section of rib 8, no 25). There is thus virtually an outboard gangway at the height of the upper deck, from which the upper-deck guns (possibly demi-culverins and sakers) could be conveniently loaded and cleaned.

Apart from iron, and occasionally stone, shot, there was a variety of special munition for harassing the rigging, hull and crew of an enemy ship (Fig 34). Monson lists the equipment entrusted to a gunner: 'A gunner is to be provided, besides his ordnance, with powder and shot of all kinds, firepikes, cartridges, case shots, cross-bar shot, langrel shot, chain shot, armed arrows of wild fire, and grenades of divers kinds.'[35]

Cartridges were small packages of material or paper, containing the right quantity of powder for each gun. This pre-packaging of powder was very important at sea, as unwrapped powder could not be handled on deck. Monson continues (Fig 35):

> Fireworks are divers, and of many compositions, as arrows trimmed with wildfire, pikes of wildfire to stick burning into a ship's side to fire her. There are also divers sorts of grenades, some to break and fly in abundance of pieces every way, as will your brass balls and earthen pots, which when they are covered with quarter bullets stuck in pitch, and the pots filled with good powder, in a crowd of people will make an incredible slaughter. Some will burn under water, and never extinguish till the stuff be consumed; some will burn and fume out a most stinking poisonous smoke; some being only of oil, anointed on anything made of dry wood, will take fire by the heat of the sun when it shines hot.

It was not for nothing that gunners and artificers were advised to go ashore, 'or otherwise into sea far from the ship' to make their fireworks. The wildfire mentioned in the quotation, with which pikes and arrows were smeared, must not, of course, be confused with the medieval speciality of the same name. The secret recipe for that substance was lost for ever in the sack of Constantinople in 1204.[36] Monson seems to know some of the other inflammable mixtures more from hearsay than from first-hand experience.

Up to this point, the names of guns of around 1600 have been culled from English sources and technical works. What names were given to guns intended for use only in German-speaking areas? We get a glimpse of these in the Artillery List for the *Adler*, a large Lübeck warship of 1566. Its keel length was 122ft (35.5m; 1 Lübeck ft = 0.292m). This ship, however, had a lifespan of over sixty years, and it is not clear from which decade the following artillery list comes.[37] The *Adler's* main artillery consisted of (continued on page 61):

Fig 37: A man poling his boat across a small harbour basin. The boat holds cannon mounts typical of the period. (Extract from an engraving by Robert de Baudous, after Cornelis Claesz van Wieringen, 1618. Rijksmuseum, Amsterdam)

8 bronze Kartaunen (cannons), for 40lb iron shot

6 bronze Halbekartaunen (demi-cannons), for 20lb iron shot

26 bronze Feldschlangen (demi-culverins), for 8–10lb iron shot

On board there were also twenty-eight evidently old, forged Steinbüchsen for stone shot of 10-30lb, with appropriate chambers.

The secondary armaments consisted of:

20 Steinbüchsen (periers), for 3lb stone shot

20 Quartierschlangen (quarter culverins), for 5lb stone shot

40 Quartierschlangen (quarter culverins), for 1½lb stone shot

These secondary guns were breech-loaders with appropriate chambers.

'Kartaunen', also known as 'Nachtigall' (nightingales) or 'Sängerin' (female singers), were first referred to as 'Kanonen' (cannons) in the *Geschützbuch für Kaiser Karl V* c.1542, an important source work for the science of arms. Emperor Charles V's cannons, with their 40lb iron shots, are comparable to English full cannons; Lübeck Halbkartaunen (Halbekanonen) to English demi-cannons. At any rate, the Lübeck Halbekartaunen fired 20lb shot; Emperor Charles V's half-cannons fired 24lb shot; and English demi-cannons of around 1600 fired shot of between 26–33lb. Any form of standardisation was virtually unknown at this time. So it is only possible in exceptional cases to classify guns with similar-sounding names, or names with similar etymological roots, as having technically similar barrels as well.

The Lübeck 'Feldschlangen' for 8–10lb iron shot were comparable to English demi-culverins. These were long-barrelled guns for 9–9½lb iron shot. Serpent or culverin-type guns were mainly found on ships. Steinbüchsen, the forged-iron breech-loaders which the Lübeck ships carried in quantity, are described as 'well-suited to ships' in contemporaneous books on artillery, as they could be reloaded in quick succession, without taking up much room. They were perier-type guns: short-barrelled with large calibre; being heavy, they were no longer carried on Dutch and English ships of around 1600. The smaller Steinbüchsen could also be loaded with Hagel (small shot) and Feuerwerk (fireworks), and were used as anti-personnel weapons in repelling boarding crews. They were described, overwhelmingly, as dangerous by their contemporaries. They were not only dangerous to anyone who found themselves in front of the barrel, but also to the person standing behind it. Daniel Speckle (also Specklin), the town architect of Strassburg, wrote in 1600:

Some people want to use chambered guns, for speed, as they can load some chambers and smear the touch-hole with wax or tallow; then when they wish to shoot, push the shot into the barrel, then the chambers, more pins, and then set fire. My reply to them is that they may well be very quick, but there is a lot of smoke; they are dangerous and inaccurate in firing, and more of a liability on ships.[38]

The Lübeck Quartierschlangen (quarter-culverins) were breech-loaders for 5lb and 1½lb stone shot, and were comparable to the smaller English perier-type guns (portpieces, fowlers and slings).

In the early decades of the seventeenth century (after the experiences of the Thirty Years War), authors attempted to simplify the multifarious, and confusing, practices concerning the naming and sizing of guns. In 1627 the engineer Joseph Furttenbach wrote in his *Halinitro-pyrobolia. Beschreibung einer newen Büchsenmeisterey*: 'The diverse names given to guns years ago have become so intermingled that I myself do not have brain enough to distinguish homers, singers, nightingales, basilisks, apes and so on'.[39]

Furttenbach reduced the proliferation of gun types, and tried to give only the shape and name 'which are used by reasonable and experienced people on land and at sea'. He divided guns into three 'genera',[40] culverins, cannons, and chambered guns:

Culverins

Name	Barrel length (calibre)	Shot weight (lb)
Smeriglio	38	½–1 (lead)
Falchoneto	36	2–3 (iron)
Sagro	32	4–6 (iron)
Moiana (particularly used on galleys)	26	8–10 (iron) (hybrid type)
Meza columbrina, or demi-culverin	32	12–18 (iron)
Columbrina, or full culverin	32	20–35 (iron)

Cannons

Name	Barrel length (calibre)	Shot weight (lb)
Quarter cannon	28	15–16 (iron)
Demi-cannon	24	25–30 (iron)
Full cannon	18	50–60 (iron)
Bastard (suitable for galleys) 1	36½	9½ (iron)
2	28	11 (iron)

Furttenbach's third genus is chambered guns. These fired 10–20lb shot, small shot and fireworks, and were 8½ calibre long.

To return once more to the *Geschützbuch für Kaiser Karl V* (Fig 36), even then, more than seventy years before Furttenbach, the classification of gun types was drastically simplified, as the following list (excluding mortars) shows:[41]

Name	Weight (lb)	Name	Weight (lb)
Cannon	40	Short culverin	12
Demi-cannon	24	Saker	6½
Culverin	12	Falconet	3
Demi-culverin	6		

The practice of naming guns according to the weight of the shot (for example, 24-pounder, 12-pounder etc) did not come into use in German-speaking areas until 1720–30.[42]

At first glance, mounts (known as Lafetten or Ramperten) of around 1600 seem to resemble those which were still to be found on ships of the eighteenth and early nineteenth centuries (Fig 37). They were four-wheeled carriage mounts of the type which had existed since the second half of the sixteenth century. But they were constructed in a different manner to that used in later centuries: the base consisted of a thick wooden bed, to which were tenoned two side-pieces. These pieces were stepped to the rear, so that a rod could be placed across them and the cannon, rather crudely, raised upwards. The two axles were bolted on under the wooden base. In the early stages, the mount's front and rear wheels were often of similar size. As the bases soon rotted away through constant dampness, they were severely reduced in size or omitted altogether. The side-pieces were then joined together with long rod-like iron bolts, and the axles were bolted directly on to them.[43] A whole row of early carriage-mounts emerged on the decks of the *Wasa* when it was raised in Stockholm harbour.

CHAPTER 4

In Battle

NUMEROUS sources tell us what a conflict between galleons and galleys or other sailing ships looked like at the turn of the seventeenth century. Battles were always rather better reported by the participants than, say, ship construction details. Knowledge about shipbuilding was the preserve of a few specialists, and was, for the most part, not written down. Sailors' deeds of derring-do were more interesting than their vessels. Unfortunately, there are no chronicles from this early period by men before the mast. Few could read and write: in any case, a life of privation would have left any literate ones with little energy for record-keeping. So virtually the only reports – official and unofficial – in existence were written by the officers in charge.

Around 1600 the highly seaworthy galleon had successfully ousted all other types of warships in the rough waters of the Atlantic. Fleets consisting of galleys survived only in the Mediterranean. But even in calm seas – the ideal weather condition for galleys – they had to have both superiority in numbers and good luck to be successful against a determined galleon attack. Even in the Mediterranean there had been, by 1609, a Spanish fleet consisting only of sailing ships, which had managed without the help or hindrance of galleys.[1] That, perhaps, indicates that galleys were already of diminishing significance even there. William Monson, to whom we are indebted for much of our detailed knowledge of seafaring in his day, reported the last occasion on which the Spanish attempted, with galleys, to engage the English and the rebel Dutch (in the Atlantic and the English Channel). Both nations ruled the open sea with their sailing warships.

In 1599 the young Genoese Frederico Spinola led a group of six galleys from Spain to the coast of Flanders, where the ships were stationed at Gravelines, Dunkirk and Sluys. Opportunities for galleys to enter these harbours were limited by the tides, and another drawback of these vessels soon came to light: they could not stay at sea for long, as they relied on human labour and could only carry limited supplies; they required a safe harbour in the vicinity.[2] Dutch sailing warships and English galleons were patrolling the English Channel. Regardless of the weather, they could remain at sea longer than the Spanish galleys with their low freeboard. That Spinola achieved any successes at all against Dutch and English merchant ships can therefore be ascribed to his personal courage.[3]

Three years later, in 1602, Spinola was leading another group of galleys against the rebellious northeners, when he was recalled by the Viceroy of Portugal to see to the protection of the richly-laden Portuguese carrack, the 1700-ton *San Valentino*. The latter had sought protection on the roadstead at Sesimbra, east of Cape Espichel. Hostile English galleons had been sighted. Not less than eleven galleys (including three from the Spanish Admiral Alvaro de Bazán), soon formed a defensive line for the treasure ship. They faced five English galleons. The English had known how to fight galleys since their second attempt on Cadiz (1596), when twenty oared boats had been unable to impede the conquest of the town. This time the 33-year-old Vice-Admiral Monson made the first attack. He anchored his large 530-ton galleon *Garland* so that the guns on both sides could fire at the galleys. We can surmise that Monson's aggressiveness was fuelled by the fact that he had spent a year (1591) as a galley-slave on one of these Spanish galleys. What was astonishing was the self-confidence of the English, and the trust they placed in their new weapon, the broadsides-armed sailing ship. The galleys were forced to withdraw when the other galleons joined the attack. Later the much-prized *San Valentino* surrendered. When the fighting was over, there were five dead on the *Garland*; on the open galleys, they amounted to hundreds.[4]

De galeyen van Frederik Spinola door 's Landts oorlogs scheepen overseilt in den Jaere 1602.

Fig 38: This copper engraving by the Master Jan Luyken shows an episode in the battle between Dutch warships and Spinola's galleys. The Mond, Vice-Admiral Cant's ship, *is ramming the Spanish galley* San Felipe, *an example of the inferiority of the light-weight Mediterranean oared ship against the robust north European sailing ships. (Rijksmuseum Amsterdam, Cat F Müller, no 1197)*

Spinola's galleys met their fate in the same year (24 and 25 September, 1602). A group of English and Dunkirk warships captured the galleys in the English Channel. The latter tried, in vain, to row against the wind. The exhausted slaves pulled at their oars for twenty-four hours, unable to make progress. Two galleys sank during the night after one of the sailing warships fired a broadside and another sailing ship rammed them (Fig 38). Out of a crew of four hundred, only forty people survived the catastrophe. Another of Spinola's galleys later sank in Calais harbour, providing the town with firewood over the following winter.[5] The end came for Spinola's capitana, the leading galley, and her commander, when they were attacked three years later by the large Black Galley, a ship which had been built by the

Dutch in answer to the Spanish galleys, and which operated in conjunction with sailing ships.[6] The sailing ships from the north triumphed resoundingly over the galleys from the south. Monson explains how a galleon should proceed against galleys:

> The chief annoyance that can be done a galley in fight is to devise the destruction of the slaves and oars, for without them galleys are of no use. And therefore be they galleys, or ships that fight with galleys, they must seek with cross-bar and langrel shot to hurt and spoil their men and oars. And in this case a ship that carries her ordnance low, and hath her hull high-built has a great advantage of a galley, for her ordnance will lie level with her, and being ahead or astern of her she may have the fortune with a cross-bar shot to take away the whole side of her oars, and if the galleys be forced by desperateness to attempt to board the ship then, by reason of her height and high charging, they shall not be able to enter her.[7]

The risk to sailing ships in attacking galleys lay in the fact that the latter attempted to row in a line, ahead or astern of the sailing ship. The galley helmsman knew he was in the right position for firing when he could see his mast and the masts of the sailing ships in alignment. Those on board sailing ships feared the shots from a galley's large, central main gun, which was usually a cannon. The large gun was built into the central gangway (coursier) at the front of the galley. The galley aimed with its whole hull, and could inflict serious damage on the sides and rigging of its opponent's ships. Galleys were often armed with four small guns in the prow, parallel to the main gun.

A galleon could reply with at most four guns from the stern: two long culverins (chasers) in the stern ports of the gunroom, and perhaps two additional guns above this room, under the deck of the upper gun room. Monson valued the open firing galleries still in existence on ships of his period. Fowlers and smaller guns could be placed there to increase the fire-power from the stern.[8] If, however, a galleon succeeded in firing a broadside against a galley, the effect on the overfilled, totally unprotected oared vessel was gruesome.

Since time immemorial the Mediterranean had been the galleys' own domain. But there, too, it was increasingly the case that oared vessels could no longer force a victory over heavily armed sailing ships, even in ideal weather conditions. On the morning of 8 August 1626, the English galleon *Sampson* was lying at the island of Malta. There was 'not a breath of winde', and the sea was 'as smooth as glasse'. The walls of the capital city Valetta were in sight. The ship was a typical, well-armed merchant-ship of the period. It was equipped in such a way that it could have found a place in any war fleet. Large merchant-ships carrying valuable cargoes in the Mediterranean only stood a chance against pirates and other attackers if they were well-armed. The *Sampson* had been built in England in the 1620s. She was a large 600-ton ship, with a crew of 200. Her ordnance consisted of thirty-two iron guns. Six of these were culverins; the remainder demi-culverins, sakers and minions.[9] Equipping a ship like this for a trading voyage was an expensive business, and the value of the cargo had to be enough to justify the outlay. On this occasion Sir Thomas Roe was on board. He had been the English Ambassador in Constantinople. Roe was on his journey home to England, accompanied by his family and suite.

At ten o'clock they saw, from the galleon, that four galleys of the Knights of Malta were coming out of the harbour at Valetta. What subsequently happened is recounted in a detailed report which was most probably written by the ambassador himself.

> They came up all abrest, right with the starre-boord quarter of our ship: which warned us to fit sailes and selves to fight, not knowing their purpose. When they came neere, the Admirall galley, without sending boat, or speaking with us, made a shot, which fell short: then rowing neerer, made another which did almost reach us. And comming still on, the Vice Admirall gave a third, all demy-cannon, that flew over us, between our masts. These we supposed they made to try the length of their ordnance, and to lie there for batterie; for they stopped, and piked halfe their oares [ie, raised them out of the water]. Whereupon we sent them a culverin shot, that grazed under the Admiral's starre-boord bow; and soe we began a sharpe fight between twelve and one.[10]

Although it was flying the English flag, with the red cross of St George, the galleon was attacked by the Christian

Knights of Malta. The Order was in a constant state of war with unbelievers, and viewed all goods from Turkish territories as its booty, and its due, even if they were being transported on Christian ships.[11]

A three-hour long artillery duel then developed between the galleys and the galleon, with its 9-pound demi-culverins on its broadsides. Both sides scored direct hits. The report continues:

> Then Captain William Rainsborow [who was in command of the galleon], finding a breath of wind to give the ship motion; considering that he was a great marke on the broad-side, and the gallies very narrow, keeping their prowes sharpe toward him, and that he could beare little [armament] upon them, trimmed his sailes before the winde, and brought them to a sterne fight . . . the *Sampson* could then beare upon them two whole culverin in her stern-chase, and two transome-culverins in the gunne-room and two sakers in the great Cabbin.

Eventually they let the ship yaw, so that the bow guns could also be fired at the galleys. Roe has this to say on the galleys' method of fighting:

> Their manner of fight was, when they were all laden [had their guns loaded], they rowed up, and brought all the masts of our ship together, and then gave all their gunnes; having fired, they fell asterne; and this in order *alternis vicibus*; but yet we reached them [with our guns]. The Admirall of the gallies gave eight pieces at once, so that she appeared all fire; one demi-cannon of twenty-five pound bullet, two demi-culverin, five Saker and Minion. All the rest were alike armed, and they plyed their ordnance very hard and often dangerously . . .they shot at the mast and yards of our ship and maimed them almost all in a line; hoping to see some fall, and then they had lain by us [would have bought the gallies alongside to board us]. But it was so calme, that the masts strained not, though they were almost spoiled.
>
> About five o'clocke they paused, and the Admirall sent [a signal] to his Fleet: whereupon they took a resolution, either to boord, dismay or sinke us; and came up on our larboard quarter all abrest, within pistole shot, and their swords drawne, and Trumpets sounding; bidding us Amaine for Malta [lower our top-sail in sign of yielding] . . .Then began a hot fight, and too hot for them, for the *Sampson* forbare, and gave them not a shot untill they were very neere, and almost under us; and then poured in two Culverin, and two demy culverin, and one Saker with a round shot and a case, that raked them fore and aft: and they having given us all their gunnes together, began to fall againe asterne. But we . . .sent them a broadside at parting.[12]

The battle lasted seven hours; the galleys fired 400 shots from large guns at the sailing ship. Over 120 cannon-balls hit the hull, masts, yards and other parts of the rigging. The sailing ship remained afloat, and was even able to continue on its way. That, however, was probably only because of the exceptionally good weather. The *Sampson* had fired fifty-six shots from its culverins, and exhausted ten barrels of powder in total. Amazingly, it suffered only one fatality – a passenger – apart from two sheep and a parrot (perhaps the Ambassador's wife's pet?). Four men had been wounded, some suffered contusions. The most dangerous things had been the galleys' 25lb stone shot: eight of which had hit the hull near the water-line. Some broke through 19in (0.48m)-thick planks and internal timbers. The Maltese allegedly lost thirty-six Knights and officers, as well as two hundred and sixty-four slaves, volunteer oarsmen and soldiers. That does not sound exceptional, as at least five to six hundred men would have been crammed into the open, unprotected galleys. The calm sea not only meant favourable conditions for the galleys, but also enabled the galleon to get away. It finally found safe anchorage on the south side of the island of Lampedusa, where the masts could be fished, the sails repaired and the leaks plugged: 'The Carpenter was forced to hang like a Tortoise upon the water, and drive many nailes under the sending of the sea, washing him over continually . . .'[13]

The terms were different when sailing ships had to fight against other sailing ships. There is an illuminating report by Alonso de Contreras (a Spanish mercenary captain) from the end of the sixteenth century. He was really a soldier, and no sailor, but the Spanish custom at this time was that the person commanding the soldiers also held the highest authority on a warship. Spanish sailors, who had no social standing, were subordinate to the military leaders, who viewed ships purely as platforms for their soldiers – in the manner of the old galley battle tactics. Ships approached one another with the sole intention of boarding and fighting man-to-man. Artillery was used during the approach. Guns were considered an ignoble weapon by the Spanish: serving only to fill in the time before boarding and fighting hand-to-hand. The objective was to aim high: to hit the rigging, and to prevent the enemy ship from fleeing.[14]

Contreras found himself on a galleon operating from Malta against the Turks and he wrote:

As the evening approached, we espied on the horizon what appeared to be a very large ship – and in fact it turned out to be just that. We sailed in its wake, so as not to lose sight of it, and approached it around midnight. We made ready our arms, and asked 'What manner of ship?' The reply came back: 'A ship on the sea!'. It was an extremely well-armed warship, and its guns had also been readied. It was manned by over 400 Turks, and festooned with heavy guns. They fired a broadside at us, which left some of our men wounded, and despatched seventeen of them into the next world. We replied with a broadside, which had no less effect. Then we boarded her. It was a murderous battle, as the Turks had control of our forecastle, and it took a lot of courage to drive them back on to their ship. We waited until daybreak and then renewed the attack; the Turks showed no signs of fleeing. Our Captain then applied a refined strategem: he allowed only a few people on deck, and had all the hatches carefully fastened down, so that people either had to fight or jump into the sea. It was a bloody confrontation. We gained the enemy's forecastle and kept it for a long time. In the end, however, the Turks drove us back. Then we changed course, and attacked the Turkish ship with our artillery, as we could sail faster and our guns were better.

On that day I witnessed two spectacles worthy of mention. A Dutch gunner was loading a gun without cover. The Turks fired a cannon-shot at the middle of his head, which burst into thousands of pieces. His brain spurted against the people standing near him, and a piece of his skull hit a sailor right on his nose, which had been crooked from birth. After the wound had healed, it transpired that the sailor's nose is now as straight as mine.[15].

The battle had started with Spanish tactics; after a single broadside the ships approached each other so closely that they could be boarded. From the large number of casualties we can infer that people kept their nerve and fired the guns at close quarters. Neither opponent seemed inclined to fire a second broadside. The to-ing and fro-ing on the decks shows how highly prized was the tactical advantage of occupying the forecastle of a sailing ship. These forecastles were constructed with sealed forward and after bulkheads for defensive purposes. People fought with swords, hand guns and small breech-loading guns. Broadside artillery was used only if the boarding fighting was indecisive: the ships would separate, and an artillery duel would start. What mattered was loading speed, good seamanship and the ship's sailing qualities. The reference to the Dutch gunner, who had to reload a gun without cover, makes it clear that they were fired without recoil, and that the guns were loaded from the outside.

Later on in the report it becomes apparent that no decisive result was going to be reached between the battling ships through artillery alone. Contemporary ship ordnance was generally not up to sinking an enemy ship, even when fired from the immediate vicinity. Significantly, not a single Elizabethan galleon was ever sunk by gunfire, in more than twenty-five years of naval conflict in the Anglo-Spanish War. The guns were there to inflict damage on the adversary by a process of attrition. The rigging would be shot down, the superstructure shattered and the boarding nets destroyed; no-one considered themselves capable of sinking the enemy.[16] The battles between English galleons and the ships of the Spanish Armada were no different. But there the English avoided boarding fights, and merely fired to render their opponents incapable of movement. They hoped to be able to overpower any ships remaining behind. The effect of the contemporary artillery is apparent from a report written in 1588, after the Armada campaign. Sir William Wynter, Master of Ordnance in the Navy (1557–89), wrote to Walsingham, the Secretary of State:

Out of my ship there was shot 500 shot of demi-cannon, culverin, and demi-culverin; and when I was furthest off in discharging any of the pieces, I was not out of the shot of their harquebus, and most times within speech one of another . . . and when every man was weary with labour, and our cartridges spent, and munitions wasted [expended] . . . we ceased and followed the enemy, he bearing hence still in the course as I have said before.[17]

As it was, at the time, current English tactics to engage with artillery and avoid boarding, this process was not crucial to the fate of the Spanish Armada. Spanish ships which had exhausted their ammunition were always in a position to continue their journey. The English Naval Reform Commission of 1618 also made the point:

> Experience teacheth how sea-fights in these days come seldome to boarding or to great execution of bows, arrows, small shot and the swords, but are chiefly performed by the great artillery breaking down masts, yards, tearing, raking and bilging the ships, wherein the great advantage of His Majesty's navy must carefully be maintained by appointing such a proportion of ordnance to each ship as the vessel will bear.[18]

The English thus took pains to avoid a confrontation with the fearsome soldiers on board the Spanish ships. So they pioneered a new type of naval battle tactic, in which the manoeuverability of the Elizabethan galleons was combined with superior force of artillery. Sir Francis Drake (c.1543–96) is credited with being the first to appreciate the significance of the broadside. Ending the medieval practice of arranging warships abreast is also supposed to have been his idea. The tactic was to sail in a straight line past the enemy, fire a broadside, tack and fire the other broadside. This group tactic, which amounts to a pure artillery duel, was the nucleus of the line of battle of the eighteenth century.[19]. The first task was to get to the weather side of the enemy: no easy matter at a time when the best square-rigged ships could not bear more than six points to windward.[20] That would be 22°–23° against the direction of the wind. Only the best sailors could manage this. Having the weather-gauge meant that they could choose their distance from the enemy. Sir William Monson wrote about the battle order of a fleet:

> The greatest advantage in a sea-fight is to get the wind of one another; for he that has the wind is out of danger of being boarded, and has the advantage where to board and how to attempt the enemy. So ought the General of a fleet to labour to compass the wind before he put himself to fight.[21]

Sir Walter Raleigh (see p 38) gave similar orders in the instructions to his captains on an expedition to South America in 1617:

> Every ship, if we be under the lee of an enemy, shall labour to recover the wind if the admiral endeavours it. But if we find an enemy to be leewards of us, the whole fleet shall follow the admiral, vice-admiral, or other leading ship within musket shot of the enemy; giving so much liberty to the leading ship as after her broadside delivered she may stay and trim her sails. Then is the second ship to tack as the first ship and give the other side, keeping the enemy under a perpetual shot. This you must do upon the windermost ship or ships of an enemy, which you shall either batter in pieces, or force him or them to bear up and so entangle them, and drive them foul one of another to their utter confusion.[22]

The number of people at the fighting stations of a galleon shows that only one broadside could be manned at a time. There was therefore some point in presenting the enemy with fully-loaded guns from the other broadside when the ship turned. The following list from the beginning of the seventeenth century shows how the crew of a 30-gun warship were arranged before battle:

18 gunners and 48 men in the battery
50 men on the small arms
50 men to manoeuvre the ship and man the tops
 4 men in the powder room
 4 carpenters below

Fig 39: Musketeer from c.1600, as
we may imagine those on board
warships would also have looked.
He is carrying a musket, forked
bracket and a match lock. We can
make out his cartridge bandolier,
with approximately ten powder
measures and a tinder bottle.
Muskets had an effective range of
100–200m. (After J de Gheyn,
(1606) in A Essenwein Quellen zur
Geschichte der Feuerwaffen,
Leipzig, 1877)

The following also served:

> 3 trumpeters
> 3 surgeons and their mates
> 4 stewards, 3 cooks and 3 boys

Contemporaries sometimes complained that almost one-third of a warship's complement consisted of officers or non-combatants.[23] But the efficiency of such a battle order was actually increased by the custom prevailing on English ships: all soldiers on board were under the command of an officer who had the rank of corporal. But the soldiers were also sailors, and could also be commanded by naval officers. That system had developed through the particular requirements arising at sea.[24] Its social background can be traced to the gradual disappearance of strong class distinctions in the England of the Renaissance and the Reformation. It was particularly noticeable amongst merchants and seafarers.

The outlook and way of life of Spanish society, was, by contrast, still purely feudal.[25] Spanish discipline at sea had entirely military forms. This meant that it was often limited in its effect. What worked on land could often be to one's detriment at sea. Spanish warships were organised like land fortresses. The crew were divided into three groups: soldiers, sailors and gunners. Soldiers occupied the highest rank; sailors the lowest. Sir Richard Hawkins, the English seaman who undertook an expedition to Spanish South America in 1593–94, had this to say (quoted by Corbett) about the crew on Spanish ships:

> The soldiers ward and watch, and the officers in every ship [make the] round as if they were ashore. This is the only task they undergo except cleaning their arms, in which they are not over curious. [In like manner the gunners were especially exempted] from all labour and care except about the artillery . . . the mariners are but as slaves to the rest, to moil and toil day and night, and those but few and bad and not suffered to sleep or harbour themselves under the decks. For in fair or foul weather, in storms, sun or rain, they must pass void of covert or succour. [Or in other words they are exactly, in a soldier's eyes, on the level of galley-slaves.][26].

Hawkins continued on the subject of the officers:

> There is ordinarily in every ship of war a captain, whose charge is that of masters with us; and also a captain of the soldiers, who commandeth the captain of the ship, the soldiers, gunners and mariners in her . . . They have their *maestros de campo*, sergeant, and master-general or captain of the artillery, with their *alfere* major and all other officers, as in a camp. . . . If they come to fight with another *armado* [ship-of-war] they order themselves as in a battle by land; in a vanguard, rearward, main-battle and wings, etc. In every particular ship the soldiers are all set upon the decks; their forecastle they account their head-front or vanguard of their company; that abaft the mast the rearward; and the waist the main-battle, wherein they place their principal force and on which they principally rely; which they call the *plaza de armas* or place of arms, which taken their hope is lost. Their gunners fight not but with their great artillery: the mariners attend only to the tackling of the ship and handling of the sails, and are unarmed and subject to all misfortunes; not permitted to shelter themselves, but to be still aloft, whether it be necessary or needless. So ordinarily those which first fail are the mariners and sailors of which they have greater need. They use few close-fights or fireworks; and all this proceedeth, as I judge, by error of placing land-captains for governors and commanders at sea; where they seldom understand what is to be done or commanded.[27]

This picture is no doubt somewhat prejudiced, but its main points are certainly accurate. The galley's military system had been transferred to sailing ships. Every system had its advantages and disadvantages, and Hawkins admits that discipline in the Spanish service was better than in his own.[28]

William Monson, the English captain and, later, vice-admiral, described the preparations which had to be made on board ship when a battle was looming:

Before ships and fleets encounter, or enter into fight, these things following are necessary to be done: to divide the company into three parts; the one appointed to tack the ship, the second to ply the small-shot, and the third to attend the ordnance; but not so precisely but that one may be assisting to the other in the three several places. The ship is to be brought into its short or fighting sails, viz. her foresail, her main and fore-topsails. For the other sails are troublesome to handle, and make the ship heel so that her lee ordnance cannot be used; besides the danger of firing her sails with arrows and other wildfire from the enemy.

The master is to appoint a valiant and sufficient man at helm and to receive his directions from his captain how to order the fight and where to board. Which must be done with most advantage, and according to the placing [of] the enemy's ordnance; and therefore it is requisite to have a captain of experience.

Every officer is to do his part; the boatswain to sling the yards, to put forth the flag, ancient, and streamers, to arm the tops and waist-cloths; to spread the netting, to provide tubs, and to command the company to make urine in them for the gunners to use in their sponges to cool their ordnance in the fight, and all other things that belongs to his charge. The gunner is to appoint his officers to their quarters, to have care to the fire, budge barrels, and cartridges, to have his shot in a locker near every piece; and the yeoman of the powder to keep his room, and to be watchful of it, and to have his eye upon any leak that shall happen in hold. The carpenters are to be vigilant, and to have their oakum, lead, nails, and what else belongs to the stopping of leaks in readiness. He must have a man always ready to sling overboard if there chance a leak. Or if there be cause to take in the lower tier of ordnance, by the sudden growing and working of the sea, he must have all things ready to caulk the ports.[29]

A continuing theme in these reports is the fear held by sailors of old of their wooden vessels catching fire. Uncontrollable fire could easily mean the loss of both ship and crew. Sooner or later, a fire of any size would reach the powder supply. Fire on board was an even greater danger than an enemy's energetic attacks. Fire prevention measures played an important part in all ship instructions – whether in war or in peace. Damping the sails, and setting out barrels of water etc was one of the most important preparations made before a battle started. Sometimes the boats were also filled with water, or wet cloths kept ready in them.[30]

Light fowlers could be placed on the galleon's high stern-galleries. Men with infantry weapons were also posted there. The galleries were highly valued, as the place from which the ship's side could be extinguished, if it was set alight by wildfire.[31] Cabin walls which interrupted the space between the decks were brought into the hold. Bedding and sacks served as shot-catchers. Last but not least, gunners were instructed to fire their first shots at point-blank range, as nothing could be more uncertain than a long-range shot at sea: merely a waste of gunpowder and munition.[32] In his advice for the protection of men in battle, Monson described what happened on the decks of ships at the onset of hostilities (Fig 39):

Several nations have several ways to preserve their men in fight at sea. The French use to stow half their soldiers in hold, and to draw them out, causing the others to retire as there shall be occasion or necessity. This I hold dangerous, troublesome, and inconvenient, when all men are otherwise busy in their several places, to pass to and again with their matches lighted which may unhappily fall on something to take fire.

The Spaniards imitate the form of their discipline by land; as namely, a head-front or vanguard, a rearguard, and a main battle. The forecastle they count their head-front for vanguard, that abaft the mast the rearguard, and the waist their main battle wherein they place their principal force. This in my opinion will breed great disorders, especially if the ship should fight with all her sails standing; for the labour of the mariners in tacking and handing their sails will confound them, that they know not what to do. But if they strip themselves into their fighting sails that a few men may handle it would be less inconvenient, but howsoever here is no provision for safeguard of men who lie open to their enemy.

The Dunkirkers use in fight to place their small-shot flat on their bellies upon their decks, that the shot, great or small, coming from an enemy, shall have only their head for their aim. This is to be allowed of in small ships that carry not many men nor ordnance, but inconvenient in greater vessels where men are ever in action running and stirring up and down in the ship.

There is a device made with a plank of elm, because it does not shiver like oak; this plank is musket proof, and removed with trucks from one part of the ship to the other, which is a good safeguard for small-shot. But in my opinion I prefer the coiling of cables on the deck, and keeping part of the men within them (as the French do theirs in hold) before all other devices. For the soldiers are in and out speedily, upon all sudden occasions, to succour any part of the ship or to enter an enemy, without trouble to the sailors in handing their sails or the gunners in plying their ordnance.

. . . Whereas I have shewed every country's manner of fight at sea, and their care to secure their men from danger and to annoy the enemy with advantage, instead of cables, planks, and other devices to preserve their men, the Hollanders wanting natural valour of themselves, use to line their men in the head by giving them gunpowder to drink, and other kind of liquor to make them soonest drunk. Which, besides that it is a barbarous and unchristian-like act, when they are in danger of death to make them ready for the devil, it often proves more perilous than prosperous to them by firing their own ships or confusing them in the fight, their wits being taken from them. Whereas if they had been sober they might have fought in good order.[33]

Once he had his opponent on his lee side, a ship's captain could decide to what extent he would use defensive tactics, or go on the attack. His position on his ship's poop or quarter-deck was extremely dangerous. If he decided on battle, chivalry bade him first ask his opponent, with drawn sword, to surrender. While this was going on, the master or first officer would have taken up his position on the half-deck, from where he could control the course of the ship and the handling of the sails.

If the enemy declined to surrender, the gunners opened the gunports and ran out their guns. Firing a broadside at anything beyond musket-range (150–200m) was uncertain and virtually pointless. So at greater distances the chasers would open fire first. They were generally unshortened long-barrel culverin-type guns, positioned at the bow and stern. When the enemy ship was nearer, the broadside battery fired one shot after another, as quickly as they could reach their target. Men with handguns were not ordered to fire until the ships were within pistol-range. If the vessel was a good sailer, you ran past the enemy and tacked, giving the stern-chasers a chance to fire. It was crucial to keep the weather side. When the turning manoeuvre was complete and the sails were still backing, the enemy was let run past and the other broadside fired. It was important to study all the enemy's manoeuvres. You had to be able to change course promptly if the opposing ship was doing so.

When the first salvoes had been fired, the captain had to decide whether to force the outcome and board the enemy ship, or to prolong the gun-battle. This became a matter of evaluating the enemy ship correctly: if it had higher sides than his own, the horizon could no longer be seen from his stern. That was undesirable. What kind of construction and shape of timbers did the ship over there have? Did the sides of the upper decks curve inwards? That meant a broader gap to be crossed by the boarding teams, if they were to go on the offensive. What kind of decks did the other ship have? Did they run straight through from the bow to the stern, or did they have bulkheads offering protection? If no-one was to be seen, that was probably because they were staying below decks to incite boarding. Then it would be foolhardy to be drawn into a boarding battle, as well-prepared, determined defenders could repel an attack. If boarding was still considered inadvisable, the battle had to be continued with ordnance. The musketeers would then direct their fire at the enemy ship's gunports, to force the gunners to move away. The guns fired at the rigging with cross-bar shot or chain-fire. In this way a ship could be prevented from firing and manoeuvering, and one's own broadside could be brought into play. By this process of attrition an enemy ship could be made to surrender, and even sunk. But to do this, the guns, and the men behind them, had to be good.

When the captain saw an opportunity to board the enemy ship, all the lee gunports would be pushed open and as many guns as possible brought to this side. Then the master had to bring his vessel right up to the enemy's. If he could place it abeam, across the hawse, the guns on his own ship could be used to advantage; whereas the other ship could fire only its bow-chasers. If he placed it amidships, at the enemy's quarter deck, people could board over the sides. The ship boys armed themselves with stones, fire pots and brass balls (which exploded on being thrown), and occupied the tops and yards. These weapons had to be thrown at the moment of boarding the deck of an enemy ship. When all the guns

were ready, and the ships lay side-to-side, a full broadside was fired. Each division boarded quietly, under cover of gunpowder smoke. A pre-selected group would then attempt to take control of the rigging, as quickly and completely as possible.

Even when the boarding parties had gained a foothold on the enemy ship, and the masts and yards had been freed from the opponent and the decks swept clean, the danger was by no means over. Sometimes the enemy had made preparations for this situation and laid powder trails leading to powder-chests or barrels below deck, to blow them up. For this situation Mainwaring recommended: 'They must be careful to clear the decks with fire pots or the like, if it be possible, from the trains of powder before men do enter, for it happens many times that there are more men lost in a minute by entering than in long fight board and board.'[34]

To get below decks, the scuttles and ladderways had to be cleared as quickly as possible. The enemy ship was taken once control had been gained of the sails and the rudder. Captain Boteler (Nathaniel Butler, the English seaman and historian, c.1577–c.1643) wrote appeasingly in his dialogues between a captain and an admiral: 'The ship is taken and the men at your mercy; wherein, nevertheless, a soldier-like quarter is always to be given, and never to be bloody in cold blood, nor cruel at any time.'[35]

We are already familiar with much of the material in this chapter from reports of battles in the next two centuries. Sailing ships' tactics, dependent on wind and weather, remained essentially the same. Reports of battles between galleys and sailing ships became rarer as the galley lost its significance as a warship. The period around 1600 saw the development of the galleon as the superior vessel; which, with the new weapon – the broadside of heavy guns – was an instrument of power capable of remaining at sea for months on end. For the first time, the significance and effect of military action in distant lands, blockades of enemy coasts, the landing of large troop contingents, was understood and made possible. The later rules and tactics of whole fleets in battle may not have been developed yet, but the necessary component part – the manoeuvrable, large sailing ship, which did not alter significantly in later centuries – now existed.

CHAPTER 5

The men

I N 1598 Richard Hakluyt, the English chaplain and geographer, wrote of the seamen of his time: 'No kinde of men of any profession in the common wealth passe their years in so great and continuall hazard . . . and . . . of so many so few grow to gray heires.'[1] The ships wore out the men who travelled on them; life on board was very hard. The oft-repeated tribulations were: 'A hard cabin, cold and salt meat, broken sleeps, mouldy bread, dead beer, wet clothes, want of fire.'[2] Most of the men had only one set of clothing for a voyage. Darkness, dampness and foul air below decks presented a lot of problems. The stench from the bilges must have been particularly unpleasant. Gravel was used for ballast at the time, and the high-sided ships needed large quantities of it. It became saturated with bilge water, beer swill and ship refuse, and was injurious to both the health of the crew and the timbers of the ship. By 1578 Sir William Wynter, the Surveyor of the Ships, was – unsuccessfully – recommending that stones should be used instead of gravel ballast, and that the galley should be relocated from the middle of the ship to the forecastle.[3]

Virtually every voyage brought serious losses through illness, accidents and desertion. Ships were therefore heavily manned, at least at the outset of a voyage. The heavy bulky equipment and crude, barely effective mechanical aids of the time demanded a lot of muscle power.[4]

Officially a galleon in war service had three crew members (excluding officers) for every five tons of its dead weight. One-third of the men were soldiers; of the rest, one seventh were gunners, the remainder were sailors. A medium-sized ship of 500 tons therefore had 100 soldiers, 28 gunners and 172 sailors – making 300 in all. For commercial voyages, ships were classified according to their freight capacity for barrels of wine (burden in cask), and had one crew member for every five such tons. A merchant ship of 500 'tons burden' would have a crew of 75, of which 69 were sailors and 6 were gunners.[5]

Not much was known about medicine, hygiene and food preservation in the seventeenth century. But long voyages were being made more and more frequently – and in tropical waters, at that. So it is hardly surprising that the mortality rates from diseases on board warships and merchant ships was very high. Dysentery, scurvy, typhoid and beri-beri were widespread, and there was also plague on board ship.[6] Sir Richard Hawkins, the English Admiral, estimated that 10,000 men died from scurvy alone during twenty years of Queen Elizabeth I's reign. But that was only one of the often fatal illnesses. During the first open campaign waged by the English against the Spanish (commanded by Sir Francis Drake, 1585–6, in the Caribbean), 600 out of 2300 men died from diseases. Almost 6000 of the 12,000 men who sailed with Drake's 1589 expedition to the Spanish coast died from illnesses due to rotten food and hunger. Sick and wounded men received no special care. When their ship went into battle, they were laid in the cable-tier or on the ballast – the safest, but hardly the healthiest, place on board.[7] After the English ships returned from the Spanish Armada, Charles Howard, Commander-in-Chief of the English fleet, wrote:

Sicknes and mortallitie begin wonderfullie to growe amongst us . . . of the 500 men which she (the *Elizabeth*) carried out, by the time she had bin in Plymouth three weeks or a month there were ded of them 200 and above, soe as I was driven to set all the rest of her men ashore, to take out the ballast and to make fires in her of wet broom 3 or 4 daies together, and so hoped therebie to have cleansed her of her infectione.[8]

Rations for the men on a meat day officially consisted of one pound of biscuits, a gallon (4.5 litres) of beer, and two pounds of salt beef. On a fish day there was one pound of biscuits, a gallon of beer, cheese and a quarter of dried cod. In addition, a pound of ham and a pint (0.56 litres) of peas were distributed one day a week.[9] Things were rather different in practice, as victuals were often distributed among groups of five or six, rather than four, men. This weakened the crew, particularly on long voyages, and made them more susceptible to illness. Beer – the quantity of which can be explained by the salt content of the food – was difficult to keep. It was brewed without hops, and soon went sour. The bad taste was less dangerous than the possibility of infection, which was a form of enteritis, particularly prevalent in tropical waters. Despite that, sailors insisted on their beer.[10] There were, of course, epidemics of typhoid and plague on land as well, which decimated the population. That was considered one of the risks of daily life. It was the same at sea, only there these illnesses were much more prevalent.[11] Life for the ordinary man on land was hard as well, and if he happened to be in the army, he probably found the discipline harsher than on board ship.

A large proportion of the crew on the warships of the English Crown were pressed, often people with criminal records, or vagabonds – mainly novices, who had been brought on to ships by the press gangs. Sir Walter Raleigh took this into account in the instructions he gave his captains on an expedition to South America in 1617: 'You shall cause all your landsmen to learn the names and places of the ropes, that they may assist the sailors in their labour upon the decks, though they cannot go up to the tops and yards.'[12] Trained seamen could bribe their way out of the press gangs. They preferred to serve on merchant ships or, even better, on privateers where discipline was less harsh, rations were better and the prize money was higher. The proportion of officers to men was not always adhered to: in 1582, 60 out of 121 men on the *Galleon Leicester*, a privateer, had a higher rank than the ordinary crew members. From the pilot to the apothecary, these people had the right to free transport of a certain amount of goods for private trade.[13] That proved a strong incentive to put up with the vicissitudes of life at sea.

Cases of mutiny and disobedience were more common amongst ordinary seamen in these harsh times than in later centuries. The mutiny on the galleon *Golden Lion* was a typical example: when Drake attacked Cadiz with a fleet, in 1587, to disrupt the Spanish military preparations against England, the *Golden Lion* left the fleet and returned to England without orders. The mutineers wrote a letter in which they tried to present their desperate position:

> What is a piece of Beefe of halfe a pounde amonge foure men to dynner or halfe a drye Stockfishe for foure dayes in the weeke, and nothing elles to helpe withall – Yea, wee have helpe, a litle Beveredge worse than pompe water. Wee were preste by her Maties presse to have her allowaunce, and not to be thus dealt withall, you make no men of us, but beastes.[14]

A seaman who had been severely wounded was returned to his parish, which was theoretically responsible for his welfare. If he was lucky, he received permission to beg for a year. The parish received a tiny allowance from the Crown for such cases; this maintenance was, however, not officially introduced until fourteen years after the battles of the Armada.[15]

We know something of the seaman's life on board a galleon from surviving instructions from English commanders to their captains, and from Captain John Smith's *Sea Grammar*, from the early seventeenth century. Smith described how the watches were selected at the outset of a voyage:

> The Captain or Master commands the Boatswaine to call up the company. The Master, being chiefe of the Starboard watch, doth call one, and his right hand Mate on the Larboord doth call another, and so forward, till they be divided in two parts. Then each man is to chuse his Mate, Consort, or Comrade, and then divide them into squadrons according to your number and burthen of your ship as you see occasion. These are to take their turnes at the Helme, trim sailes, pumpe, and doe all duties each halfe, or each squadron for eight Glasses or four houres, which is a watch.
>
> But care would bee had that there be not two Comrades upon one watch, because they may have the more roome in their Cabbins to rest. And as the Captaine and master's Mates, Gunners, Carpenters, Quartermasters,

Trumpeters, etc. are to be abaft the Mast, so the Boatswaine and all the Yonkers or common Sailers under his command is to be before the Mast.

The next is, to messe them foure to a messe, and then give every messe a quarter Can of beere and a basket of bread to stay their stomacks till the Kettle be boiled, that they may first goe to a prayer, then to supper; and at six a'clocke sing a Psalme, say a Prayer, and the Master with his side begins the watch. Then all the rest may doe what they will till midnight; and then his Mate with his Larboord men, with a Psalme and a Prayer, releeves them till foure in the morning. And so from eight to twelve each other, except some flaw of winde come – some storm or gust – or some accident that requires the helpe of all hands, which commonly, after such good cheere, in most voyages doth happen.[16]

Discipline was maintained by harsh means. Ships rules list the punishable offences, large and small. Fear of fire on board is always uppermost:

You shall make in every ship two captains of the watch, who shall make choice of two soldiers every night to search between the decks that no fire or candlelight be carried about the ship after the watch be set, nor that any candle be burning in any cabin without a lantern; and that neither, but whilst they are to make themselves unready. For there is no danger so inevitable as the ship firing, which may also as well happen by taking of tobacco between the decks, and therefore [it is] forbidden to all men but aloft the upper deck . . . The steward shall not deliver any candle to any private man nor for any private use.[17]

You shall give especial charge, for avoiding the danger of fire; and that no candles be carried in your ship without the lanthorn: which if any person shall disobey, you shall severely punish.[18]

The things that made life worth living were forbidden: 'No man shall keep any feasting or drinking between meals, nor drink any healths upon your ship's provisions . . . No man shall play at cards or dice either for his apparel or arms upon pain of being disarmed and made a swabber of the ship.' Even on dry land, one had to take precautions: 'You shall take especial care when God shall send us to land in the Indies, not to eat of any fruit unknown, which fruit you do not find eaten with worms or beasts under the tree.'[19]

Special laws for the punishment of serious offences on board English ships were passed during Queen Elizabeth's reign. There was more differentiation between punishments for the various misdemeanours than a few centuries later, when virtually every transgression was atoned for by hanging or the cat o' nine tails. Monson gives a summary of the punishments which a captain could inflict:

Put a man in leg-irons. Withold his food. Duck him in the water. Haul him under the keel. Tie him to the capstan and whip him there, or at the mainmast. Hang weights around his neck, until his 'heart' or spine begins to break. Stop up his tongue or cut out a portion of it, as a punishment for blasphemy or swearing. That should be sufficient to subdue the roughest seamen in the world.[20]

Draconian penalties threatened anyone who created a disturbance on board:

There is no man that shall strike any officer, be he captain, lieutenant, ensign, sergeant, corporal of the field, quartermaster etc.[21] . . . Nor the master of any ship, master's mate, or boatswain, or quartermaster. I say no man shall strike or offer violence to any of these but the supreme officer to the inferior, in time of service, upon pain of death.[22]

A murderer was tied, hand and foot to the body of his victim, and thrown overboard. A cannon shot was fired at the same time, as a warning to others who might be so inclined.[23] Even thieves risked a lot: 'If any man steal any victuals, either by breaking into the hold or otherwise, he shall receive the punishment as of a thief or murderer of his fellows.'[24]

A thief who had been caught was ducked in the water three times from the bowsprit; allowed to stay alive, he was 'dragged at the boat's stern to the next shore, and there left with a loaf of bread and a can of beer.'[25] Sleeping on watch on board a warship was a serious offence at this time. The old rule ran:

If anyone slept in his watch; for the first time he was to have a bucket of water thrown upon his neck, which is called heading with a bucket of water; for the second time he was to be haled up by the wrists and to have two buckets of water poured into his sleeves; for the third time, he was to be bound to the mainmast with iron plates, and to have some gun-chambers or a basket of bullets tied to his arms and so to remain during the Captain's pleasure; for the fourth time, he was to be hanged at the bolt-sprit [bowsprit], with a can of beer and a biscuit of bread, and a knife, and so to hang, and choose whether he would cut himself down, and fall into the sea, or hang still and starve.[26]

Cowardice in the face of the enemy was treated surprisingly mildly: 'Whosoever shall show himself a coward upon any landing or otherwise, he shall be disarmed and made a labourer or carrier of victuals for the rest.'[27] The ship boys also came off relatively lightly. Their 'waggery and idleness' was punished by the boatswain's rod. This took place on Monday mornings, and was such a regular occurrence that 'some mere seamen and sailors believe in good earnest that they shall not have a fair wind until the poor boys be duly brought to the chest; that is, be whipped every Monday morning.'[28]

A payroll from the year 1582 gives us a summary of the officers, non-commissioned officers and their mates serving on board a medium-sized English galleon of 500–800 tons:[29]

A Master	A Yeoman of the tacks	A Master Carpenter	Their Mates
Two Mates	A Coxswain	A Mate	A Surgeon
A Boatswain	His Mate	Another Mate	His Man
His Mate	A Purser	A Swabber	Two Trumpeters – three, if the
Four Quartermasters	A Cook	A Master Gunner	ship is a flagship (admiral)
Their Mates	A Steward	Two Mates	A Drum and Fife
A Yeoman of the jere	Two Mates	Four Quartermasters	A Pilot

I have been unable to find any further reference to the function of, and the range of duties performed by, the two yeomen for parts of the tackle.

The hierarchy of officers on board an English galleon like this began with the captain. Initially he was often not a naval officer but a gentleman, a courtier with little sailing expertise, whose naval proficiency was not the grounds for his appointment to the post. He was, however, in control of the voyage. Many contemporary Officer Lists do not even mention captains by name. These Lists start with the master, who was always a professional seaman, and who sailed the ship. He arranged the watches, had rights of punishment, and supervised the people working on the tackle.[30] On smaller ships he was often also the navigation officer, and measured the height of the sun or stars with his astrolabe or Jacob's staff.[31] He had to be aware of the distance the ship had travelled and its course. He obtained his data from the traverse board,[32] from which the course run in a watch could be reckoned.[33] Dead reckoning was an important part of this, requiring a lot of experience. The master of a merchant ship might be the owner or a shareholder, as ships were often owned by a group of investors, each of whom was rewarded with a percentage of the proceeds.[34] On large ships the master shared the navigation duties with the Pilot. The latter had specialist knowledge of shallows, coastlines and harbour approaches. Monson describes the pilot's job with polished conciseness: 'The principal thing in a pilot . . . is to know where he is.'[35]

The boatswain communicated the master's orders to the crew. He led a watch, and amongst his numerous duties was the supervision of the tackle forward of the mainmast. Masts and yards had to be well painted, dressed and equipped; sails had to be patched and adequately supplied with reef bands, clewlines and gaskets. The shrouds had to be tightened, the deep-sea line and lead prepared, the anchor cables and buoys secured, the ballast checked. The boats were another of the boatswain's specialist areas. He was in charge of the long boat, and had to ensure that the boats were well equipped with sails, oars, thwarts, tholes, a windlass and a rudder. Before a battle he had to secure the yards with chains, rig the arming cloths, and hoist the flags and pennants. He was responsible for seeing that, overall, every man performed his duty. For this purpose he carried a silver whistle as a sign of his officer status. As the ship's provost-marshal he was responsible for punishing malefactors.[36]

The master gunner had one of the most responsible positions on board a ship of this time, whether it be a merchant ship or a warship. Monson describes his duties in detail:

A gunner at sea ought to be skilful, careful, and courageous, for the strength of the ship is put into his hands.

A principal thing in a gunner at sea is to be a good helmsman, and to call to him at helm to loof, or bear up, to have his better level, and to observe the heaving and setting of the sea to take his aim at the enemy.

A gunner is to be provided, besides his ordnance, with powder and shot of all kinds . . . [see p 59]. He is to furnish himself with a horn, a priming-iron, lint stocks, gunner's quadrant, and a dark lanthorn; to make his choice of his mates, his quarter gunners, yeoman of the powder room, and his company in the gunner-room, who are privileged from the labour before the mast unless by his sufferance.

A gunner must know the names of his pieces [Monson lists fifteen types of guns, with their dimensions], their bores or height, their weight, the weight of the shot, the weight of the powder, the goodness of powder, and how far every piece will carry, both at random and point-blank, which is fittest for a ship . . .[37]

The gunner had to ensure that his guns were well lashed and secured, as there were serious consequences if they broke loose in heavy seas. He was also responsible for ensuring that the lower gunports were well stopped; this was important not only in rough seas, but also in a harbour or estuary, as a ship could take in too much water very quickly if another ship sailed past suddenly.[38]

The carpenter, wrote Monson:

is the man who gives life to the ship . . . all the works that iron or timber is used in pass through his hands and skill. He looks to the hull of the ship, that there be no damage by leaks within board or without, but that all be tight and staunch; likewise to the strength of the masts and yards, and repairing of the boats, cabins or partitions of plank, deal . . .[39]

He had to have material available to strengthen the round timbers and for a reserve rudder. Spare spars, which were lashed outboard, were part of his stores. His workshop on the orlop deck had to include a well-equipped toolbox. His materials included pintels and pump parts, together with oakum, lead sheets, softwood, spare canvas and tallow, for stopping leaks and caulking seams. Finding leaks was one of his tasks. If he could not see the water coming in, he relied on a sounding pot, which he held with its opening against the planking. By listening through a hole in the base of the pot he could deduce the direction from which the water was entering. He could also use an ear trumpet as a sounding tube. He had to maintain the pumps and report daily to the captain how much water the ship made.[40] English ships of this time already had chain pumps as well as the normal suction pumps. Röding[41] describes them in his *Allgemeines Wörterbuch der Marine* as a type of paternoster. They were, however, susceptible to problems and their repair posed a difficult task for the ship's carpenter.

On large ships there was also a joiner, who worked under the carpenter's direction. We can learn something about his duties from the *Dialogues* of Nathaniel Boteler, the English seaman and historian who (see p 73) has left us a collection of details about contemporary naval life in the form of a fictitious conversation between a captain and an admiral. The joiner was responsible for the ship's decoration, and so had, amongst other things, to fit wainscot in the large cabin; Boteler however thought that this was going out of fashion, as lots of rats hid behind the wainscot, and besides this it creaked terribly if the ship was on heavy seas. With regard to the ship's interior, the joiner was concerned with the bed boxes and chest benches in the officers' cabins; making fast and repairing the tables; with parrels of all sorts, and with the bench in front of the poop bulkhead. Inserting small windows and light holes round the large cabin was also one of his tasks.[42]

On merchant ships the purser was the owner's repesentative. Sometimes he too was a shareholder in the ship. He purchased the cargo and supervised the loading. He undertook financial transactions, like customs duties and the wages of the crew, for which he kept a muster roll.[43] He supervised the provisions and checked the daily rations given to the steward and the cook. At the end of a voyage he had to account for the remaining supplies.[44]

The steward shared with the purser the responsibility for keeping the provisions stored in good condition. He organised the supply of candles etc and kept the bread room in good order. For distributing the victuals at each meal he had his own room at the bottom of the ship, where he also ate and slept.[45]

The cook's task was to prepare the meat and the dried fish, and to distribute them at every meal. Prior to doing so, the salted pieces had to be adequately soaked and turned.[46] He could, at his discretion, allow, for example, a wet boat crew to dry themselves at the fire. He might also have to put up with invalids there – and could earn tips by doing so.[47]

A trumpeter also had duties to perform on warships, especially if the ship was an admiral (flagship). He then carried a silver trumpet with a silk pennant in the admiral's colours. His place was on the poop, where he had to announce boats with important visitors. He also had to give clear signals in the noise of a battle, as well as at the start of the eight o'clock watch in the evening and at the end of the morning watch.[48]

A surgeon travelled on warships. He was expected to have the necessary qualifications for his profession. His medicine chest had to be well equipped with instruments and medicine, and was inspected at the beginning of a voyage. During battle his place was in the hold.[49]

The soldiers and sailors who had to circulate in battle with hand guns were under the direction of the corporal. He was responsible for seeing that the weapons, from the muskets and pistols down to the swords, were in good condition. On calm days he had to exercise his men. Before and during a battle he had to deploy them and ensure that they stayed at their posts. He had to stand ready at a sheltered place on deck, with a small powder barrel and shot, to refill the soldiers' bandoliers and to supply them with bullets and lighting fuse. His biggest concern was to ensure that, in the excitement of the battle, no-one came up to him with a burning match.[50]

The coxswain was in charge of the captain's boat. He had to have a gang of presentable, reliable men for this job, who might sometimes have to wear uniform or livery (which was otherwise an uncommon practice). He sat, with his silver whistle, at the rudder of the boat, which was often furnished with cushions and carpets. It was important that he was familiar with the harbours and knew the tides, and it was to the captain's advantage if the coxswain could speak foreign languages.[51]

The cooper belonged to the lowest ranks of service and was responsible for all types of barrels etc. Last in rank on the Officers' List was the swabber. He had to keep the ship clean, from the large cabin to the decks. From time to time he had to burn pitch or similar 'wholesome smells' between the decks to prevent an outbreak of infection. The exterior of the ship had to be cleaned as well, in particular the gunwales, the rails and the beakhead; the latter served as the crew's latrine. But the swabber did not have to clean it himself: that task was reserved for the first man to be named a liar on a Monday morning. He was pronounced 'A Liar, A Liar' at the mainmast, and remained the lowest member of the ship's hierarchy for the rest of the week.[52] All these ranks on board had their mates and assistants. An officer's prestige increased if his men could be excused from routine duties. As might be expected, this was a source of frequent disputes.

The situation on board the Portuguese vessels travelling to India was somewhat different to that on Dutch or English warships. The former were either galleons or the rather larger 'naos' (carracks). We can find a comprehensive portrayal of the Portuguese voyages to India in the works of the historian C R Boxer, in particular in his *Tragic History of the Sea*, a new edition of reports of Portuguese naval disasters from the sixteenth and seventeenth centuries.[53] Also in G Schurhammer, S J's opus on the life of Francis Xavier, the great missionary in India and Japan, which contains a detailed description of the 'Carreira da India'.[54] Missionary Jesuits, Franciscan friars, veterans and other chroniclers on board the galleons and carracks all sent back reports. Amongst the interesting descriptions are those of the French seaman François Pyrard[55] and the Dutchman Jan Huygen Linschoten (1563-1611).[56]

The galleons sailing to India were of 700–800 tons in size; carracks could be from 1500–2000 tons, or even larger.

They were the largest ships of the period. These tonnage figures and the formulae by which they were calculated cannot, however, be compared with the methods used by the Dutch and English for measuring their ships. They merely enable us today to compare individual ships of similar construction (see p 25). An 800-ton galleon had a maximum breadth of approximately 14m, a straight keel length of around 29m, and measured about 42m between the perpendiculars. The height in the hold was 3.8m.[57] A ship of this type could have a crew of over 200 people, although officially there were only 120 men. Some of the crew were not professional sailors, but grumetes – boys, and inexperienced men. A sufficiently large number of experienced seamen for the voyage to India could never be raised in a country the size of Portugal, so tailors, cobblers, servants and all sorts of riff-raff went on board. It was difficult for the professional sailors to teach such people the elements of seamanship, even the difference between port and starboard. We hear of one master, who, in despair, hung a string of onions on the starboard rail, and a bunch of garlic on the port rail, to help the new hands distinguish the sides of the ship. One reason for the shortfall in manpower was the enormously high rates of illness and death on board these ships. Trained Portuguese seamen were so rare in India that galleons sometimes sailed in the Indian and Pacific Oceans with the captain being the only European on board.[58]

The sailor's calling received little respect in Spain and Portugal. Seamen here, as everywhere, were a class apart, with a reputation for selfish coarseness, boorishness and lack of discipline. The reason for this was possibly that sailors with more worthwhile qualities did not make such impressive reporting subjects. At any rate, life for the average seaman at that time was nasty, brutish and short. Men were exposed to many hardships, as well as being badly paid. The 'free chest' system (see p 11) compensated for this underpayment, which also applied to the other ranks on board. Officers and crew had the right to bring back a certain quantity of goods duty-free, on their own account, in standardised chests, the number of which was distributed according to rank.[59] One ulterior motive behind this scheme was that a ship would be defended better if people were defending their personal possessions. But it was common knowledge that even large Portuguese ships would surrender at the first cannon-shot from a Dutch ship, as the Dutch spared life, and were content with booty. Of course, there were also exceptions, and many a ship was defended heroically. But the galleons and carracks of the India fleet were equipped by the King; their cargo, mainly silver coinage for trade and administration in India, belonged to the Crown, for which no-one wanted to die.

Soldiers ranked higher in the social hierarchy than sailors. A ship might have 400–500 men on board for engagements in the Far East. Pyrard reports that the soldiers were mainly uneducated young men: farmers' sons and the sons of the lower orders. As yet they had no war experience. As soon as they had rounded the Cape of Good Hope, they all gave themselves new, impressive-sounding aristocratic names on the muster roll, and became noble gentlemen, so that they would not be disdained by the Portuguese in India. From the royal instructions for the voyage to India we learn that these men had to exercise with harquebuses and muskets during the crossing, 'whereby it is important that the soldiers do not retain any gunpowder after such exercises'. Ordnance and hand-weapons had to be cleaned once a fortnight, and all weapons were to be surrendered on arrival in Goa, before the soldiers went on land.[60]

Boys and pages came below even the seamen in the hierarchy of the official ship's crew. They were commanded by a petty officer and strictly controlled. Anyone failing to obey the second blow from the petty officer's silver whistle felt the rod or the end of a rope. The boys carried messages on the ship, saw to the lamps, served on the pumps, and had to lend a hand supporting the seamen. They were not allowed on the tackle, but had to stay day and night on the deck of the waist. They were not allowed to leave the deck, even in wind or rain, although their only protection there was from ox-hides. Three to four small boys, called pages, sang out the watches every four hours, and they would cry out from the foot of the mainmast if, for example, the goods and chattels of a deceased person were to be auctioned.

The officer posts on board the Portuguese East India ships were bestowed by the Crown on favourites, or as a reward for services at court. They were negotiable. If a man to whom such an office had been given died before the voyage started, his wife or children inherited the title, and could sell it to the highest bidder. No special aptitude was required.

At the apex of the hierarchy was, as captain, a gentleman from a good background, who did not need to understand anything about seamanship. He thus often only co-operated unwillingly with his colleagues in a convoy fleet. That could lead to situations where a ship, separated from the rest of the fleet, became easy booty for the Dutch. However, men like this had the highest powers of command, sufficient to punish boys and ordinary seamen by death. This right, however, did not apply to the fidalgos (lower nobility) or to gentlemen who were sentenced in Goa if they were guilty of 'swearing, witchcraft, blasphemy, perjury, sexual immorality, or reading prohibited books'. In such cases the captain could impose a fine instead. If anything very important had to be decided, he had to seek the advice of all officers, gentlemen and merchants, for which a certain protocol was to be followed.

After the captain, the pilot was the most important man on board. He actually steered the ship. The pilot sat on his seat on the quarter deck and watched the compass needle. Navigation was his subject, and he had to remain at his post day and night. His deputy took his place when he needed to rest. These men were the real experts who preserved and furthered the traditions of Portuguese seamanship. Below deck, the master watched a second compass and conveyed the pilot's orders, via a middle man, to the men on the tiller. The latter had no direct view of the course and the sails. On large ships it was not possible to move the rudder by means of a whipstaff. So the tiller was moved, on call, by men with tackle – in bad weather it might take nine to ten men. Orders on large ships may also have been given through wooden tubes: the first mention of such an arrangement comes from the year 1639.[61]

The stern of the ship as far as the mainmast, the waist amidships and the forecastle were the three areas commanded by the master, the quarter masters, and the master's mate. They remained there on duty day and night. They split the scant deckspace under their command between crew and passengers – the latter had to pay for it. In contrast to ships from other countries, the Spanish and Portuguese had no deck which was common to all. The smallest sheltered space was allocated: either apportioned or traded. So it could happen that a poor fellow, who, as a passenger, was not in a position to buy a space, had to spend the entire voyage of nine to fourteen months on an upper deck. He stayed there, regardless of the wind and the weather, and, at night, sailors trampled over him; his treatment, together with the other privations, could easily cost him his life.

A merinho (petty officer) carried out the captain's orders in matters of justice. Serious offenders were clapped in irons on the stinking pump-well. No-one, other than the merinho, could go near them. There were also places on deck where malefactors could be held in stocks. The merinho also kept all weapons, munitions and gunpowder under lock and key, and was responsible for every open fire on board the ship. No-one dared run around with a naked light or flame. If anyone needed a light below in the hold, the merinho himself enclosed a candle in an iron lantern there.

Two estrinqueiros (rigging masters) occupied additional posts on the East India vessels. They were responsible for mending the sails and for bringing down the main yard. Their duties were probably similar to the English yeomen of the jere.

A ship's scribe, or secretary, was an important, respected man on board. He was nominated by the King, and represented his power on board. Everything which came on to, or left, the ship had to be noted by him. His duties ranged from drawing up a last will and testament to noting which provisions had been distributed. He had the key to the lower hatches on the ship, and if anyone – even the captain – wanted to go down there the secretary had to accompany him. There were two additional stewards on the ship, who were subordinate to the secretary, and a whole range of apprentices, as were required on all ships.

One post, however, is missing – that of the cook, which sometimes proved fatal. The King, who victualled the ships at his own expense, saw to the basic care of the men. Each received the same quantity of wine, water and bread on a daily basis, and salt meat, oil, vinegar, salt and onions once a month. All these groceries were supplied raw, and everyone had to prepare his own meals. For this there was one stove in the waist, at the foot of the mainmast. The merinho lit the fire there at eight or nine o'clock every morning. Two sentries watched over it, to ensure that no-one spread it round the ship. The fire was put out at four o'clock in the afternoon. We have to imagine eighty to a hundred earthen pots standing on this smoking stove, and the same number of people pushing and struggling around it – sailors, soldiers, the servants of the fidalgos and the passengers. Invalids unable to cook for themselves suffered tremendously under this system; they were badly cared for, and for some that meant death. Many people had brought their own supplies on board, and there was a lively trade and barter in groceries.

A ship's chaplain also belonged to the ranks of the officers. He conducted the church ceremonies and read a 'dry' mass on Sundays and holy days – communion wine was not allowed on the swaying deck of the ship.[62] The royal instructions regarding order on board ship state: 'Great attention must be paid to ensure that God is not blasphemed and His divine wrath thus incurred.' Portuguese Catholics accordingly observed their religious customs meticulously on board ship. The chaplain took confessions, prayed, and there were 'Masses, Vespers, holy water, processions and fasts' on board, as one Protestant traveller, the Frenchman Pyrard, reported. There were also chapels with 'wonderful' holy pictures, where everyone could say their prayers. Religious life intensified when the East India vessels were becalmed in the doldrums in unbearable heat. Vows were made, and left for safekeeping with the ship's scribe; processions of penance were held around the mainmast; supplications were made to all the saints with prayers. For people on the ship, this was the only way in which they could counter the unyielding power of the forces of nature. There was an hour of worship every Saturday on the India voyages – the sailors' prayer (Salve). Chaplain and pilot sang in honour of Our Lady in the traditional manner, trumpets sounded, the saints were invoked and litanies were recited.

The master gunner was answerable only to the captain. He commanded a number of gunners and was responsible for the guns on the ship, as well as, surprisingly, for the two sheets of the mainsail.

A barber dealt with blood-letting and enemas. Blood-letting was a universally applied therapy. It was possibly inappropriate for dysentery, which occurred particularly frequently, and may have hastened an invalid's death. One and a half quartilhos (one quartilho = 0.4–0.55 litres) of blood was tapped at a session. Some invalids let their blood be taken twenty times .[63]

The surgeon presided over a copious medicine-chest, which, as one inventory shows, might contain up to 230 preparations.[64] The captain's written instructions obliged him to ensure that both the barber and the surgeon performed their duties free of charge.

In a chapter entitled 'The men', some space must also be devoted to the women and children who were to be found on the Spanish and Portuguese voyages to the East Indies. Some accounts of voyages mention a number of children on board galleons. Fathers were occasionally permitted to take their children (this almost certainly meant sons) to India with them, so that they could become familiar with the seaman's life from an early age. But one ship, which held over 600 men, also carried some women; not many, around fifteen to twenty, but the scenes which their presence caused incurred the disapproval of the officials and missionaries on board. The most respectable would have been wives of officers, colonial officials and merchants. Some naval officers, however, brought women of 'easy virtue' to India with them, and prostitutes were occasionally found amongst the stowaways.

Single women also travelled to India in an official capacity, as the 'Crown's orphans'. These were respectable girls of marriageable age, whose future husbands could expect a post in the colonial service. This does not seem to have been a popular lifestyle, as these young women would probably die in childbirth in the tropics.[65] White women on the return journey from Goa to Lisbon posed no particular problems, as they were invariably accompanied by their husbands or other relations. But the Portuguese were also always trying to bring coloured slave-girls back to Europe. How successful they were cannot be established; such activity was strictly prohibited.

The ships of the India fleet would leave Lisbon around the end of February or the beginning of March, and aimed to reach the Cape of Good Hope without stopping. From then on, if the voyage went well, there was no further landing before Goa. In emergencies they would land at Bahia de Todos os Santos in Brazil (Salvador), or, on the other side of the Cape, at Mozambique – the Portuguese graveyard. There the ship's crew would be decimated by the unhealthy climate, and by venereal diseases. Experienced and well-off people could prepare themselves for a voyage to India such as this; poor wretches, in contrast, went on board and relied solely on the care provided by their king. An Italian Jesuit travelling in 1574 was amazed:

> It is astonishing to see with what lightness and in what numbers the Portuguese embark for India . . . Many act as though setting off on a journey of not more than a mile from Lisbon. They just bring one shirt, and one or two slices of bread; further provisions consist of nothing more than some cheese and a pot of jam.[66]

Stowaways gradually surfaced after the Cape Verde islands had been passed and they had no further fear of being left on land. They swelled the ranks of the have-nots on board. The ship would reach the dreaded doldrums, a zone of frequent calms, where they might languish for thirty to sixty days, at seven or eight degrees of latitude north of the equator. If people were not already suffering intensely, they would start to do so now: the air would be still, and the heat on board the poorly ventilated ship would be unbearable. Sailing manoeuvres would be carried out several times a day, to make the most of the lightest breezes. The heat would cause cracks to appear in the waling, and the hot, tarred wood would have to be sprayed with water. Pyrard reports:

> The heat is strong and oppressive in the extreme. It destroys most of the provisions, the water is foul and full of worms. Even very carefully salted meat and fish go rotten. Butter melts to oil, as do the tallow candles. Pitch and tar melt as well. It is impossible to stay below deck, as it is like an oven down there. . ..[67]

Even elementary hygiene was lacking on board the overfull ships. By the time they had reached the equator they resembled floating plague-houses, whose inhabitants were dying like flies. Carriers brought infectious diseases on board. Dysentery and scurvy spread rapidly during the month-long absences of fresh provisions. Most people of the time were completely unaware of the health-preserving properties of cleanliness and hygiene; in contrast with the practice on Dutch and English ships, little attempt was made to clean the decks on board Spanish, French and Italian ships. It was not necessary to go to the beakhead ('el jardin') to relieve oneself; pots and jugs fulfilled the same function. The weak and sick were often left lying for days in their own excrement, and the smell between decks was so appalling that people almost fainted when they came in from the fresh air and climbed down a hatchway. There are accounts of voyages where half the passengers and crew died, and Pyrard described even worse cases:

> When I was in Goa, I saw some ships coming in with less than two hundred men on board, out of the one thousand or twelve hundred men with which they had set sail from Lisbon. They were ill with scurvy and so enfeebled that they could scarcely bring themselves on to dry land.[68]

Pyrard does not, however, mention that these ships had broken their journey at Mozambique, where invalids and other people were sometimes left behind. A corpse on board was – as in later times – sewn into a piece of sailcloth and weighted down with a stone. When the master gave a signal with his silver whistle the chaplain said prayers and the dead person was thrown overboard. For the survivors there were only three cures: 'Blood-letting, enemas and faith in God'.

But not all voyages had such disastrous results. They finished increasingly quickly, without making stops on land. Then there would only be a few deaths on board to report. We also find acts of humanity to invalids being made by ships' officers and missionary voyagers. The missionary's duties did not exclude resolving the numerous quarrels which broke out as a result of so many different people living together in such a small space. Mozambique was known for being the place where, within days of a ship's arrival, the soldiers and fidalgos would avenge their quarrels and insults in a most blatant manner; the captain's writ no longer applied. Of course life on board these ships was more than just the quest for a better life, marred by illness and stench. There were also modest pleasures, like cards and games of chance. Don Quixote, Cervantes's hero, had popularised the excesses of chivalrous romances amongst the Spanish and Portuguese, and these were avidly read and passed around. The sailors caught birds, turtles and sharks, and held a rowdy celebration when they crossed the equator.

Once the ship approached the stormy Cape of Good Hope, the company could consider themselves free from attack by enemy (mainly Dutch) ships. The guns were raised from their mounts and brought down to the hold. The sailors redistributed the ship's ballast, and augmented it with drinking-water barrels, now filled with sea water. They brought down the topgallant masts and hoisted new, smaller sails. All movable items on deck were secured, and the joiner dismantled the light-holes, nailing boards over the openings. Passengers had to remain below decks, and the fire was put out. As long as the weather was bad, the pilot (at his seat), the master (on the quarter-deck) and the captain, all stayed awake. There was no sleep or hot food to be had; only ship's biscuit and some wine. Those who had complained of the heat in the doldrums now froze and produced their wraps. The poor wretches whose single pieces of clothing now hung in tatters suffered as well, and some paid with their lives for their missing kit. Many despaired at such times, cried out 'Misericordia' and made vows. Relics were dipped in the sea; holy water sprinkled; and stormy winds exorcised by the ship's chaplain from the poop – a procedure which necessitated his being held fast by strong men, to prevent him from falling overboard. When the Cape had been successfully rounded, the tension in many people dissolved into happiness. The weather improved; passengers rejoiced and held a celebratory meal (whatever that might be), as there was once again hope that they might reach Goa after all.

The ships returning from Goa to Lisbon were only occasionally galleons: more often large carracks. Many galleons remained behind in India, where they served on trading routes to Indochina, Japan, China and the Spice Islands. The homeward voyage was no less hazardous than the outward one; the risk was even greater owing to the unfortunate custom of overloading the ships. Pyrard, who boarded a returning ship in Goa, wrote:

> When you board one of these ships, which looks like a fortress with a huge quantity of people and merchandise, the effect is astonishing. The deck of our ship was so laden with goods that they reached halfway up the mast. Outboard as well – on the railings and ledges on either side, you could see nothing but goods, provisions and bunks [berths], that is, little cabins where the sailors and other people lie down, covered with ox- or cow-hides. In short, the whole deck was so arranged that you could hardly move around on it . . .[69]

To the bedbugs, lice, fleas and rats, which the passengers had encountered during the outward journey, were now added Indian cockroaches: 'They are numerous, and found on everything coming from India. If you squash them with your hand, they stink horribly' On the other hand, it was also true that the returning ships smelt pleasantly of all the spices in the cargo.

Bad weather and high seas could be dangerous to the overladen ships as they approached the Cape of Good Hope. Jan Huyghen Linschoten, the Dutch explorer and traveller who made the return journey in 1590, recorded how a storm announced itself on the coast of Natal with a St Elmo's fire on the yardarms of the mainmast. The crew strengthened the ship's masts and hull with rope and cable which was passed under the keel. Everyone doubted whether the ship would be able to ride the huge waves. The sea flooded the entire upper deck and the men worked day and night at the pumps. Only the foresail remained hoisted: a strong brace had been rigged from the yardarms of the fore yard aft of the pilot, who sat rigidly on his seat. Fifteen to sixteen men stood ready at each of these mainbraces. The deputy helmsman watched the mountainous seas from the poop. He would warn the pilot of an approaching wave; the latter then gave orders to the men on the braces, and – via a middle man – to the ten or twelve men standing by the rudder below deck. No one slept for days at a time. There was no rest and no hot food. The psychological tension on the people on board the tossing ship was enormous: 'for if the seas had washed over us from the sides, it would have all been over: requiescant in pace' wrote Linschoten. He survived the journey round the Cape – only to be shipwrecked a little later, at Terceira, in the Azores.[70]

CHAPTER 6

The Stockholm galleon model

O NE of the loveliest exhibits in the Stockholm Maritime Museum is the galleon model which used to hang in Stockholm Cathedral (the Storkyrka). Nothing is known about the model's origins, or its date of construction. A church inventory list of 1830 describes it as 'a somewhat older ship, which used to hang in the organ loft, and is now kept in the tower'. In 1937 the model was transferred to public ownership in the Maritime Museum (Fig 40). The model has, unfortunately been badly damaged. The beakhead is missing, as are the galleries and other parts of the stern. The rigging has disappeared without trace. But what has survived of the 1.27m long × 0.39m high × 0.26m wide hull over the centuries is worth a second glance. The intricacies of the model's construction and its decoration are impressive. By comparing it with contemporary pictures we can date it at around 1600.

*Fig 40: Side view and plan view of the Stockholm galleon model, now displayed in Stockholm Maritime Museum. (*Photo: Statens Sjöhistoriska Museum, Stockholm*)*

STOCKHOLMS STORKYRKAS GAMLA VOTIVSKEPP
PLAN OCH SIDOVY UPPMÄTNING. I VOTIVSKEPPETS SKALA (1:32?)

1--18 = fästpunkter för vant, vid några finnas rester av röstjärnen

S. 96/97

Plan 1: Plan view and side view of the Stockholm galleon model,

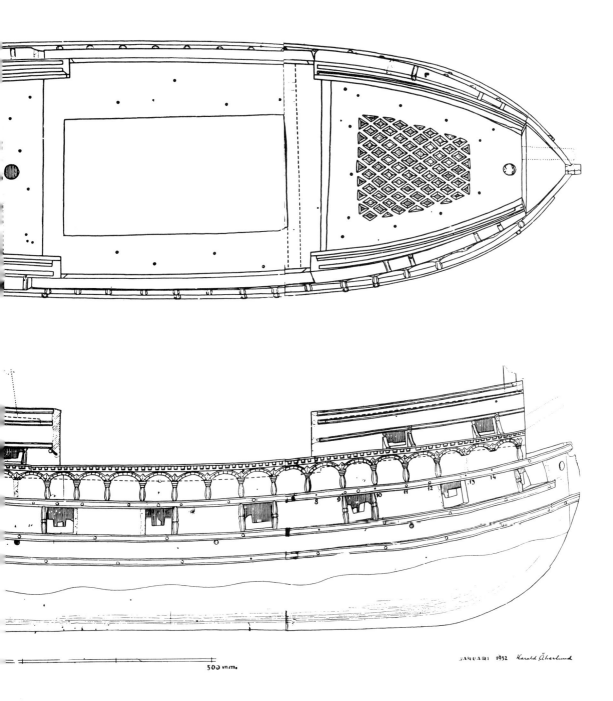

500 mm.

JANUARI 1952 Harald Åkerlund

*a large sailing ship from around 1600. (*Drawing: H Åkerlund*)*

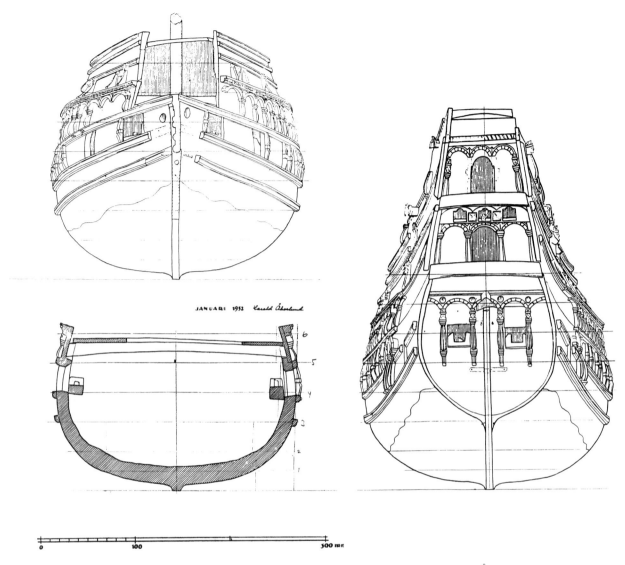

JANUARI 1952 *Harald Åkerlund*

Plan 2: Bow and stern view, together with mid-ship section, of the Stockholm galleon model. (Drawing: H Åkerlund)

The Stockholm galleon, as I call it, is a typical votive ship. Until the beginning of the seventeenth century, ship models were generally votive gifts, made by artists, sailors and, perhaps, ships' carpenters. Not until later in the seventeenth century did shipwrights in England, France and the Netherlands occasionally prepare demonstration models and samples before commencing construction of an actual ship. The Stockholm galleon was built to hang in a sacred place. Perhaps someone commissioned it as a proof of piety; perhaps it was originally a thanksgiving for a successful voyage. The congregation would see the model from below, in the same way as, today, we see the replica which hangs in an aisle in Stockholm Cathedral. The full-bellied roundness of the lower part of the ship with the 'correct' proportion jars when seen from this perspective: one's glance should be directed to the places where old ships might have had decoration – the sides, or the painted sails. We have to imagine the missing rigging above the hull to compensate for the foreshortening in perspective. Like many votive ships, the Stockholm galleon is too narrow. Its builders evidently intended to show only the presentable side view of a large galleon of its time. This part of the model seems to have been based on an original, and that vindicates the attempt made in this book to reconstruct the hull proportions of a ship of this type.

The part of the model which would lie below the water has soft, round lines (Plans 1 and 3). They become almost sheer at the stem. The underwater part merges harmoniously into the upper part of the ship. All in all, the hull is a pleasing structure with the kind of ideal shape a contemporary shipbuilder could only dream about. The Peller model, which is, chronologically speaking, not so very far apart from the 'Stockholm galleon', is a similar example of a pleasing, rounded, ideal shape.[1] In actual fact, the lines of ships' hulls from around 1600 were not as rounded as we find in some models and reconstructions today. The shape of the underwater hull, which the model builder of almost 400 years ago gave to his block of wood with a rasp and a carving knife, omits one thing in particular: a distinct floor. It is most unlikely that the floor timbers of a real ship had an angle like this as their baseline, or that the floor head was as rounded and ill-defined.

Around the beginning of the seventeenth century we can see two characteristic styles emerging in the shape of large ships' midship frames constructed in north European waters with substantial tidal differences. On the one hand, the English method of construction, appropriate for those with the advantages of deep water harbours; on the other, the Dutch method, which had to allow for shallow water (Figs 67 and 68). The English gave their midship frame a relatively narrow floor, and the first futtocks of the ribs projected obliquely outwards from the floor head. Ships with this rib shape had a considerable draught. The Dutch used a broad floor for the midship frame, and the futtocks went upwards steeply from the sharp floor head. Shipwrights from both countries assembled the ribs from pieces of wood which were straight or curving, in varying degrees, in a recognisable sequence. Our model's underwater hull, however, has none of these features, so we cannot classify it as belonging to either of these traditions.

Side view

In 1952 Harald Åkerlund took the measurements of the Stockholm galleon so that he could construct a replica which would include the missing parts (Plans 1–3). (See Fig 45 for the names of the parts of the Stockholm galleon in the following description.) If we look at the side view, we can see the typical silhouette of a galleon: the stern of the ship is low-lying, in comparison with the large carrack-type ships built in the sixteenth century (Figs 2, 7, 14). On the stern the two curved sections above the counter indicate two open galleries. The sternpost has an angle of 18°, in keeping with contemporary shipbuilding practice. The model's forecastle is low and short, with only one deck. It is closed off forward with a front bulkhead, ahead of which there was another small deck. The beakhead (unfortunately no longer extant) was structurally separated from the forecastle by this bulkhead. Most carracks still did not have a forward bulkhead like this – the forecastle continued straight on to the beakhead.

The lower row of gunports and scuppers gives a clue as to the position of the lower deck. Ports and hawse-holes on the bow show that the deck was continuous to this point. Scuppers and ports on the stern show that the lower deck dropped down and continued as the deck of the gunroom. Lower deck was the term used around 1600 for the first watertight deck above the ship's waterline (see pp 21 and 29), on which was placed the lower tier of guns.

A glance at the waist area of the model shows that it has a continuous upper deck. It continues forward under the forecastle, following the run of the first wale at this height. Two guns stand on the upper deck, their ports (2 x 1.5cm) cut into the sides of the forecastle. On the aftermost third of the model's hull, the upper deck does not run in the way we would expect on a real ship, or as indicated by the second tier of five gunports (Fig 42). The reason may well be that the modelbuilder did not have enough curvature in the boards he was using. There is a halfdeck above the upper deck, which, as its name implies, runs sternwards for half the length of model. The remains of a gunport can be distinguished from the arming cloths. A quarter deck and a poop deck, all leading to the stern, follow. All these decks are curved and follow the camber of the deck beams, as they would have done on a real ship. The longitudinal curve of the decks closely follows the run of the adjacent planking and wales.

From the side view we can see a noticeable run on the three lower wales. At the stern, this differs only slightly but at the bow it varies significantly from the flatter course of the wales which was conventional English shipbuilding practice at the beginning of the seventeenth century. The curve of the wales there consists of a large arc (see p 183). The strong

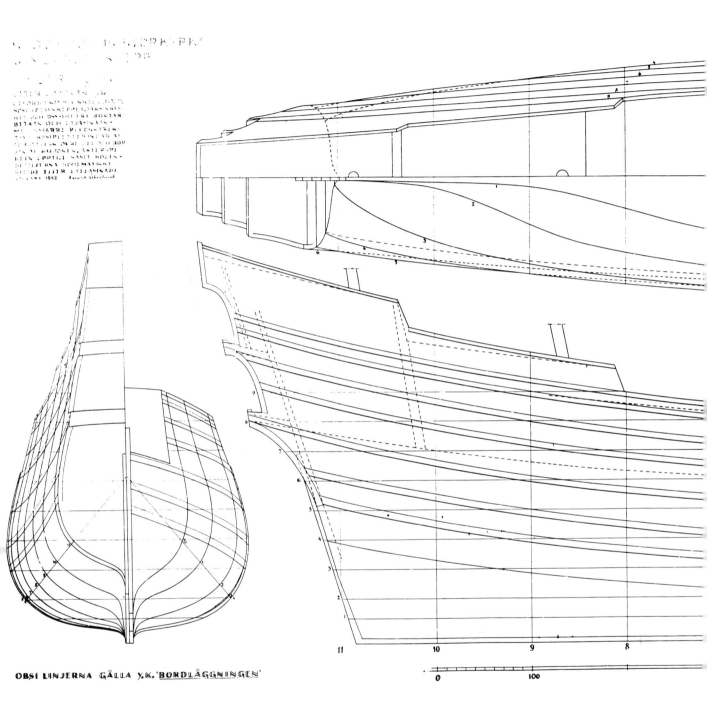

OBS! LINJERNA GÄLLA Y.K. "BORDLÄGGNINGEN"

0   100

Plan 3: Reconstruction of the lines of the Stockholm galleon model,

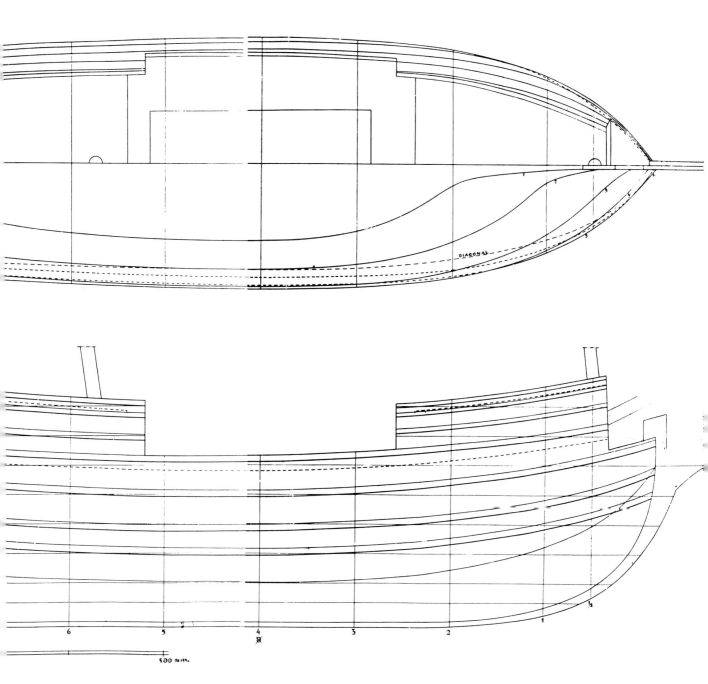

*made by Harald Åkerlund for a replica. (*Drawing: H Åkerlund*)*

upwards curve of the wales in the forward part of the Stockholm galleon would be improbable in a real ship. A little digression is necessary here to clarify this statement. The breadth line was an important element in ship construction around 1600.[2] It was a construction line which passed through all the ribs at the point of their greatest breadth. Amidships, the breadth line lay somewhat above the waterline (Figs 41, 65, 74). If this line, viewed from the side, lay deep and had only a gentle curve, then the maximum breadth also lay deep. A ship had its maximum displacement at this point, and consequently its greatest buoyancy.

If we reconstruct our model galleon's breadth line from Åkerlund's drawings, it becomes clear that it rises sharply upwards towards the bow of the ship (Fig 41). If a real ship had had a breadth line like this, its buoyancy at the bow would have been very low indeed, perhaps too low for the pressure of the large sails and for the weight of the long-barrelled chasers which galleons carried at the forward ports of the upper decks and, occasionally, on the forecastle. On the other hand, a breadth line which is high at both ends suggests older shipbuilding traditions, and perhaps an earlier construction date for the model – before the beginning of the seventeenth century, say. The increasing weight of guns carried in that century meant that the breadth line became deeper and flatter. This augmented the load-bearing capacity of the warships.

It was conventional shipbuilding practice to construct the stem in the shape of an arc; the stem merged harmoniously into the keel. The low underwater part of the Stockholm galleon imposes too strong a curve on the stem.

Eleven gunports pierce the display side of the model, above the first two wales. The two sternports are set lower down and pierce the second wale. The ports are very large (3 x 2.5cm) to accommodate the (proportionally) over-sized guns which old votive ships often carried. In the interior of the model we can make out the remains of upright stanchions with which these guns (no longer extant) were secured. We can also see a row of round scuppers – a rare detail – below the first wale. These also indicate the position of the deck.

The main rail, which lies somewhat above the height of the upper decks is interesting, from the point of view of the ship's construction. In the waist area, between the superstructures, it forms the upper end of the ship's side. Its width varies: at the waist it is 10mm. Just in front of the mainmast it becomes 3–4mm wider towards the stern. Its width decreases at the aft upper deck gunport, and it runs inconspicuously down to the stern. In the direction of the forecastle the main rail is 13mm wide, decreasing to 5mm at the bow. The lower side of this broad item is decorated with a toothed strip to prevent it from appearing too heavy. In contrast with traditional shipbuilding practice of this time, broad wood was used for the channel for the yards of the foremasts and mainmasts. We can still see the nail heads for

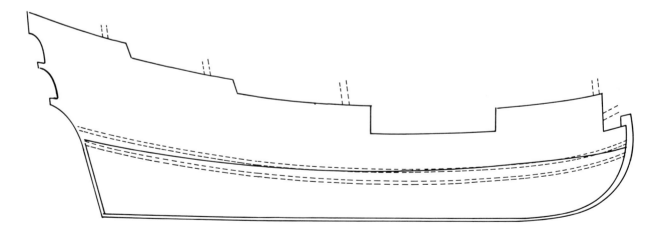

Fig 41: Diagram showing the Stockholm galleon model's breadth line. It is the solid line running through the two lower wales, shown as dotted lines. Here the breadth line curves upwards at the bow relatively sharply: most probably an overstatement on the part of the modelbuilder, if we compare it with known ship-building practice from the early decades of the seventeenth century. In an actual ship this would indicate low buoyancy at the bow.

the chains of these shrouds on the third wale. This noteworthy arrangement of the rails fits elegantly into the structure of the ship's hull, and we can infer that a ship based on this model would have been similarly constructed. Knees decorated with crowned heads flank the gunports and support the rails against the upper sides of the ship. One such wale, broadened into a channel, has the qualities of a gangway. It made work on the tackle easier, and allowed easy access to the gun muzzles on the upper battery. We know that towards the end of the sixteenth century, and in the early part of the seventeenth century, ships' guns were often cleaned and loaded from over the ship's side. They could be fired without recoil (see p 59).[3] Incorporating the rails into the construction of the ship's side does not, however, seem to have been general practice. In most contemporary pictures we find rails which were placed individually on the wales. Perhaps an arrangement like that found on the Stockholm galleon posed problems in practice: possibly it created too much wind resistance, or provided boarding parties with an inviting foothold.

From an examination of the third wale we can infer from the missing sternpiece that a gallery was originally attached there. It ran round the stern, and was entered from the stern bulkhead via an arch-shaped passage. A knee supported each side of the deck against the side walls. Its position can be identified by an unpainted area in the decoration of the sides (Fig 49). Above it we can see traces of a second gallery, situated on the upper edge of the second wale. The front outer edge of the gallery deck was decorated with a toothed strip. The upper gallery railing seems to have been attached to the ship's side by a wooden bracket (Figs 47 and 49).

Plan view

Forward and aft of the main rib, or midship frame, of a galleon were a number of similarly-shaped ribs. The ratio of keel length to maximum breadth was 2½–3:1. Features like this cannot be observed from a plan view of the model. The whole hull is too narrow, in comparison with the proportions of real ships. From the plan view it is clear that the forward end of the forecastle, with its lines running inwards, is narrow. The forward bulkhead does not yet have the projecting shape it had on ships of a later period. From that we can assume that the Stockholm galleon did not have a cathead. Shipwrights of the time arranged the row of the upper futtocks of ribs according to the toptimber line (Figs 66, 74), a construction line which defined the shape of the hull at the tops of the ribs. As is clear from the plan view, this line merges into the stem, forcing the galleon builders to construct narrow superstructures. They overcome this to a certain extent, however, by accentuating the curve of the line.

The modelbuilder never intended the decks to be viewed from above, so these have been left with almost no detail. The upper deck has been cut away in the waist area, allowing us to see inside the hold; the foredecks and halfdecks have two gratings with a diagonal pattern. Wickerwork-type patterned gratings like this are occasionally found in contemporaneous pictures of ships (see Fig 6). Some drawings show ships with diagonally-patterned gratings as well as ships with rectilinear-patterned gratings. We can assume, in such cases, that the artist was acquainted with both types. The diagonal grating seems to have been the less common form of construction at the turn of the seventeenth century, and was later discontinued. We can count four mast holes on the decks, so this was clearly meant to be a four-masted ship. The sternmost mast, the bonaventure mast (see p 36 ff), was a characteristic feature of large ships of the period. This was the case until the third decade of the seventeenth century, when bonaventure masts could still be found on ships which had been built at the end of the sixteenth century. W L Clowes, the British naval historian, says: 'By 1618 one-half of all the king's ships were four-masters . . . while by 1640 the use of four masts had entirely disappeared from the English Navy'.[4]

The triangular mizzensail and the sheet belayed to a mast positioned as far aft as the bonaventure mast must have projected over the poop deck. This made a boom necessary: the outlicker. Unfortunately the part of the upper stern with the hole for this round timber has not survived on the model. The mizzenmast, which is situated on the forward third of the quarter deck, was, like the bonaventure mast, rigged with a lateen sail. A knighthead with two sheaves was used on the tackle required for lowering this spar (see the rigging plan for the reconstruction, no 36). On the model it is located on the halfdeck, in front of the mast. The knighthead is positioned slightly to starboard, and leans gently aft.

Fig 42: For a votive ship, the external appearance is of primary importance; the internal construction is only a means to this end. The hull of the Stockholm galleon, up to the height of the third wale, was constructed from a hollowed-out block of wood (shaded portion of sketch). The upper ship's side, on each side, is made from a single plank of coniferous wood. The decks and bulkheads (shown in black) indicate the supports and crosspieces between the two sides.

The mainmast and foremast are situated on the forward parts of the halfdeck and forecastle deck respectively. Both are unusual positions, as in most contemporaneous pictures these masts are unmistakeably forward of the relevant bulkheads. The bowsprit runs on the side of the forecastle, past the foremast. The extreme forward position of the foremast on galleons did not allow sufficient support for the heavy bowsprit, which had the same circumference as the mast nearby. So it ran past the mast into the ship's interior. The sprit curved towards the centreline and met it with its head. This compensated for its offset position.

In its present state the Stockholm galleon model has mast stumps, which are possibly not original. So we need to exercise caution in considering the angles at which these round timbers meet the keel floor. Unfortunately we cannot establish any further details about the original rigging, or the ship's construction, from the decks.

Construction of the model

The simple construction of the model results in a shell, which has, externally, the shape of a ship's hull. The inner structure bears no resemblance to the construction of a real ship.

The model is a block model from the keel up to the third wale (Plan 2 and Fig 42). Even the keel has been worked from the same block. In the middle, at the main beam, the floor of the hollowed-out block is 20mm thick. The width of the sides diminishes to approximately 13mm at the top. The wood is conifer. The upper edge of the block, at the height of the third wale, ends in a groove. On this rests, on each side, the piece of construction which forms the entire ship's side from bow to stern: a single piece of coniferous wood which has been carved into the correct shape. The ship's side is about 5mm thick at the groove, narrowing to about 3mm at the upper edge of the superstructure. The third wale covers the seam between the lower block and the side walls of the model except for the part where the lower gallery used to be. The three lower wales are held fast with thick nails. In the third wale we can still see the nails below the channel of the mainmast which were used for fastening the chains. We can see seven chain nails for both the foremast and the mainmast.

No lower deck has been built for the guns at the lower row of ports, althought scuppers have been bored for it. Instead of being mounted on a deck, the guns are held by plugs on a 15 x 10mm strip which runs round the inside of the model at the height of the lower edge of the gunports. The upper deck consists of three adjoining parts: as already mentioned, the stern area does not correspond to the run of a real deck. All the decks, and the remaining parts of the model, are made from coniferous wood. They lie across deck-beam type cross-timbers, and support the upper part of the hull of the model. The front bulkhead of the poop leans aft, and leads down inside the model to the upper deck, where it serves as a construction support.

The stern part of the lower block of wood has been hollowed out to give thin sides. A small board has been fitted for the lower part of the stern (Fig 43). It runs right up to the poop, at the same angle as the stern post, and stabilises the sides of the model at the stern. The hole for the tiller has been cut into this board, as has, higher up, the arched passageway to the gallery. Below, there is a floor for the stern part of the gallery. The floor for the second gallery is above the passageway. As it projected further astern, there is a bulkhead here containing an arched passageway to the second gallery. The richly-decorated upper part of the stern of our galleon would at one time have been closed off with a further bulkhead which is no longer extant.

All wales, timbers, arches, columns and decorative elements are nailed on to the ship's side. Close observation – particularly where the lower block joins the sides – shows that at some stage coarse nails were used to prevent the separate sections of the model from falling apart. The nail heads of this safety measure are not painted, and can therefore be considered a later addition.

All in all, the model is a very simple, functional, robust construction. It consists of a few large pieces, probably one of the reasons why the core of the old hull has survived until the present day.

Fig 43: This view of the stern of the model shows the two stern gunports of the gun room, below the first counter. The two passageways, one above the other, visible on the upper portion of the stern, lead to the upper and lower galleries.

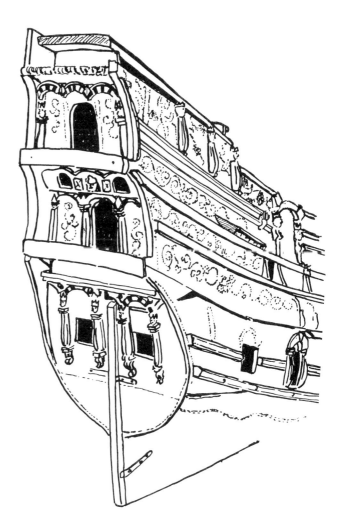

Fig 44: This fine specimen from the Museo Naval in Madrid is one of the few remaining model galleons. It was presented to King Philip II in the Netherlands in 1597. We can recognise the characteristic features of the classical galleon. An upper deck, running the length of the ship, lies above a continuous lower deck carrying the lower guns. The halfdeck starts unmistakably aft of the mainmast. This model has no quarter-deck. The poop is a light barrel-type construction without its own deck, reminiscent of superstructures on Mediterranean galleys or galleasses. The short forecastle with a front bulkhead, in front of which the foremast leans gently forward, is also typical. The forecastle is lower than on a carrack. As here, many galleons also had the fourth (bonaventure) mast at the stern. The angle of the open gallery and the beakhead correspond harmoniously – the model builder evidently paid scant regard to the actual proportions of the hull. The model has been ineptly restored; the rigging in particular yields such misleading conclusions that it has been omitted from this sketch.

Façade

The upper part of the ship's side is the *pièce de resistance* of the model. In keeping with contemporaneous taste, it is decorated with a renaissance façade. The Stockholm galleon is peerless – no other ship model from this period is so richly decorated and painted. Even the beautiful ornamental painting on the Flemish galleon of 1593 (Fig 44) in the Maritime Museum in Madrid is not so imaginative or so varied. Landström has reconstructed this galleon in his book, *The Ship*.[5] The English galleons of this period, depicted in the shipwright Matthew Baker's drawings of c.1586, are also more functionally, and more modestly, decorated.[6] However, we will never know which elements of these decorations on models and drawings were actually used on a real ship. The decoration on the sides is further emphasised by the arrangement of the wales, planking and gunports (Fig 45). The white-painted underwater portion of the ship ends – far below the place where an actual waterline would be – in a wavy line, which is further adorned with a thin black scroll decoration. This element in the decoration has its full effect when we view the hanging model from below. The scroll decoration is repeated between the two lower wales: this time in orange-red on a lime-green background.

Polygonal columns 'knotted' with shaft rings flank the gunports of the lower battery deck. Between the ports there is a panelled frieze, with representations of zoomorphic creatures, which I will discuss later. The two aft lower gunports have a portal-type frame consisting of two full-bellied, fluted columns with fascia capitals and a toothed arch segment. The first rail, which has for the most part been broadened into a channel, is decorated with a toothed strip, and lies like an architrave over a similarly-sized row of arches. These consist of arch sections which are decorated with a toothed strip, and supported by bulging columns with three-tiered capitals. The distance between these columns corresponds to the distance between the columns flanking the lower row of gunports, and continues their line upwards. Where they cannot be decorated with open gunport lids, the arches contain curved panels painted with pairs of mirror-image male

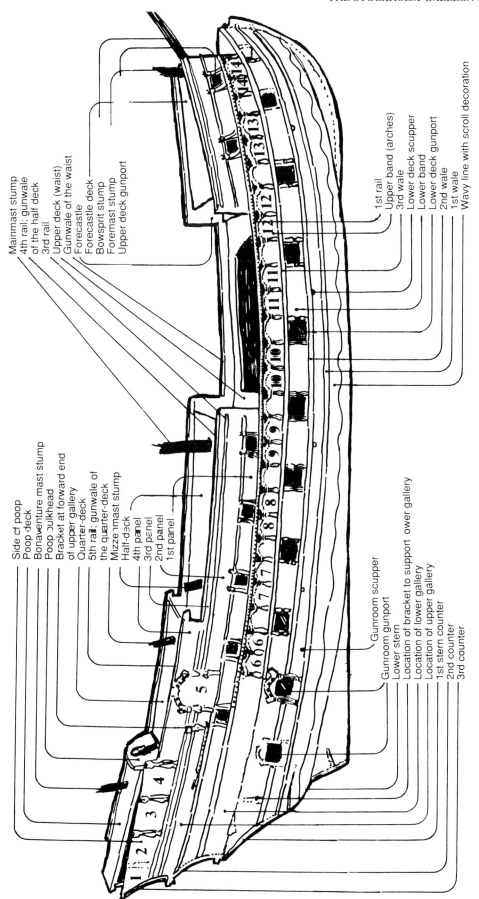

Fig 45: *Technical terms for the individual parts of the Stockholm galleon, with numbers identifying the spaces containing pictorial representations. (After a sketch by W Jaeger)*

Mainmast stump
4th rail: gunwale of the half deck
3rd rail
Upper deck (waist)
Gunwale of the waist
Forecastle
Forecastle deck
Bowsprit stump
Foremast stump
Upper deck gunport

1st rail
Upper band (arches)
3rd wale
Lower deck scupper
Lower band
Lower deck gunport
2nd wale
1st wale
Wavy line with scroll decoration

Side of poop
Poop deck
Bonaventure mast stump
Poop bulkhead
Bracket at forward end of upper gallery
Quarter-deck
5th rail: gunwale of the quarter-deck
Mizzenmast stump
Half-deck
4th panel
3rd panel
2nd panel
1st panel

Gunroom scupper
Gunroom gunport
Lower stern
Location of bracket to support lower gallery
Location of lower gallery
Location of upper gallery
1st stern counter
2nd counter
3rd counter

busts, on a light-blue background. The arches end aft where the lower gallery began. The ship's side there is painted with its characteristic scroll decoration – this time in white on a black background.

The first row of upper deck gunports is in the panels above the first rail. They are flanked by strong knees with carved, crowned flesh-coloured heads as finials. The crowns are gilded, as are the other elements in the façade: wales, rails, columns, arches, etc. The white scroll decoration on a black background reappears in the first panel between the upper gunports (Figs 46 and 47). The next highest space – the second panel – contains, in the forecastle, a vine tendril motif on a white background (Fig 46). Aft, in the halfdeck area, we find an architectural painting (Fig 52): fluted pilasters with abutments and curved arches are painted in various shades of blue-grey. Here the artist is using a form of decoration containing elements of land-based architecture to ornament the sides of his ship. Painted scroll decorations and rows of arches were often to be found on contemporaneous galleons, as many of the pictures in this monograph show.

At the stern the architectural painting gives way to plastic elements again. A large section in the ship's side (Fig 45, no 5) even demands the sacrifice of the rails running through it. It is framed by an arch segment with a toothed decoration, supported by caryatids in the form of female upper bodies with crowned heads (Fig 47). Under the arch a seated, female figure is painted on a black background. And we find the vine tendril motif from the forecastle again on both sides of the arch, in the fourth panel.

The model ship's side is extremely beautiful at poop height (Figs 48, 49). The starboard side has not been completed, but we can imagine how it would have looked from the port side. The latter is divided into four panels by a series of arches. Fluted half columns bear crowned heads, above which are arch segments with a toothed decoration. All

Fig 46: The forecastle of the Stockholm galleon model. The second panel of the ship's side shows a vine tendril motif of blue grapes and green leaves on a white background, a symbol of the body of Christ. Underneath, between the gunports of the gun deck, is a line of scrollwork – a stylised acanthus motif on a black background. In the arches of the upper band below that are the portrait panels 12, 13 and 14. Then comes the lower band, with the frieze of mythical creatures.

Fig 47: Two wales at the height of the quarter-deck are interrupted for panel 5. A large toothed arch is supported by two caryatids. The panel shows a seated woman playing the harp, and a stag's head. The woman may represent music, one of the fine arts. In Christian symbolism the stag represents rebirth through baptism – perhaps also perseverance. The picture has a black background. The woman's skirt is painted in yellowish-green shades, the sleeve blue-green; the bodice crimson. There is a vine tendril motif in the fourth panel; a symbol of the body of Christ. To the left of the panel we can see the remains of a wooden bracket which may have led to the railing of the upper gallery.

the columns and arches here have been gilded as well; the heads have been painted flesh colour. Each panel of the picture holds a seated female figure, on a black background.

The Stockholm galleon's high-projecting stern, with its five decks, offers a rich opportunity for architectural decoration (Fig 43 and Plan 2). We find the elements used in the decoration of the stern bulkheads elsewhere on the model. The fluted columns with abutments in the area of the stern gunports are further adorned with heads supporting the toothed arch segments mentioned earlier. The columns on the lower gallery bulkhead are overlaid with an architrave-type structure, resembling a row of barred, open windows, from where three crowned heads used to gaze out at the gallery railing. Only the middle one is still there. Images like this are a common feature of renaissance façades.

Since the earliest times the decoration of an object with figures or ornaments has also implied the wish to express a hidden meaning. A ship's decoration was no exception: some overtly political concepts lie behind the allegorical figures decorating imposing State ships of the seventeenth and eighteenth centuries.[7] A historic ship model is itself a symbol with a predominantly religious character.[8] We will never know the precise reasons for which the Stockholm galleon, like most other old ship models, was conceived and built. The rich symbolism of its iconography indicates general Christian and pre-Christian beliefs, seemingly reaching from hell to heaven and encompassing our world in between. The painting is good folk art. The unknown artist completed his task with skill and expertise. Was he also the person who built the model? We will never know. If the model was the work of two people, then they must have co-operated very closely. Close examination of the details shows that in some places the colouring has been continued below the parts which were at one time nailed on but are now lost. That means that some of the wales, galleries, columns etc were only attached after the model had been painted.

In the spaces between the lower gunports we find a group of fabulous animals, arranged in mirror-image on the left-hand and right-hand sides of each port. The springing creature at the bow, where the row begins, has the body of a lion, complete with mane and tail (Figs 46, 51), and the head of a dog, out of which hangs a large red tongue. In Christian symbolism the lion represents the devil, and the dog, in this context, anger.[9] Next come two basilisks: mixtures of bird and reptile (Figs 50, 55, 56). On a green, winged body sits the head of a cock with a red comb and a long, red arrow-headed tongue. The body has cock's feet, and ends in a pointed, ringed, red serpent's tail. The basilisk, the king of the

Fig 48: The side of the poop is taken up with four large panels (1–4), the upper part of which is missing on the starboard side. The port side, however, which is shown here, is intact. Its figures vary only slightly from those on the other side. The four seated women are all endowed with symbolic attributes, and may be taken to represent vanity, virginity, wrath and inconstancy. The portraits are painted on a black background. The woman in Panel 1 (starboard) is wearing a blue skirt and a yellow-green bodice. The monkey is brown, the fruit light red. The woman in Panel 2 is wearing slightly different clothing from the picture on the starboard side. There she is wearing a yellow-green dress, with an orange-red underskirt. The flowers are red and white; there is no vase in the picture. The woman in Panel 3 is wearing a crimson skirt and a blue-green bodice. The parrot is green with touches of red. The woman in Panel 4 is wearing a yellow bodice with a light red skirt. The eagle is dark brown. (Photo: Stockholm Maritime Museum)

Fig 49: The Stockholm galleon's aft starboard side. We can see the symbolic pictures of women on the side of the poop (Panels 1–4). Beneath them there is a scroll decoration in the upper band and the first and second panels. In the lower band, which runs under the (missing) lower gallery, we can make out basilisks and griffins.

reptiles with the Medusa-like, fatal glance, symbolised the devil. The next group consists of two griffins, figures from classical mythology (Figs 53, 54). These bird-lion hybrids are painted in green on a black background, and have long red arrow-headed tongues. The hybrid creatures depicted in the lower area of the heavy ordnance seem to represent the evil, threatening part of the hull. The projecting red tongues of these monsters echo the tongues of fire emanating from the gun barrels. Fabulous creatures like these had their origins in magic and animism.

A group of busts of various men has been painted in the row of arches above (Figs 46, 50-58). They are looking at each other, as though in mirror-image. Some of the heads are clean-shaven; some have magnificent red, white and black beards. We find monks, Moors and Renaissance men wearing ruffs. Classifying this group is not a simple matter. We can perhaps see them, in terms of Christian symbolism, as representatives of the races through which the message of the Holy Spirit will be spread throughout the whole world. They could also be people who had witnessed the miracle of the 'Effusion of the Holy Spirit'. The vine tendril motif on the model's forecastle and in the panel of the quarter deck also

Fig 50: The ship's side in the quarter-deck region. To the lower left of the picture is the portal-type framework for the side gunports of the gunroom. On the lower band, between the lower deck gunports, there is a frieze of painted hybrid, or mythical, creatures. A basilisk, consisting of a bird's body and a cock's head with an arrow-headed tongue, and symbolising the devil, is depicted on a black background. Its body ends in a reptilian, arrow-headed tail. The body, head and tail are painted in shades of olive to yellow-brown; the comb, tongue and tip of the tail are light red; the feet and beak yellow. In the upper band is a row of arches, above which lies the first wale: broadened, architrave-like, into a rail. The panels numbered 6 in the upper band show the bust of a bearded man in a yellow jacket with a dark-blue cap-like head covering, on a light blue background. On the first panel, between the gunports, there is a scrollwork decoration in white on a black background.

has Christian symbolism (Figs 46, 47): it represents Christ himself. Vine leaves, which are often depicted in connection with the Good Shepherd, were the most important of all botanical symbols.

The feminine sphere rises above the masculine world. The large arched panel (no 5) contains the picture of a seated woman playing a seven-stringed harp (Fig 47). A stag, whose head projects into the picture, appears to be listening. Perhaps this woman symbolises music, one of the seven fine arts, which is often depicted by a harp. In Christian symbolism the stag may represent rebirth through baptism. According to medieval physiology (a synopsis of allegorical interpetations of nature, which was widespread in the medieval period), the stag treads on an outstretched snake and devours it, and so as not to die from its poison, it looks for a spring with fresh water. There it loses its antlers, but is reborn. The stag is both the enemy and the conqueror of poisonous snakes; and sometimes also a symbol of perseverence. In classical mythology it also represented Actaeon, a young and beautiful huntsman mentioned in one of Ovid's metamorphoses. Actaeon had the misfortune to be caught observing the goddess Artemis

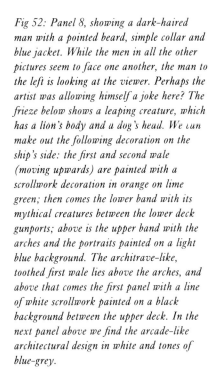

Fig 51: Panel 7 shows a red-haired, bearded man with a renaissance ruff and a blue jacket. The hybrid creature in the frieze below has a lion's body and a dog's head, with a long, red tongue. In Christian symbolism the lion and the dog represent the devil and anger.

Fig 52: Panel 8, showing a dark-haired man with a pointed beard, simple collar and blue jacket. While the men in all the other pictures seem to face one another, the man to the left is looking at the viewer. Perhaps the artist was allowing himself a joke here? The frieze below shows a leaping creature, which has a lion's body and a dog's head. We can make out the following decoration on the ship's side: the first and second wale (moving upwards) are painted with a scrollwork decoration in orange on lime green; then comes the lower band with its mythical creatures between the lower deck gunports; above is the upper band with the arches and the portraits painted on a light blue background. The architrave-like, toothed first wale lies above the arches, and above that comes the first panel with a line of white scrollwork painted on a black background between the upper deck. In the next panel above we find the arcade-like architectural design in white and tones of blue-grey.

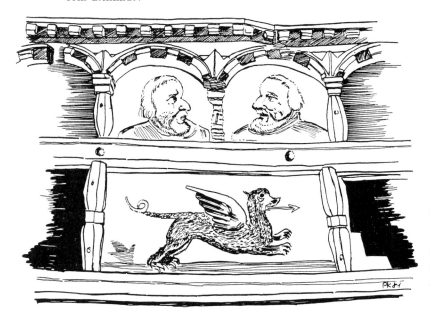

Fig 53: In Panel 9 we find a bust with the profile of a white-bearded old man. He is wearing a simple, purple jacket. The space below shows a leaping griffin with a long, arrow-headed tongue. The griffin, a creature from classical mythology, is painted in yellow-green tones on a black background, with a red tongue and tail-tip.

bathing herself. He was turned into a stag as a punishment, and torn apart by his own hounds.

The group of four women pictured on the side of the poop (Panels 1–4, and Fig 48) is similarly rich in symbolic meaning. Panel 4 is decorated with a picture of a young lady, whose décolletage reveals an ample bosom. She is seated, viewing herself in a mirror with evident satisfaction, and being watched by an eagle, a symbol of Mary – just as an eagle directs its young towards the sun, so does Mary lead us to the true Light of Christ. The mirror is another Marian symbol; but in the case of this young lady, who is obviously pleased with her appearance, it seems to be more a symbol of vanity.

The seated woman in Panel 3 has a similar décolletage, and holds a parrot with red and green plumage on her outstretched arm. The bird symbolises virginity – unlike the green parts of plants, its green feathers never become

Fig 54: Panel 10, showing a portrait of a tonsured monk. The space below holds a leaping griffin.

Fig 55: Panel 11, showing a portrait of a Moor in a light red jacket. The space below holds a basilisk.

Fig 56: Panel 12, showing a portrait of a man with a light brown beard, ruff and mid-blue jacket. The space below holds a basilisk.

Fig 57: Panel 13, showing a portrait of a dark-haired man with a white, upturned collar and an ochre-yellow jacket. Below is a leaping hybrid creature, with the body of a lion and the head of a dog. The large, red, projecting tongue of the mythical creature in this frieze is reminiscent of the tongues of fire emanating from the nearby gun barrels.

Fig 58: Panel 14, showing a portrait of a clean-shaven, dark-haired man in a green jacket. In the space below there is a lion/dog hybrid creature with a projecting red tongue.

wet in the rain, but remain quite dry. A tortoise – a cosmic symbol, linking heaven and earth and also the symbol of chaste reticence – is crawling up this woman's skirt.

Panel 2 shows another seated woman, who is holding a bunch of flowers in her left hand, and a single red bloom, which she seems to be smelling, in her right hand. The head of a large dog projects into the picture. This picture is slightly different on the port side of the model; there the woman is holding a single flower in her right hand, and there is a vase of flowers nearby. On this side a dog's head also projects into the picture. The attributes of the dog and the plucked flower indicate the vice of anger.

In Panel 1 the artist has blended the third counter of the stern elegantly with the composition of his picture. A woman leans comfortably against the curve of the counter, as though on a divan. A light red fruit, perhaps an apple, is lying in her lap. On the port side we can see her bringing the apple to her mouth: a monkey eating a similar piece of fruit is sitting on her knee. The apple, like the pomegranate, symbolises the Fall of Man; the monkey symbolises inconstancy. Art, virtue, and (overwhelmingly) vice are thus depicted in the upper part of the model, via the feminine world. The worthy men below are free of positive and negative values: they speak for themselves. The lower part of the ship is the domain of devils and demons. A whole world is spread out before us in a small space by the artwork on the galleon. It reaches from the tortoise, who symbolises the cosmos, to the devil in the form of a basilisk. A ship, which often sailed the seas for months on end, formed a similarly enclosed world in itself.

This depiction of decorative figures rich in symbolism is, in my opinion, non-commital in character. Its patterns seem to be based on one of the collections of figures and decorative elements for architectural or graphic ornamentation which was widespread at the time. Nothing more can be drawn from the elements selected and their sequence than a general statement about their symbolic content. And, unfortunately, we are left none the wiser about the votive ship itself.

CHAPTER 7

Early methods of ship construction

S HIPBUILDERS of old, and people supervising the work carried out in dockyards and arsenals, had to be extremely good craftsmen. They needed to have 'a good eye', plenty of experience and a solid understanding of woodworking techniques; in short, shipbuilding required mainly practical craftsmanship. If a master shipwright (one who was able to write, that is) actually reached for his quill pen and committed something of his craft to paper, there was always a specific reason. No-one was particularly interested in penetrating shipbuilders' trade secrets; apart, perhaps, from one group of people – those in administrative and managerial positions, who had reached this level in the dockyards or the navy through their careers at court, and needed to find out about the world in which they found themselves working. In this respect, these people were comparable to present-day ministers, who are put in charge of a ministry for political reasons, without necessarily having more than a vague idea of its operations. It is no accident that there are important source works in the library of Samuel Pepys (1633-1703), one of the leading men in the English Royal Navy, who toyed with the idea of writing a history of the institution he served. Manuscripts in his library include parts of the *Anthony List* (Anthony Roll, see p 14), the Master Shipwright Matthew Baker's *Fragments of Ancient English Shipwrightry*, (see p 14), and the *Doctrine of Naval Architecture*, 1670 by the Master Shipwright Anthony Deane, which was written at Pepys's request (see Fig 75 and p 126).

A career at court could take an officer out of the saddle and put him on the quarter-deck of a ship. Henry Mainwaring wrote his *Seaman's Dictionary* for just such people (see p 40). For most sources on shipbuilding we are indebted to lay people who were interested in the craft and wrote down what they had learned about it. The rules of thumb and systems of proportion which were used in the steps of creating a ship were the closely-guarded, tried and tested, knowledge and secrets of an occupational group, or guild, who protected themselves from outsiders. There was, however, another impediment to publication: the problem of how to present, on paper, a complicated three-dimensional artifact like a ship's hull. How could it be depicted, so that it could be unambiguously interpreted and constructed?

Venice

In the Arsenal at Venice we do find early attempts at setting down shipbuilders' rules and the methods of construction used in the Mediterranean. From the archives there, the historians F C Lane and R C Anderson have unearthed some treatises on ship construction from the fifteenth century and the early decades of the sixteenth century.[1] These treatises are very difficult for us, today, to understand, and are little suited to helping us envisage the steps by which a ship took shape.

In 1526 a new type of sailing ship, called a galleon, was built in Venice, for use against pirates. Matteo Bresan, a supervisor in the Arsenal, had built a model of it to demonstrate his ideas (see p 3). The galleon was a successful ship. When she was broken up in 1547, the shipbuilders carefully took her measurements, so as to be able to reproduce them on other ships.[2] A model and the main measurements were thus sufficient to describe a ship's hull. Even at the time,

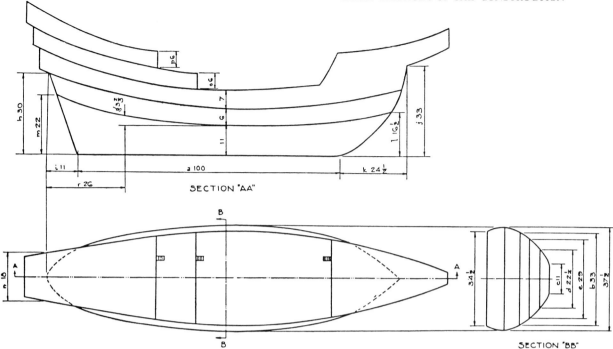

Fig 59: The dimensions of a large Venetian galleon from around 1550, reconstructed by F C Lane from a text by Pre Theodoro de Nicolò. In contrast to the Venetian merchant ships, this early galleon had a long straight keel, and the curved stem did not project so far forward. The maximum breadth was smaller in proportion to the straight keel, and of the order of 1:2.6. The galleon had a keel length of 100 Venetian ft (34.7m), and a maximum breadth of 37.5ft (13.01m). The maximum breadth was very high up on the futtocks of the midship frame, with its narrow floor. The galleon here does not yet have the later, lower silhouette. (From F C Lane, 'Venetian Naval Architecture about 1550', Mariners Mirror, vol 20, 1934)

people did not put much faith in this sort of documentation: in a manuscript from Venice from the early sixteenth century we read of eight trustworthy galleys, which were kept by for emergency use and should be used as models for new constructions. But the contemporary state of the art meant that, even with an actual ship as a model, no-one could guarantee an exact copy.[3]

It is interesting to note how the Venetian shipbuilders of the sixteenth century solved the problem of portraying curves with changing radii. Pre Theodoro de Nicolò was one of the chief shipwrights at the Arsenal in the 1540s; we are indebted to him for a treatise on the draughting of galleys, galleons and merchant ships (Fig 59). He gives us a little insight into the means by which the forms of ship construction were depicted in his time. Firstly, one had to draw the ship's curved stem, and, in the case of the galleys, the curved sternpost. To do so, the Venetians used a system of right-angled triangles (Fig 60). Vertical lines, the gauges, led up from the hypotenuse. The points of the triangle and the ends of the gauges were the points through which the builder drew his curve. Together with the straight keel, these stem and sternpost curves gave the outline of the side view of a ship's hull.

Another important part of the construction was the shape of the midship frame, and its position on the keel. The shape was determined by the fact that the ship's depth in hold (that is, the height from the keel to the first deck beam) was divided into three equal portions (Fig 61). The four dividing lines were: the floor, the trepie, the sepie, and the deck beam. They divided the space in the hold into thirds. The length of these four dividing lines then determined the curve of the frame. The proportions of the lines to each other had to be established. When this had been done, proportionally correct frames (and ships) of varying sizes could be constructed. Once the midship frame had been constructed, the next task was to find the correct inward curvature of the longitudinal lines of the hull from the midship to the stem and the sternpost. That was achieved by setting up a line of marker ribs fore and aft of the midship, indicating the narrowing, or inward curvature of the ships' sides and the height of the floor to the stem and sternpost.

This procedure was called partison, and involved using the meza luna (Fig 62); the radius of the semi-circle gave half the breadth of the ship at the midship. The horizontal lines corresponded to the ribs fore and aft. The intervals between them, looked at from top to bottom, gradually decreased, in the series 1, 2, 4, 7, 11, 16, 22, 29 etc. The curve of one of the quadrants of the meza luna was divided into as many equal portions, and hence horizontal lines, and ribs, as were required. The decreasing breadths showed, from the plan view, a slowly flattening curve.[4] In his *Architectura Navalis* (1629), Furttenbach also describes this technique for the construction of the inward curving lines of galleys.[5]

Techniques like this did not help with making drawings of a ship prior to its construction; there was, at that time, no method for doing this. We have to assume that the shipwrights applied these geometric techniques at the dockyards, marking directly on to the construction timbers the shapes into which they were to be cut and sawn.

Netherlands and Portugal

The standard work on Dutch shipbuilding in the second half of the seventeenth century was written not by a shipbuilder, but by a layman, Nicolaes Witsen (1641–1717). A politician and scientist, he was Burgomaster of Amsterdam no less than thirteen times; in this capacity he accompanied the Tsar Peter the Great, who was interested in shipbuilding, during his visit to Amsterdam. In his work *Aaloude en Hedendaagsche Scheeps-Bouw en Bestier* (1671),

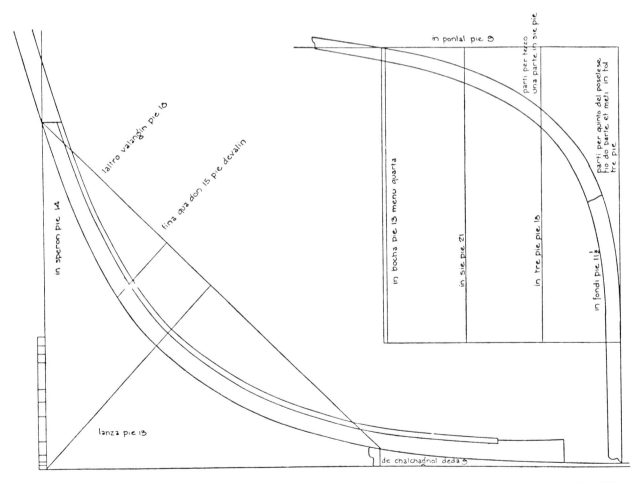

Fig 60: The method of depicting curved ship parts, in this case the stem and the midship frame of a large Venetian galley from the middle of the sixteenth century. (From F C Lane, 'Venetian Naval Architecture about 1550'; Mariners Mirror, vol 20, 1934)

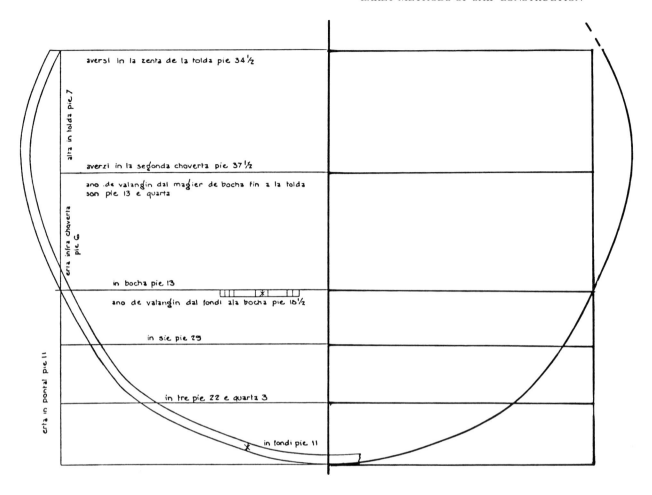

aversi in la zenta de la tolda pie 34½

alta in tolda pie 7

averzi in la segonda choverta pie 37½

ano de valangin dal magier de bocha fin a la tolda son pie 13 e quarta

erta infra choverta pie 6

in bocha pie 13

ano de valangin dal fondi ala bocha pie 16½

in sie pie 25

erta in portal pie 11

in tre pie 22 e quarta 3

in fondi pie 11

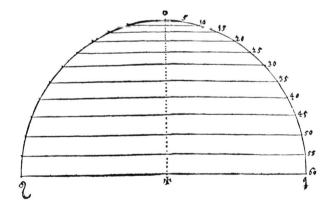

Fig 62: The meza luna served in the construction of the 'narrowing lines' of the hull, so that the ribs narrowed towards the ends of the ship. In this case there are twelve guiding ribs out of a total of sixty in a galley, numbered from the midship to the stern. The two quadrants were divided into as many portions of equal length as there were guiding ribs. The points were connected by means of parallel lines. (From Furttenbach, Architectura Navalis, 1629)

Fig 61: The midship frame of a large Venetian galleon, c.1550, from a sketch by Prе Theodoro de Nicolò, one of the master shipwrights in the Arsenal at Venice. The shape of the ribs, with the narrow floor and widening futtocks, is comparable with the midship frame of an English galleon from around 1600 (see Fig 67). (From F C Lane, 'Venetian Naval Architecture about 1550', Mariners Mirror, vol 20, 1934)

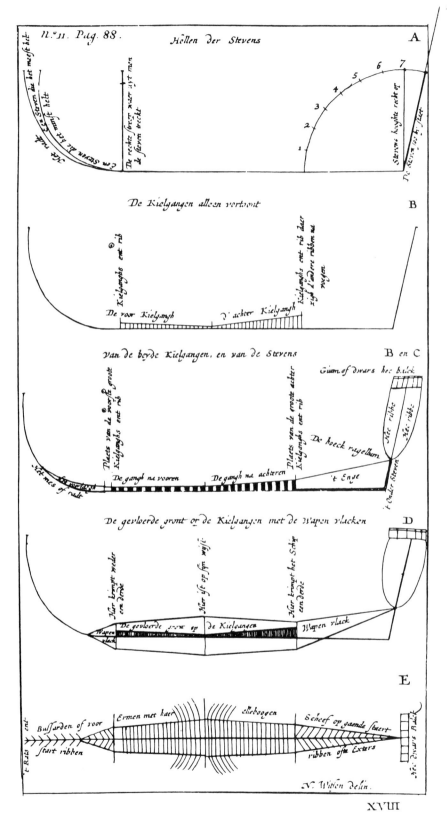

Fig 63/1

*Figs 63/1 and 63/2: These sketches by the Portuguese Fernando Oliveira, from the middle of the sixteenth century, are examples of early attempts at depicting a ship's hull by means of technical drawings. (*From N Witsen, Aaloude en Hedendaagsche Scheeps-Bouw en Bestier, *1671)*

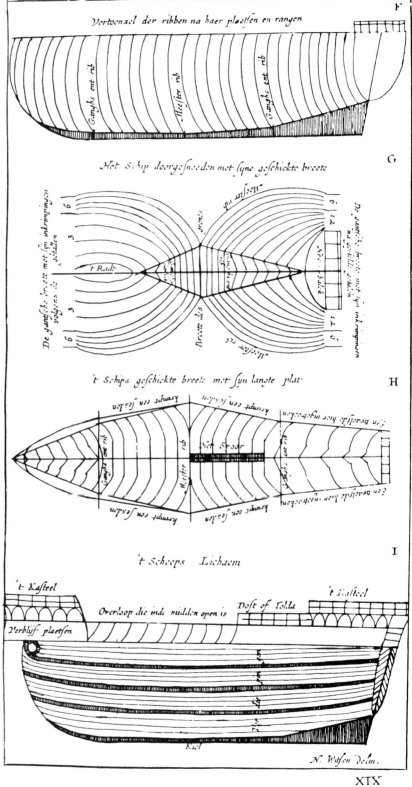

Fig 63/2

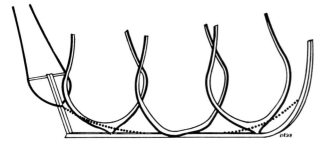

Fig 64: The (dotted) lower rising-line is a construction line which runs along the ship's axis below the floor timbers, and on the upper edge of the deadwood – that is, the blocks of wood which lie fore and aft on the keel at increasing height. This line is one of the guidelines in the rib construction, and represents the height of the ribs above the base line or the keel.

Witsen shows the contemporary methods of drawing a ship's hull. But he also quotes copiously from the works of Fernando Oliveira, a Portuguese layman, to illustrate shipbuilding methods from an earlier period, c.1520. Oliveira published his book *Ars Nautica* around 1560.[6] His descriptions and drawings contain elements in the depiction and construction of ships' hulls which we will find in later English treatises on shipbuilding.

The stem of the ship portrayed by Witsen and Oliveira was constructed as a sector of a circle (Figs 63/1 and 63/2). A vertical line is drawn at the forward end of the straight keel, on which lies the mid-point of the stem curve (Fig 63/1 A). At the aft end of the keel, the sternpost has an angle of 12° from the vertical: steeper than in later galleons. The midship frame is roughly at the end of the first third of the keel (Fig 63/1 D). Oliveira's drawing shows various heights for the deadwood: that is, upright pieces of wood at the bow and stern above the keel. This means that the course looks like a rising-line, a concept to which I will return later (see p 123 and Fig 64). From the plan view we can see a floor, called the vlack. Its breadth was one-third of the breadth of the ship's hull. The height of the stem and sternpost of Oliveira's ship amounts to one-third of the ship's keel length. The ship's hull has been built very full aft, as the gallery is half the breadth of the ship.

Witsen explains that the ship is split at the midship frame, the meester rib (Fig 63/2 G). The ribs fore and aft are projected flat to show their width. We do not learn much about the rounding of the ribs, but we can infer that, like the ribs on Portuguese galleons and carracks a century later, they were designed from only one or two arcs (see Fig 8). Oliveira admits that the shipwrights were unwilling to divulge anything about the construction of the ribs, so that not even their own sons would discover these secrets.[7] We can see from Fig 63/2, however, that the curvature of all the ribs is fairly uniform; they all seem to have been derived directly from the midship frame.

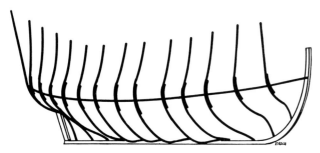

Fig 65: The breadth line (line of maximum breadth) was an important line of construction in the whole-moulding technique. It can be seen here in this perspective drawing of the guiding ribs of a hull side, running past each rib at the point of its maximum breadth, where it had its greatest buoyancy. In terms of the rib construction, the sharply curved breadth sweep lay on this line, which is line B in the rising-line plan (see Fig 74).

Fig 66/A and 66/B: Perspective drawing of some elements of construction mentioned in the English Treatise on Shipbuilding (c.1620). The detailed description (see Appendix) allows us to reconstruct the shape of a medium-sized galleon of approximately 550 tons; with a length of almost 40m (at the waterline), a breadth of almost 11m and a depth of 4.5m. It is a typical English design with a narrow stern and floor and a sharp sweep in the midship area. The upper line connecting the ribs is the toptimber line. The line running along the ship at half height is the breadth line.

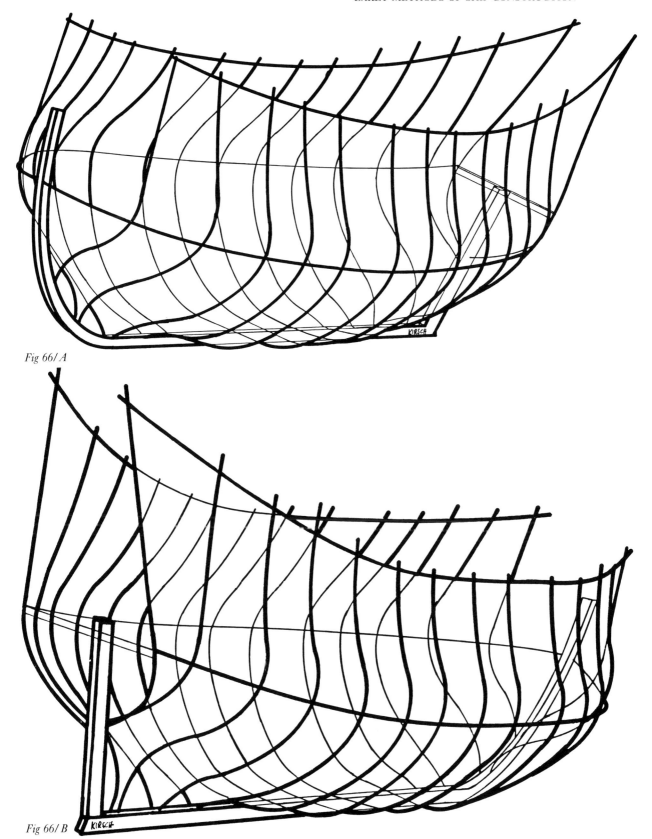

Fig 66/ A

Fig 66/ B

England

We can thus identify, for the first time, a process by which the largest rib of a ship, the midship frame, serves as a template for all the rest. Later, this method would be developed and refined. In the early seventeenth century, in England in particular, this was the most common method used in the construction of ships up to the size of galleons, and in the first three-deckers. It was even used in the construction of boats. The method was called whole-moulding, and involved constructing the shape of the midship frame from various different arcs. This shape was then re-used in the construction of the remaining ribs.[8] The term moulding comes from mould, a large template nailed together from thin boards of wood, with which shipwrights would transfer particular specific shapes on to the construction timbers.

A ship's hull consists of a base, and shapes reaching up to the bow and the stern from the keel. Viewed from above, the ship's sides run together to the bow and the stern. The result is that each rib has a different height from the keel, and that the curves of each rib are at a different distance from a central plane. The rising-lines (curved, auxiliary construction lines), were needed to construct the mould for each rib. The rising-line plan is the arrangement of lines for a ship's hull (Fig 74). This meant that the rib moulds could be arranged in whatever way was needed to produce the desired shape of hull. Only later did 'risings' come to mean the thin planks nailed together by shipbuilders on a ribbed hull to test its fairness; and the 'lines' on a modern ship-construction drawing have nothing to do with the construction lines of the seventeenth century.

The shipbuilders of old used three classic rising-lines to determine the shape of a ship's hull: the lower rising-line lay at the bottom of the hull (Fig 64), and gave the height of individual ribs above the keel. The breadth line was about halfway up, where the ship's hull had its maximum breadth (Fig 65). The toptimber line (Fig 66 A and B), which was usually twice the height of the breadth line, determined the course of the upper ends of the ribs and their arcs. Most ships' hulls had a flat base, the floor, which was of varying breadths and ran to a point fore and aft. Ships rested on it if they went aground.

We first find some progress in the draughting of ship construction and the system of whole-moulding in a manuscript attributed to the English Master Shipwright Matthew Baker (1530–1613) (see p 19); Samuel Pepys preserved it in his library. These *Fragments of Ancient English Shipwrightry* are the first example in England of the portrayal of ship construction by plans but we do not know whether this construction technique was developed in England. Did it come from Italy? King Henry VIII (1509–47) invited experienced shipbuilders over from Venice at the beginning of his reign. If we compare the midship frame of a Venetian galleon from 1550 (Figs 59, 61) with that of an English galleon from c.1586 (Fig 67), we can see a common pattern: wide futtocks are based on a narrow floor. The maximum breadth of the ribs lies above the waterline. The midship frame was constructed by different methods in Venice and England, but the result is similar. The Venetian-English frame demonstrates a different principle from that employed by the Portuguese (Fig 8). A Dutch midship frame looks different again (Fig 68); there the shipbuilders used box-shaped cross-sections. They valued minimal depth and high loading capacity in their ships.

Matthew Baker's drawings show many elements of ship construction which are to be found in England, and probably in other north European countries, until the first decades of the seventeenth century. I would like to examine one of Baker's drawings (Fig 69) more closely. It shows how far the method of whole-moulding was already developed in

---

Fig 67: Midship frame of an English galleon from the manuscript by the Master Shipbuilder Matthew Baker (c.1586). The outline of the rib shows Italian influence when compared with the midship frame of a Venetian galleon (see Fig 61). As strengthening elements we can see, amongst others, the dark-shaded rider on the floor timbers and floor heads of the rib. The deck supports are anchored in them, which keep the hull secure when it has run aground. The lower deck, called the false orlop deck, was built below the waterline on large ships. It lay amidships, and often supported the galley. Standing knees supported it against the rib. The lower deck follows, then the upper deck, the halfdeck, and, highest of all, the quarter-deck, with its 'clamp'. The draughtsman here shows the decks one on top of the other; in reality, the upper ones did not all run in the midship region. It is a typical feature of the English method of construction that all the deck beams taper by one-third at the ends. (By permission of the Master and Fellows, Magdalene College, Cambridge)

116

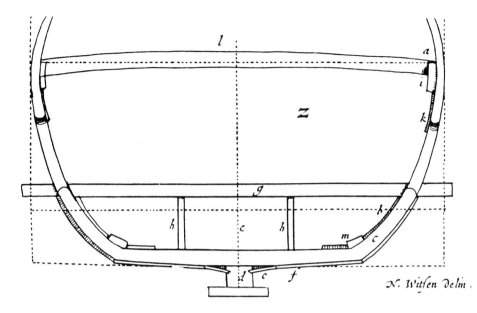

*Fig 68: The Dutch method of constructing the midship frame of a ship of approximately 37.5m in length, as portrayed by Witsen in his work on shipbuilding. The extended floor of the ship and the steep position of the futtocks are a noteworthy contrast to the English design. The Dutch reduced the draught of their ships with rib-shapes like these, to allow manoeuverability in the shallow coastal waters. (*From N Witsen, *Aaloude en Heedendaagsche Scheeps-Bouw en Bestier,* 1671)

England in the 1580s. From this drawing we can learn the most important elements of this system of construction. It is also possible to compare it with the *Treatise on Shipbuilding* (c.1620) which is discussed in the Appendix.

The keel is delimited by the sternpost which projects aft at an angle of 20°. The curved stem consists of two arcs. We have to imagine the midpoint of the lower, more sharply curved arc on a vertical line at the forward end of the straight keel. The radius of the upper curve corresponds to the greatest breadth of the ship. On the keel are three completed guiding ribs. The middle one, at the end of the forward third of the keel, is the midship frame. This position evidently applies only to the drawing in hand, as other drawings in Baker's manuscript show the midship frame at 30.8%, 36.2%, 36.8% and 38.8% of the keel length, as measured from the bow.[9] The other ribs are numbered fore and aft of the midship frame. There are twenty ribs aft and fifteen forward, spaced at equal intervals.

We can identify some of the elements in the construction of the midship frame: firstly, the rectangle in which the curves of the lower portion of the ribs were constructed. Two lines run parallel to the centreline, defining the breadth of the floor. They stand on the floor timbers which lie horizontally at the midship frame (for the names of the individual pieces of timber in a rib see Fig 95). On the vertical lines which delimit the floor, we find the midpoints of the first, or lower rib curves. They join the floor in the floorhead region. A somewhat smaller rib section, curving outwards, leads from the rabbet of the keel to the floor timbers. From that we may infer that the keel plank did not meet the rabbet at right angles, but was led upwards at a gentle angle (hollow keel). The shape of the ribs is continued above the floorheads by a flatter curve, the reconciling sweep. Its midpoint lies on the outer curve of the rib opposite; its radius is very slightly shorter than the breadth of the ship. This curve is continued up to the point where the rib is at its greatest breadth. Then the rib continues upwards in straight sections, the toptimbers. Matthew Baker's ship had, from midship frame to stern, topsides which curved evenly inwards – the s-shape came later. The longest, heaviest deck beam of the ship lay above the construction rectangle, to support the lower deck.

On both the other guiding ribs in the drawing we can see the same curvature for the upper parts of the timbers; in other words, the same mould was used as for the midship frame, a typical feature of whole-moulding. The forward guiding rib is clearly distinguished from both the others: it has a sharply curved arc at its maximum breadth. The toptimbers above are curved sharply inwards, to make the ship's forecastle narrower and lighter. The rib looks very advanced.

The first wale runs the entire length of the drawing. It lies somewhat below the maximum breadth. We have to imagine the waterline on the lower edge of the wale. The hull above it would be rather broader. If the sailing ship was heeling in the wind, it would receive additional, stabilising buoyancy from the broader ship's side.

A construction line curves upwards from the midship frame base to the stem and sternpost. This is the lower rising line, one of the guidelines of the drawing. It ends at the stem at the point where it changes from being sharply curved to being flatter. Aft, it ends at the tuck (that is the lowest point of the stern). The shipbuilders derived the height of a rib above the keel from the lower rising line.

Below Matthew Baker's drawing of the side view, we can see two curved lines viewed from above. The inner one corresponds to the forward part of the lower rising line in the side view. The aft portion is not shown. If it had been shown, it would have to run from the midships to the lowest point of the stern. This line describes a flat arc, which at first glance looks like the floor of the ship. It is, however, broader than the ribs are at the base. Its edges are outside, and not inside, the ship's hull. The shipbuilders needed this line to find the point where the first sharply curved floor sweep merges with the second sweep (Fig 70 and p 123ff). This 'flat area' is characteristic of the 'whole-moulding' method of ship construction. Last, we can see the breadth line on the plan view: a curved line which runs from stem to sternpost and links the ribs at the point of their greatest breadth; this line is not shown by Matthew Baker in the side view of his design.

The *Treatise on Shipbuilding* (c.1620) is our most detailed introduction to the design of English galleons (see Appendix, p 163ff). From now on I will refer to it merely as the *Treatise*. We do not know who the author is: his ideas are related to those of the Master Shipwright Matthew Baker (1530–1613), Phineas Pett (1570–1647) and the mathematician Thomas Harriot (1560?–1621). The original manuscript and any drawings which may have belonged to it are lost. An incomplete transcript is all that survives (Fig 92); the missing parts probably contained instructions for fitting out the ship, and for its rigging. The instructions are so clear that it would be possible to reconstruct the drawings. The historian W Salisbury has succeeded in doing so.[11] Given the conservatism in construction techniques for which the shipbuilders of old were renowned, we can assume, particularly after analysing Matthew Baker's design, that the method of whole-moulding described in the *Treatise* was already in use around 1600 or 1610. This method would not have resulted in the slimmer 'modern' galleons which already existed at that time: that is, ones with a keel length to maximum breadth ratio of 3:1. The length-to-breadth ratio of the designs described here is 2.7:1.

The manuscript shows the steps in the construction of an English galleon of medium size. According to the old English rules of measurement (see p 25), it is a ship of 550 tons burthen.

Length at the waterline	39.77m
Length of the straight keel	30.40m
Greatest breadth	10.80m
Draught	4.50m

In a later period the ship would have been termed a two-decker, as it has a continuous upper deck. The design is typically English: narrow stern and floor, sharply curved ribs in the midship area (Fig 101 and Plan 6).

As the first part of the process of designing a new ship, the shipwrights and their employers would agree on the main dimensions (Fig 71). This meant that certain details could be calculated right at the start: the ship's tonnage and its freight capacity, the quantity of building materials required, and the labour costs. The shipbuilders would then go off to the forests to seek out the trees for felling. The first important dimension was the length of the straight keel (excluding stem and sternpost). The second was the breadth, which generally meant the length of the midship beam of the lower deck. The third dimension, the depth in hold, was measured in various ways; at one time it meant the distance between the upper edge of the keel and the lower edge of the midship lower deck beam; at another the distance between the upper edge of the keel and the height of the greatest breadth at the midship frame.

The relationship between these main dimensions decided the character of the ship. As we have seen, various ideas were still current in 1600 as to the ratio of keel length to breadth. English shipbuilders settled on the '3 x breadth' rule around the beginning of the seventeenth century. This was distilled from the shipbuilding experiences of the Elizabethan era, and became the trademark of a 'pure' galleon.[12] But there were also broader galleons in existence which had been constructed according to traditional designs.

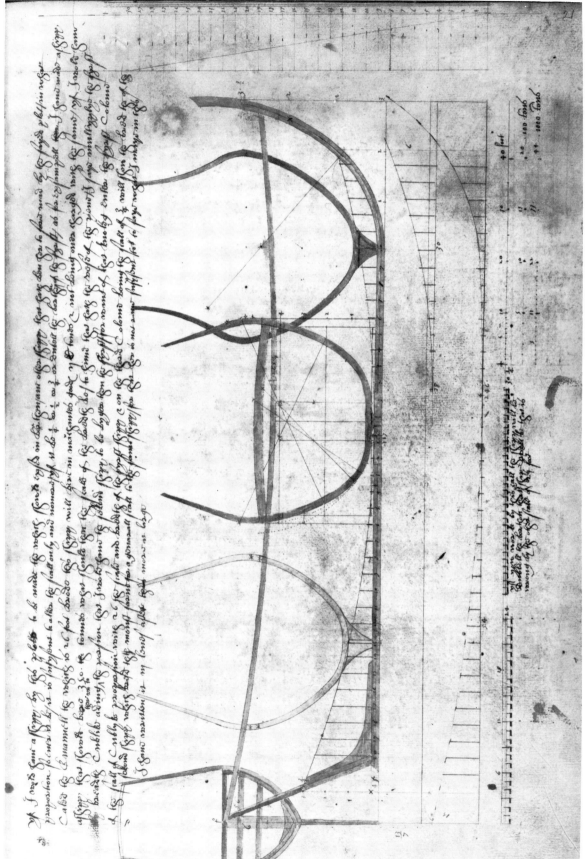

Fig 69: This design by the English shipbuilder Matthew Baker (c.1586) is the earliest example of the construction technique of whole-moulding by means of rib templates (moulds) and rising-lines, which continued to be used until after the middle of the following century. (By permission of the Master and Fellows, Magdalene College, Cambridge)

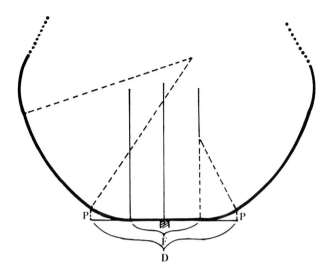

Fig 70: Two different sectors can be seen in this rib-section, which are both called the floor, the base of the hull. They played an important role in the construction of early ships. The bracket, F, comprises the actual floor of the rib – in this case the straight portion of the floor timber. The bracket, D, shows the floor we can see in the plan view of the rising-line plan (see Fig 74, line D). From there we can construct two vertical lines upwards, P. That was the point at which the shipbuilders of old had to set one futtock on another. The narrow and broad floors both climbed upwards towards the ends of the ship along the lower rising-line.

The shipbuilders' system meant that all the remaining construction measurements could be derived from a planned vessel's main dimensions. That meant the stem, the sternpost, and the radii of the curves from which the midship frame would be assembled. The specification of the proportions of the main dimensions to each other meant that, by changing the measurements of the design, different-sized ships of the same type could be constructed. In fact, some of the drawings in Matthew Baker's manuscript are for different measurements.

In the *Treatise* the stem and sternpost are drawn in a similar manner to the preceding examples (Fig 72). The sternpost was placed on the straight keel, at an angle of 18°–22°. The length of the sternpost was a specific fraction of the length or breadth of the ship. The stem consisted of a single arc, the midpoint of which lay (as usual) on a vertical line at the forward end of the straight keel, and the radius of which was the same as, or a fraction of, the greatest breadth. Here, too, the midship frame was an important clue to the ship's shape and character. It was situated at the end of the first third of the keel. Its shape was constructed as a rectangle, of which the following dimensions were specified: greatest breadth, height (and double the height) of the greatest breadth, breadth of the floor (Fig 73). The shape of the midship frame was then constructed from arcs, these being the simplest curves to reproduce. Since Matthew Baker's time this procedure had become a little more complicated, and the author of the *Treatise* uses up to five arcs, with different radii, for this purpose. They are all derived from dimensions which have already been specified. The individual component parts of the midship frame and the other guiding ribs were:

1   The floor timbers were straight, and lay horizontally. (Figs 95, 97c); their length was determined by the width of the floor.

2   The floor sweep, the first arc, came next; it had a small radius.

3   The next rib arc consisted of the reconciling sweep, which was constructed from the first and second rib futtocks.

4   The reconciling sweep merged into a sharply curved arc, the breadth sweep, at the height of the maximum breadth. The ship's side began to curve inwards again after this arc.

5   The toptimber sweep, constructed from the toptimbers, formed the upper part of the rib. These futtocks formed the ship's sides in the area of its superstructure. They could be drawn straight, or given a curve inwards (see the rib outline for the reconstruction of the Stockholm galleon). The toptimbers could also have an s-shaped curve inwards. If the futtocks were straight, the heavy guns were positioned further out, thus impairing the vessel's stability and burdening the timbers. If the futtocks were curved inwards, the weight of

the guns was also transferred inwards, allowing a more elegant-looking ship's hull – in contemporaneous eyes, at least.

6   The forward and after ribs which were positioned on the deadwood rather than the straight keel met an arc curved inwards at the base. It led from the rib to the keel or the deadwood (Fig 100, curves N–G and H–S). This arc had the same radius as the floor sweep. There are no instructions regarding its construction in the manuscript. It was probably built by eye, by the Master Shipwright.

After the midship frame had been constructed, the other guiding ribs of the ship's hull could be drawn from its arcs. This process was called whole-moulding. In practice, it seems as though not all the guiding ribs were constructed on paper. In the dockyards, the shipbuilders used thin boards to construct the arcs of the midship frame in the original size. That was the mould. It had marks and gradations showing how each rib would be assembled (as each was different). The rib curve was drawn directly on to the construction timbers from this mould. The method by which the moulds were graduated and assembled cannot be carried out in practice from the instructions in the *Treatise*. Perhaps the unknown author was not a professional shipbuilder at all – but, like some of his predecessors, an interested layman writing about ship construction?

We find the three classic rising-lines again in the *Treatise*: the lower rising-line, the breadth line, and the toptimbers line (Fig 74). I would like to elaborate a little more on these important construction lines.

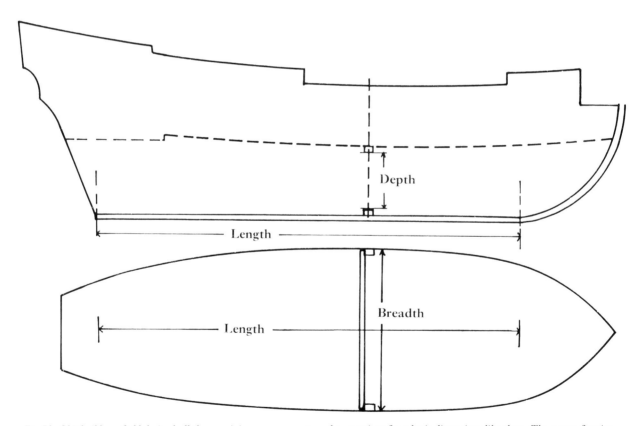

Fig 71: Shipbuilders of old derived all the remaining measurements and proportions from basic dimensions like these. The curves forming the shape of the ribs also came from these basic measurements. It was even possible to derive all the remaining proportions for a particular ship-type from only one of these dimensions, for example the length of the straight keel. Every shipwright had his own secret variations on these proportions. The 'depth in hold' shown here would probably be used when a finished ship was being measured according to the rules. The tonnage thus calculated served to determine the costs of construction, the amount of timber used and the load-bearing capacity.

Fig 72: The first step in the construction design for a galleon was drawing in the curved stem at the forward end of the straight keel. Its radius was a fraction of the greatest breadth of the ship; its midpoint was on a line perpendicular to the forward end of the keel. The midship frame was positioned one-third of the way along the keel. The straight sternpost was at an angle of 18° to 22° from the stern.

Fig 73: The overall shape of the ship's hull was largely determined by the midship frame, which was developed by the shipbuilders within a rectangle. The horizontal line in the middle lies on the greatest breadth of the rib. The upper horizontal line indicates the height of the toptimbers line. The width of the base, the floor of the rib, was already known. The shape of the rib then consisted of various arcs which were joined together in a single curved line.

The lower rising-line (Fig 64, and Appendix Plan 4)

Amidships the lower rising-line ran at the height of the upper edge of the keel, giving the height for the lower edge of the rib floor timbers. (Later, when the method of whole-moulding was discarded, it became the upper edge of the floor timbers.) At the bow and the stern the lower rising-line ran along the deadwood, rather than the upper edge of the keel – that is, the blocks of wood of increasing height which were placed on the keel (no 9 in the longitudinal cross-section of the reconstruction. The numbers which follow refer to this cross-section). Aft the rising-line met the tuck, where the aftermost ribs (Fig 94) met the sternpost. They ran to a point at the curved stem where the knee of the head (no 34) began.

It is interesting that the rising-line plan of this galleon is clearly divided into two portions, one forward and one aft of the midship frame. The two parts of the lower rising-line were constructed in a different mathematical manner (see Appendix, p 182ff). Different intervals were also possible between the ribs fore and aft of the midship frame.

The outline of the rising-line plan (Fig 74 and Plan 4 in the Appendix) contains a feature peculiar to the whole-moulding method of construction, which we find on all rising-line plans of this period: to the right and left of the centreline we can see two curved lines running inwards, enclosing a pointed oval space. In contemporaneous drawings this is termed floor, but it has nothing to do with the floor of the ship. If we measure the floor of the midship, that is, the length of the horizontal floor timbers, we can see that this is much narrower than the pointed oval floor of the rising-line plan. Viewed from the side, this area runs at the same height as the lower rising-line and curves in the same way at the bow and the stem. If we draw the floor in the rectangle used in the construction of each of the ribs, we obtain a horizontal line at the height of the lower rising-line (Fig 70). If we draw a vertical line at each of the end points of this

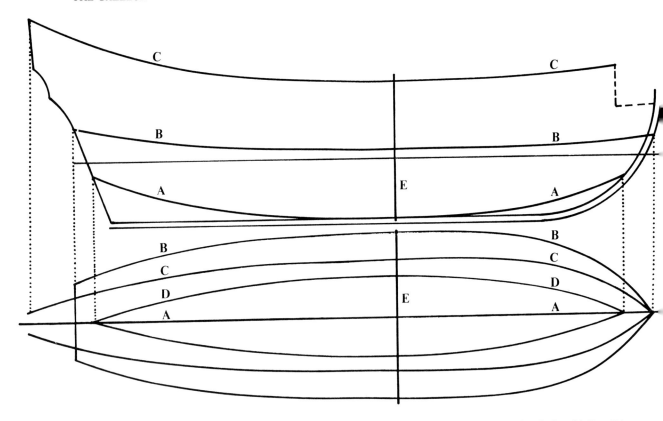

Fig 74: Side view and plan view of the rising-lines plan of a galleon. The side view shows the lower rising-line (A), the breadth line (B), and the toptimbers line (C). The top view shows the rising line (A) on the ship's axis. The curved lines are, from the inmost outwards: the lateral edges of the floor (D); the toptimbers line (C); the breadth line (B). Together with the midship frame (E), these are the guidelines for the curves used in constructing the ribs.

line, we find that these touch the rib at the point where the first arc merges into the second (floor sweep and reconciling sweep). This procedure showed the shipbuilders where they were to join one piece of moulding to another. The side line of the floor was an important element in the construction of the shape of the underwater hull. Like the lower rising-line, it was constructed in a mathematically different way fore and aft of the midship frame.

The breadth line (Figs 65, 66 and Appendix Plan 4)

The breadth line lay on the ship's hull's girdle line, joining together the points where the ribs had their maximum breadth. To us, that means the arc of the rib formed by the third curve. Like the other curves of the rising line plan, the breadth line was constructed from two portions: one forward of, and one aft of, the midship frame. Viewed from the side, it lay parallel to the keel, in midship, then curved gently upwards towards the bow and stern. The fullness or sharpness of the hull's extremities depended on the degree of this curvature. During the seventeenth century the curve of the breadth line became progressively flatter. The reason for this was that ships required more load-bearing capacity at the bow and stern, due to the increasing weight of their guns. Bows and sterns capable of carrying loads also prevented the dreaded phenomenon known as hogging of the keel amidships, which was really caused by the bow and stern sinking.[13]

Although shipwrights were continually flattening the breadth line, they still could not manage to give the hull sufficient buoyancy by using the whole-moulding method of construction, and were forced to transform the process.

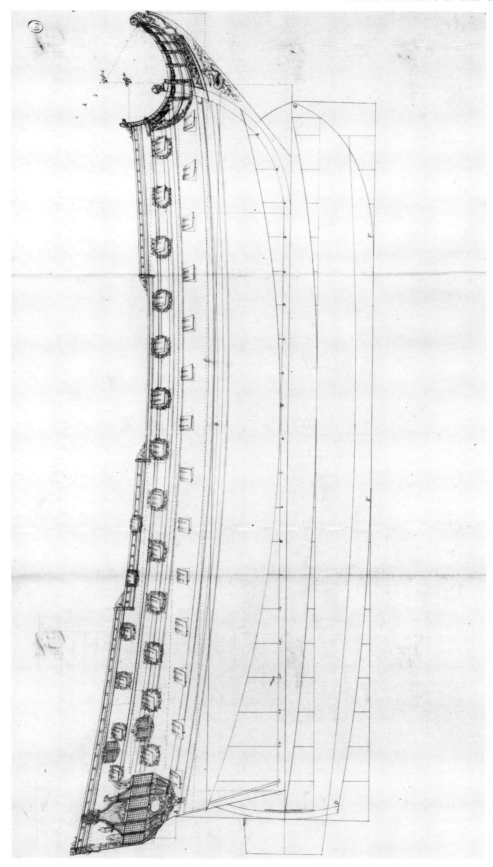

Fig 75: English two-decker, from Deane's Doctrine of Naval Architecture, 1670. Deane developed his ship's hull from a rising-line plan fifty years after the Treatise on Shipbuilding (c.1620). However the improvements of a shape which had been made in the intervening years rendered this construction technique impracticable. Deane mentions the use of waterlines in his Doctrine, but does not show them in the drawing. The floor shown in the top view here corresponds to the actual base of the ribs. The 'greater floor' (cf Fig 70) is no longer appropriate, as Deane was already modifying the curvature of the individual ribs to achieve more buoyancy at the bow and stern of the hull. On the toptimbers line we can see that large ships were now being built lower and broader at the bow and stern. The stern balcony is wide and curved: the ship no longer has a flat transom stern but a round stern, a typically English construction feature of this period. The ship's hull is slender, with a breadth-to-length ratio of 1:3. The two lower decks are continuous. All in all, this is no longer a galleon, but a true ship-of-the-line, comparable to those constructed in the eighteenth and nineteenth centuries. (By permission of the Master and Fellows, Magdalene College, Cambridge)

They started by no longer adhering rigidly to rib arcs of the same radius, but rounded out the lower portion of the rib. That was the first step towards a new method of construction. We find it mentioned for the first time in the sketches of Anthony Deane (1670), the English shipwright.[14] He used almost the same rising-line plan as the galleon builders had done. However the breadth of his floor corresponded to the actual floor of the ship (Fig 75).

The toptimber line (Fig 66 and Plan 4)

The toptimber line joined up the upper parts of the ribs, the inverted futtocks. It consequently affected the shape of the inward-leaning part of the ship's side. The *Treatise* recommends that the ship's sides should curve inwards by about one-sixth of the breadth of the ship on each side. Thus, viewed from above, the toptimber line ran one-sixth of the breadth inwards of the breadth line. Viewed from the side, the toptimber line ran parallel to the breadth line, at twice the height. As already mentioned, shipbuilders at the start of the seventeenth century were able to make the inverted futtocks of their ribs either straight, or s-shaped, curving inwards. If they were curved, the radius of this curve corresponded to the maximum breadth of the ship. This curve became flatter towards the bow and the stern. At the aftermost ribs of the ship, and the forecastle bulkhead, the toptimbers became quite straight.

In drawing the toptimber line with the side walls curving inwards by one-sixth of the breadth (Plan 4), we find a point fore and aft where this curvature can no longer be sustained: the superstructures would be too narrow. We can compensate for this deficiency in the manuscript by ensuring perfect lines in a – completely anachronistic – reconstruction of the waterlines of the ship's hull. These are shown as dotted lines on the top view in Plan 4 and the waterlines outline in Plan 6. The course of the toptimber line, as described in the *Treatise*, causes the peaked bulkhead of the forecastle to lean gently inwards. Only later did the ship's side become rounded out here, to support the function of the cathead.

The fact that we do not know the height of the head of the toptimbers causes a further difficulty in reconstructing a galleon from the *Treatise*. The run of the wales (no 101–103) cannot be determined. That shows another limitation in the old construction technique: the part of the hull lying above the water seems, for the most part, to have been left to the shipbuilder's eye. We do receive some assistance from the position of the decks, which give us a rough idea where the upper edge of the ship's side came. It is shown as a dotted line in the side view in Plan 4.

The waterline

Once the shipbuilder had drawn the longitudinal outline, with the stem, sternpost, rib divisions and rising-lines, the next thing to do was to determine the ship's waterline. Experience alone mattered here. There was, at that time, no scientific technique for calculating the displacement of a ship's hull. That must have caused many a shipbuilder a sleepless night before the launch of a new ship. The worrying questions were: how deep does it go, how much ballast should it have, and how many guns can it carry? The author of the *Treatise* courageously gives a waterline. The custom of increasing a ship's buoyancy by girdling was still widespread; this involved attaching thick planks at the waterline. In our case, the waterline is given as being at the point where the reconciling sweep merges into the breadth sweep (Fig 98). It was an important line of construction, and the shipbuilder needed to know it, as the basis for the position of the decks and their gunports. The height of the lower deck and its guns above the water was a decisive factor in the quality of a ship.

The lower edge of the first wale rested on the waterline (Plan 5), so this wale can be drawn as the arc of a large circle. The height of the points at which it cut the stem and sternpost was in proportion to the height of the breadth line above the keel. The method of finding these points is typical of all old construction techniques, in that all the lengths were calculated from fractions of other lengths. The lower edge of the wale met the waterline some feet before the midship frame. In theory the curve of the other wales should follow that of the first. More precise instructions about the breadth and position of the remaining wales have evidently become distorted in a transcript of the manuscript. It was therefore necessary to make a correction in the reconstruction drawing (Plan 5).

The decks

Now the shipbuilder had reached the point where he could draw the decks. For the position of the lower deck (no 17 in the longitudinal cross-section of the reconstruction) he had to bear in mind two considerations: the distance between the gun muzzles and the surface of the water; and a height for the gunports which did not involve cutting into the wales. In the *Treatise* a height of about 6ft (1.82m) is aimed at for the gun muzzles above the waterline (Fig 98). That is relatively high. Other sources give only 5ft.[15] In 1670 Deane considered guns only 4ft 10in above the waterline to be at a sufficient height.

The deck beams are arc-shaped. They taper towards their ends to approximately one-third of their strength (Figs 67, 98). This shape seems to have been abandoned later on. The mighty midship lower deck beams were approximately 36ft long (10.9m) and had a camber of 14in (0.35m). Their lower (external) edge lay 2ft (0.61m) above the waterline. It was by no means an immutable law in shipbuilding that decks had to run continuously from bow to stern. The lower deck could continue fore and aft on a different level to that which it had amidships. That was necessary to ensure that the wales were not cut by the lower deck gunports, and the hull weakened as a result. Aft, the lower deck was generally positioned lower down, and formed the gun room deck (no 13). Guns pointing aft, and those which formed a part of the broadside, stood here. At the forecastle the lower deck might be higher, continue straight through, or even be positioned a little lower.

Large galleons had another deck amidships, below the lower deck: the false orlop deck (Fig 67, no 22). This was where the ship's kettle was situated. The deck consisted of a row of beams which might remain unplanked. They were positioned somewhere in the middle of the first futtocks. In his outstanding source work, Oppenheim gives ten such deck beams in a ship which was only slightly smaller than our galleon. They were situated approximately 8ft above the keel.[16]

The second deck, the upper deck, ran continuously through from bow to stern (no 44). In doing so, it (like the other decks) followed the rise of the wales. The distance between the lower deck and the upper deck (deck plank to deck plank) was 7ft 3in (2.2m). The deck heights were proportionately lower in smaller ships. The halfdeck (no 67), and probably also the forecastle deck (no 80), had a height of 6ft (1.82m). The *Treatise* specifies that the length of the deck in the forecastle should be two-thirds of the rake of the stem (ie, its radius). The quarter-deck was 6ft above the halfdeck. The lengths of the half- and quarter-decks were not specified in the manuscript, and doubtless varied from ship to ship.

A width of 2½ft (0.67m) is specified for the gunports; the distance between the ports (from timber to timber) was between 7–8½ft (approximately 2.1 m). The ports of the upper decks were supposed to lie, as far as was possible, between two lower ports, and as the guns were lighter, the gunports were not so wide.

Our galleon had only one gallery. This of course had little effect on the quality of a ship, but the author of the *Treatise* considers it important that its proportions are in keeping with the ship's hull. He specifies the radius and the arc length of the counter below the gallery (nos 57, 58 and Plan 5). The length of the gallery should be one-sixth of the ship's length between the perpendiculars. Its angle from the horizontal (depth in the steeving line) was supposed to be one-fifth of its length. The beakhead was also expected to have certain aesthetic and fashionable qualities. From the stem to the figurehead it was supposed to measure one-fifth of the keel length, and to project at an angle of 12° to 13°. The arc for the beakhead half-railing is even specified (Plan 5).

We only know in the most general terms how the internal space was divided up on English galleons. In the *Treatise* the ship is divided into seven rooms: the hold under the lower deck, the main deck, orlop deck, halfdeck, quarterdeck, the forecastle and the poop (no 96). The hold between the floor timbers (no 11) and the beams of the orlop deck (no 17) is separated into five parts by bulkheads; forward, ahead of the bits are the powder magazines, the carpenter's store and the boatswain's store (no 27). Provisions are stored aft of the bits. (There is no mention of a cable tier). Gravel ballast lies on the floor timbers. This is followed, sometimes, by the false orlop deck, and ends aft in the bread room (no 12) and the steward's room.

The heavy artillery stood on the lower deck. At the fore peak, right at the bows, was the manger (no 36), to take up the water which came through the hawses (no 33). The pumps (no 46) were in the mainmast area. The gun room was aft of the lower deck, and was usually positioned somewhat lower (no 51). The cabins for the ship's surgeon, the boatswain and the ship's carpenter were on this deck. The deck had hatches amidships for access to the hold (nos 41, 43, 49). There were also small scuttles to the rooms in the hold (no 38). The upper deck also carried artillery, and served as the crew's recreation area. Bulkheads divided it into four portions. Two bulkheads separated off the forecastle (nos 75, 82). Sometimes the galley would be situated there. A ladderway led down to the lower deck (no 76). There were hatches and gratings (no 66) in the waist area, in the middle of the upper deck. There was a bulkhead (no 71) aft of the mainmast, behind which were the officers' quarters (no 70) and the steerage and steering gear (no 62). A ladderway led down to the lower deck (no 64) and up to the halfdeck. There was an additional bulkhead aft of the steerage (no 61), behind which was the captain's cabin (no 60).

From the *Treatise* we discover that there were additional cabins on the halfdeck and the quarter-deck. Like the poop, they were designed for specific purposes and followed no particular rules. The following incident, related in the autobiography of Phineas Pett (1570–1647), the English Master Shipwright, shows the extent to which, at the beginning of the seventeenth century, the quality of a ship was judged by its proportions: the carcass of an unusual, large ship lay on the blocks in the dockyard at Woolwich, on the Thames, early in the year 1609. It was the *Prince*, the first three-decker ship. Pett had designed the ship and supervised the construction. A group of doubting shipbuilders considered the dimensions of its mighty hull somewhat risky; it had a keel length of 115ft (34.69m), a breadth of 43ft (13.07m) and a depth in hold of 18ft (5.46m). They petitioned King James I, criticising some details in the new construction, and their arguments show the standpoint from which a ship's construction was judged at that time:

> Her mould is altogether unperfect, furred in divers places; she hath too much floor; the lower sweep and the upper [1st and 3rd futtocks] are too long [this refers to the radius of these arcs], and the middle [2nd] sweep too short.
>
> Her depth is too great and her side too upright, so that of necessity she must be tender sided and not able to bear sail. Her breadth [breadth line] lieth too high, and so she will draw too much water, and thereby be dangerous and unfit for our shoal seas.

They complained further:

> Her Harpings [breadth line] are too round and lie too low, which maketh a cling at the after end of it, and makes the bow flare off so much that the work is not only misshapen but the ship dangereous to beat in the sea either at an anchor or under sail.
>
> Her workmanship is very ill-done, and thereby the ship made weak, as first the limber-holes are cut so deep in the midship floor timbers that they are less thickness upon the keel than toward the rung-head; whereas they ought to be thicker and stronger in the midst, to bear the weight on the ground.[17]

Pett had experimented with new proportions, with which his fellow shipbuilders were not familiar. Amongst other things, he had increased the breadth of the floor, and both rounded out and lowered the breadth line at the bow. Following the criticism of his design, he actually altered the shape of the ribs during construction, which shows that he was not quite sure of himself.

When the various parties could not agree, the King himself, the ultimate owner, became involved. Pett reports how on Monday, 8 May 1609, the royal coach arrived in Woolwich. The King was accompanied by Prince Henry, and the principal Lords of his Council. He was soon installed ceremoniously under a magnificent baldachino in the dockyard workers' dining hall. Old Anglican tradition meant that when the monarch sat on the seat of justice, he did so as God's representative. In a case like this he had the last word, even though it really only concerned the specialists in the field. The Prince, the Lords and all the others who wanted to speak in Pett's favour stood on the King's right-hand side; Pett's opponents on the left. Pett was summoned, and knelt before his monarch. He had to give details on three points: his experience as a shipbuilder, the quality of materials used, and the costs of construction. He relates:

> Much time was spent in dispute of proportions, comparing my present frame with former precedents and dimensions of the best ships, for length, breadth, depth, floor, and other circumstances . . . One point of proportion was mainly insisted upon and with much violence and eagerness urged on both sides, which was the square of the ship's flat in the midship, they affirming constantly upon their oath it was full thirteen foot, we as constantly insisting that it was but eleven foot and eight inches; but because this difference was long and could not be tried upon the small plates, His Majesty referred the trial to be made upon the great platform, which was purposely framed of planks, to the full scale of the ship, where all the lines of the midship bend were drawn, and the square of the flat truly described, with their centres, perpendiculars and sweeps.[18]

It transpired that the breadth of the floor which Pett had cited was correct. Then the quality of the wood and its joins were put to the test. Soon the King, who certainly did not wish to endanger his prestige ship, had heard enough, and the charges which Pett's opponents had raised were dropped. Interestingly Pett mentions in his autobiography that he had made a model before building the ship: a procedure which later became common practice in the construction of large ships.

At this juncture we should mention another manuscript on ship construction: the author is the English mathematician Thomas Harriot (1560?–1621). The manuscript dates from 1609 and resembles, in large part, the *Treatise*, but is less detailed.[19] It does, however, show us that the construction techniques of whole-moulding were known to the leading mathematicians of the time. Whole-moulding survived as a construction technique, in various forms, until the beginning of the eighteenth century. But a modern method of construction, with waterlines and complete rib outlines, began to be developed simultaneously, in the seventeenth century.

Whole-moulding was easily learned and reproduced. But it had a number of disadvantages: the hulls produced by this system were very similarly shaped. There were some ribs amidships which had the same shape as the midship frame. Even the ribs at the two ends of the ship were very similar in shape. The run of the lines at the bow and stern was a particular weakness of the system. The shipbuilders could not get fair lines there if they stuck to the radius of the rib curves. They had to work by eye and reach for an axe to coax the planks into a better run.[20] As the *Treatise* makes clear, there were no hard and fast rules for the construction of the curves which led from the floor of the ribs higher up to the keel and to the dead wood. So it was quite possible for two shipbuilders, working from the same design, to come up with different results. Every shipbuilder had his own secret for handling these problems.

In 1604 the English Captain, George Waymouth, an authority on shipbuilding and navigation, wrote: '. . . yet could never see two ships builded of the like proportion by the best and most skilful shipwrights though they have many times undertaken the same . . . because they trust rather to their judgement than their art, and to their eye than their scale and compass.'[21]

Waymouth also complained that the ships were 'too high out of the water, crank, and cannot carry their canvas or work their guns in a seaway; that they will not steer, and sometimes their sides are not of equal proportion the one to the other.'[21]

The system of whole-moulding was still being described in its original form – with rising and breadth lines running parallel – in shipbuilding tomes of the nineteenth century, for example, David Steel's *The Elements and Practice of Naval Architecture* (1805), and E Bobrick's *Handbuch der praktischen Seefahrtskunde* (1848). But there it is only applied to boatbuilding. This construction technique, now over 300 years old, has still not disappeared completely from boatbuilding. In 1982 the author was shown moulds by a boatbuilder on the Greek island of Symi in the Dodecanese. The moulds were being used in the construction of caiques, and gave these traditional, elegant fishing boats their shape. The boatbuilder had no technical drawings, just moulds for the stem and sternpost, and two to three movable moulds for the middle and ends of the ship's hull.[22]

CHAPTER 8

The reconstruction

TWO main sources are used for the reconstruction of a galleon of 1610 described in this chapter: first, the rising-lines, the outline of the sides and the ribs which can be deduced from an anonymous English manuscript from the beginning of the seventeenth century (Plans 4, 5, 6); and second, the galleon model in the Stockholm Maritime Museum (see Chapter 6). The English manuscript is the *Treatise on Shipbuilding* (see Appendix and Chapter 7), which is referred to as the *Treatise* in the following passages. The manuscript is dated around 1620, but it is reasonable to assume that, in the seventeenth century, a technical process would have been known and used for ten or more years before it was written down. That would have been particularly true of ship construction, which was, historically, a very tradition-bound procedure. This means that we can date our reconstruction at around 1610. We do have a manuscript from around 1610 by the English mathematician Thomas Harriot (1560?–1621), (see p 129). Harriot takes issue with the current theory of shipbuilding, and describes principles of ship construction like those which appear in the *Treatise*; it is, therefore, clear that the refinements to the technique of whole-moulding used in the following reconstruction were already known by 1610.

I have transformed the rising-line plan and rib outline, which were reconstructed according to the *Treatise* (Plan 4 and Fig 101), into a modern outline (Plan 6). This gives us reliable proportions for the hull of a medium-sized English galleon, from the keel to just above the height of the breadth line. The side of the ship above this, in the area of the top timbers, is not very reliably documented (see p 126). The unfinished upper part of the ship from the *Treatise* can be completed from the galleon model in the Stockholm Maritime Museum, the Stockholm galleon, which shows the structure of the upper sides of a very similar, contemporaneous ship. From it, we can deduce the positions of the decks and the gunports, the height of the gunwales and many other details. The Stockholm galleon cannot be attributed to any one particular regional shipbuilding tradition. The fact that it comes from a Swedish church does not automatically mean that Swedish shipbuilders constructed an original prototype of the model in Sweden, using Swedish shipbuilding techniques.

I have used the two sources, the *Treatise* and the Stockholm galleon, to complement each other. The construction which results from this process is not the ship which an English shipbuilder would have built by following the *Treatise*; nor is it the ship which was used as a prototype for the Stockholm galleon. It is, however, a vessel which complies with all currently known building rules and rules of proportion used by (English) shipbuilders of old. Moreover, these rules leave a little room for individual play. The result of the reconstruction is logical, and coherent within itself. The reconstructed ship is of interest to modelmakers as it broadens the narrow range of serious reconstructions of ships from around 1600.

The problem of how to combine two so very different sources was difficult to overcome. Slides of the side view of the Stockholm galleon and of the outlines from the *Treatise* were projected on top of one another. This gave a realistic, common basis: the lower edge of the first midship wale (Fig 76). In the *Treatise* this line is given as the height of the water-line. Here it serves as the ideal basis for projecting both sources vertically on top of one another. The common outer edge of the stem and sternposts was used for aligning both sources horizontally. Differences in the measurements of the two sources do not matter very much, as both represent a large ship of a similar type. Vessels of varying sizes

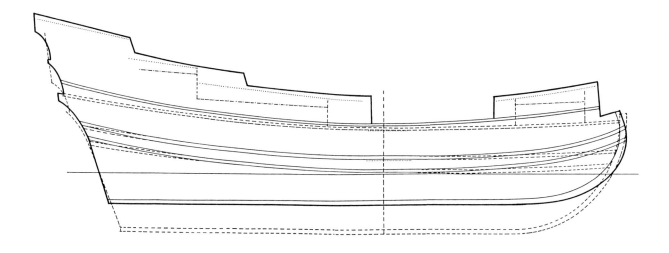

Fig 76: Projection of an English rising-lines plan (broken lines) superimposed on the Stockholm galleon (continuous lines). The two sources for the reconstruction converge at the waterline on the lower wale, and on the outer edge of the stem and sternpost at the height of this line. We can see where the courses of the wales tally, and where they vary. The sides of the two lower decks (dotted lines) correspond exactly amidships. The decks of the superstructure of the Stockholm galleon (dotted lines) are higher than those of the English design (shown as dash-dot lines).

could be built around 1600 from the same rising-line plans and rules of proportion – within limits, of course, which allowed a sufficient deck height etc. The master shipwright only had to modify the dimensions on his design (see Appendix p 186).

If we now look at the result of the superimposed projection, we can see that aft of the midship frame the run of the lower wales in both sources,and the distance between them, largely coincide. The wales of the Stockholm galleon in the forward third of the hull curve sharply upwards, as distinct from those of the *Treatise*. We can assume that the modelbuilder exaggerated the curve there. The upper wales and rails of the Stockholm galleon's forecastle have a realistic curve. According to the instructions given in the *Treatise*, all wales should run parallel with each other. In this respect the run of the lower wales aft of the midship frame in the reconstruction follows that of the Stockholm galleon. But the run of the lower wales at the forward end of the model becomes so steep that it has been made the same as that of the wales at the forecastle.

It is, of course, dangerous to use the term realistic about the reconstruction of a historical artifact. But the results of this correction are so convincing that I have yielded to the temptation; redrawing the side view of the Stockholm galleon with the forward lower wales repositioned results not only in the same silhouette, but also in the same forecastle height and deck angle. At the same time, the deck is a realistic height above the lower deck. The run of the wales in the reconstructed ship turns out to be somewhat steeper than that desired by the author of the *Treatise*. We can thus assume that the breadth line lies correspondingly higher at the ends of the ship. That reveals an older, more traditional shipbuilder's view (see p 124). The reconstructed ship has rather less carrying capacity at the bow and the stern than had the English galleon. This probably explains the narrow bulkhead in front of the foremast (see Fig 85, no 82), and the narrow, and consequently light, beakhead. Heavy bow chasers could not even be considered on this ship.

Apart from the run of the wales amidships, the superimposed sources have other coinciding features: the lower and upper deck are in the same position amidships. If we apply the contemporary rules for the size and intervals of the gunports (see p 188ff), we find that the ship from the *Treatise* has the same number of gunports on its decks as has the Stockholm galleon (Plan 5). From these points of coincidence, we can infer that the two sources concern ships of

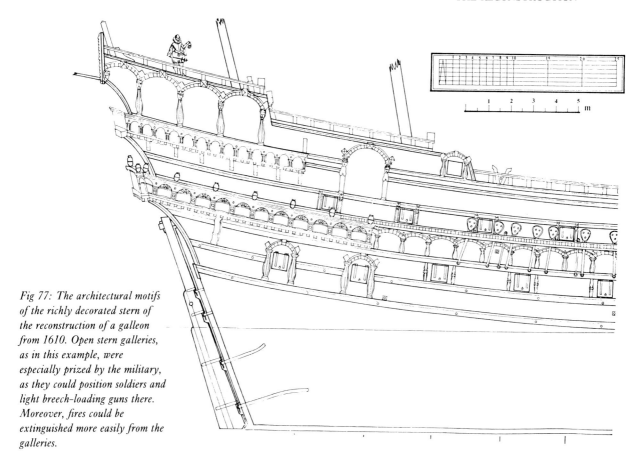

Fig 77: The architectural motifs of the richly decorated stern of the reconstruction of a galleon from 1610. Open stern galleries, as in this example, were especially prized by the military, as they could position soldiers and light breech-loading guns there. Moreover, fires could be extinguished more easily from the galleries.

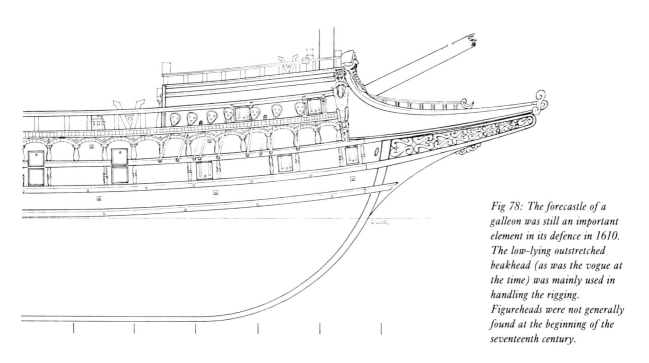

Fig 78: The forecastle of a galleon was still an important element in its defence in 1610. The low-lying outstretched beakhead (as was the vogue at the time) was mainly used in handling the rigging. Figureheads were not generally found at the beginning of the seventeenth century.

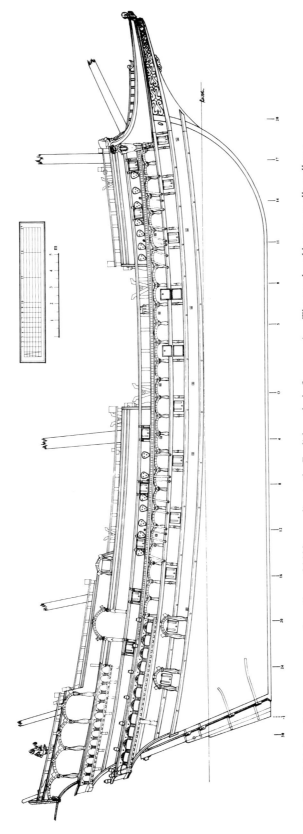

Fig 79a: Side view of the reconstruction of a galleon of 1610, according to the English method of construction. The vessel could serve equally well as a merchant ship or as a warship. It had a carrying capacity of 576 tons and an overall length of 52.5m. The maximum breadth was approximately 11m; the draught 4.5m.

Fig 79b: Stern view of the reconstruction of a galleon from 1610. The high, narrow, light stern was a typical feature of these ships, which were designed according to the method of whole-moulding, and had little buoyancy at the bow and stern.

Fig 79c: Bow view of the reconstruction of a galleon from 1610. The low forecastle, with sides leaning inwards at the forward bulkhead, was a typical feature of this type of ship. This resulted in a narrow base for the light beakhead. This method of construction can be explained by the small amount of buoyancy in the bow region.

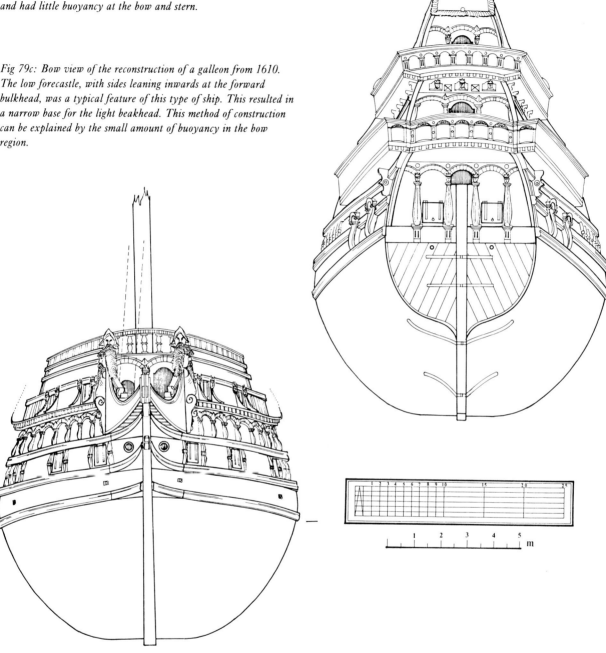

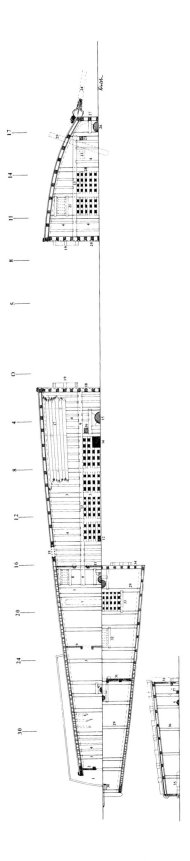

Fig 80: The poop deck, quarter deck, halfdeck and forecastle deck of the reconstruction of a galleon from 1610.

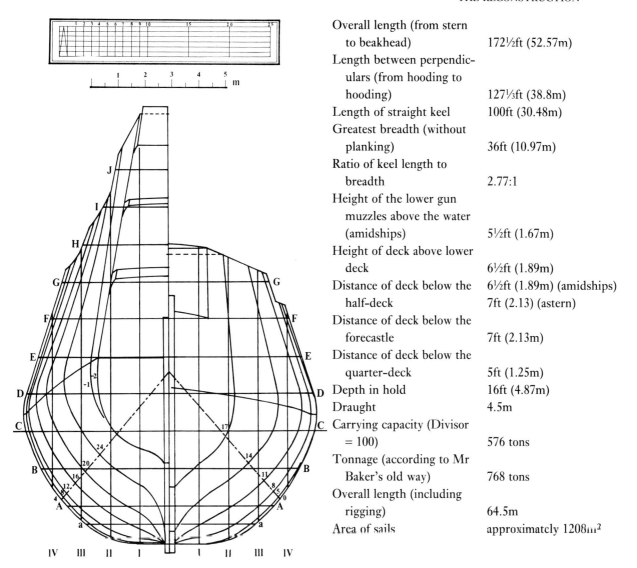

Overall length (from stern to beakhead)	172½ft (52.57m)
Length between perpendiculars (from hooding to hooding)	127⅓ft (38.8m)
Length of straight keel	100ft (30.48m)
Greatest breadth (without planking)	36ft (10.97m)
Ratio of keel length to breadth	2.77:1
Height of the lower gun muzzles above the water (amidships)	5½ft (1.67m)
Height of deck above lower deck	6½ft (1.89m)
Distance of deck below the half-deck	6½ft (1.89m) (amidships) 7ft (2.13) (astern)
Distance of deck below the forecastle	7ft (2.13m)
Distance of deck below the quarter-deck	5ft (1.25m)
Depth in hold	16ft (4.87m)
Draught	4.5m
Carrying capacity (Divisor = 100)	576 tons
Tonnage (according to Mr Baker's old way)	768 tons
Overall length (including rigging)	64.5m
Area of sails	approximately 1208m²

Fig 81: Rib plan of the reconstruction of a galleon from 1610. In this design the toptimbers, which define the shape of the upper part of the ship's sides, are still straight, and not curved inwards, as was to be the case later on (cf Fig 101).

practically the same size. This solves the problem of finding the right measurements for the reconstruction; we can take those from the *Treatise*.

The reconstructed galleon is a spacious, comfortable trading and fighting ship from around 1610 (Fig 79 A–C), built to English design. Its measurements are (see above):

From the measurements we can infer that the headroom below the halfdeck and the lower deck of the forecastle is rather larger than the English builders suggested. There was less height below the quarter-deck. Perhaps the space below was used only for cabins and storage. The 1m-high space below the poop deck was uninhabitable; but even on the large *Wasa* the height of the room below the poop deck was only 1.4m in places.

I would now like to discuss some of the points in the reconstruction in more detail.

Fig 82: This picture from Furttenbach's Architectura Navalis *(1629) allows us to deduce details about the rigging, and so serves as a useful example for a model. The low forecastle with the wide front bulkhead is a noteworthy feature; as with the Stockholm galleon it results in a narrow base for the beakhead. The ship had no cathead at the forecastle. A crossbeam above the beakhead was used in raising the anchor.*

Toptimbers

As the Stockholm galleon's toptimbers are straight and not curved inwards (as in later ships), the reconstruction could have been treated in this way too (Fig 81). This would enable us to avoid certain obscure parts of the *Treatise*, like the gradual decrease in the curve of such timbers towards the ends of the ship. But fair lines will only result if the futtocks are curved inwards for only one-eighth of the greatest breadth, and not for one-sixth (as is suggested, but not required, in the *Treatise*).

Forecastle

The shape of the futtocks and the curve of the toptimber line to the stem mean that the forecastle is very narrow at the bow. Neither source shows an outward curvature of the side wall at the beakhead bulkhead, as was found on later ships to relieve the function of the catheads. The Stockholm galleon probably did not have a cathead. The anchors were brought back to the ship's side by means of a movable davit or a crossbeam which lay above the beakhead rail. On all contemporary pictures of comparable ships, the foremast is shown as being forward of the front bulkhead of the forecastle. However, that is not the case on the Stockholm galleon, where the forecastle has been brought forward and is consequently narrower. The foremost bulkhead (Fig 85, no 82) is forward of the foremast; this means that the beakhead has a narrower base. Perhaps the narrow forecastle, with limited space for bow chascrs, and the light beakhead constituted a shipbuilder's attempt to reduce weight in the bow area. We find a comparable forecastle shape in the – admittedly smaller – three-masted merchant ship in Furttenbach's *Architectura Navalis* (1629)[1] (Fig 82), and in the so-called Peller Model of 1603, described by W Jaeger.[2] It is possible that there were equally cramped forecastles on the large English galleons; in September 1588 the Master Shipwrights Peter Pett and Matthew Baker inspected and approved all the galleons and smaller ships at Chatham, to where they had returned after the engagement against the Spanish Armada. Amongst other things, their report concludes that the forecastles of the *Elizabeth Jonas* (built in 1559) and the *Triumph* (built 1561) should be strengthened and the shape altered so that they could carry more guns at the bow. Did these ships perhaps have a narrow forward bulkhead, like the Stockholm galleon?

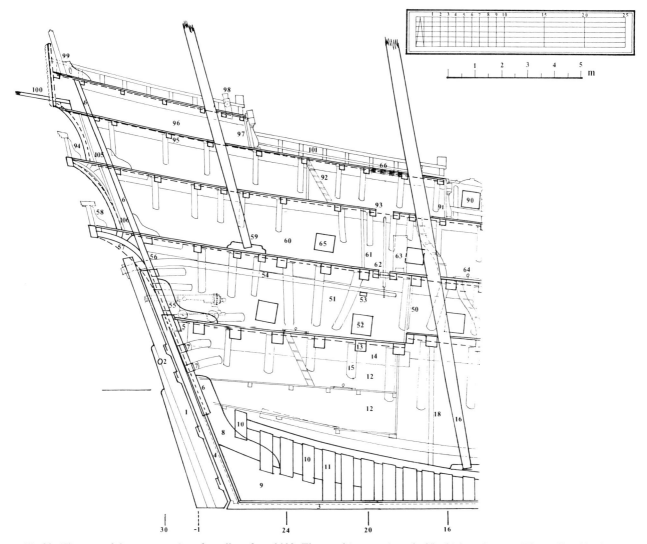

Fig 83: The stern of the reconstruction of a galleon from 1610. The vessel is approximately 15m high at the stern. The small rudder (no 1), typical for ships of this time, which had to manoeuvre a lot by sail is noteworthy. The rudder was moved by means of a long tiller (no 54) in the gunroom (no 51), which was pushed to and fro on a sweep (no 53) by a whipstaff (no 62).

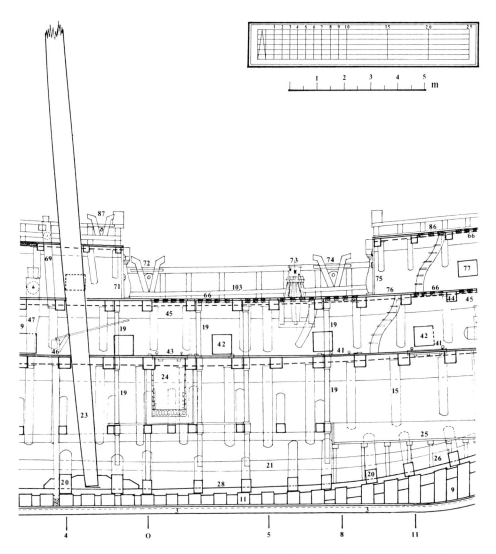

Fig 84: Part of the longitudinal section of the reconstruction of a galleon from 1610. The waist, the space in the upper deck between the fore and aft superstructures, is shown forward of the mainmast (no 23). Below the lower deck, the first continuous watertight deck, we can see the fireplace for the kettle (no 24). It is located on a row of beams amidships, which was called the false orlop deck.

Rib spacing

The reconstruction retains the same intervals between the guiding ribs as in the original manuscript. That means that the distance between the ribs aft of the midship frame is 2½ft (0.76m), and increases to 3ft (0.9m) forward of the midship frame. We can imagine that there would have been filling frames in an original ship, perhaps at the height of the waterline and the lower wales. It is possible that the ribs did not continue in a straight line from the keel to the gunwales, but were linked by contiguous parts. For simplicity, the drawing is based on an even keel. In reality there would have been a trim, causing the stern of the ship to lie deeper in the water than the bow. This was intended to improve the response of very small turns of the rudder, and to result in better sailing qualities.

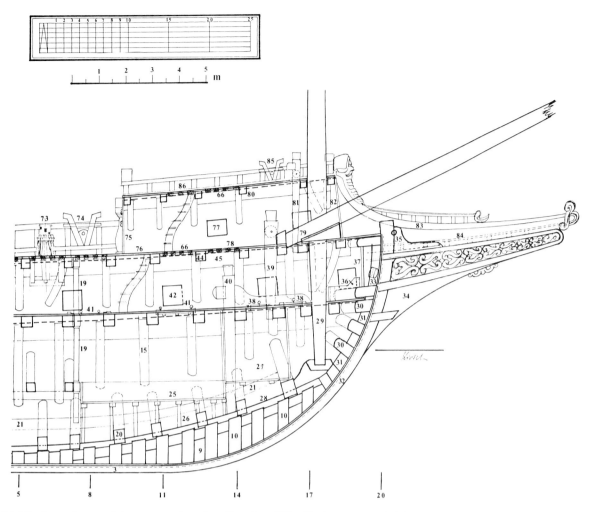

Fig 85: The forecastle area of the reconstruction of a galleon from 1610. The long, outstretched beakhead, the foremast (no 29) located on the front stem, amd the heavy, sharply projecting bowsprit (no 19) running past the mast, are all typical features of ships from this period. The forward position of the foremast and bowspritsails was supposed to balance the ship's high aft superstructure. In contrast with most other galleons, the front bulkhead here is forward of the mast.

Keel

Unfortunately the *Treatise* gives no details on the breadth of the keel, so we have to turn to a Dutch rule from the seventeenth century, according to which the keel should be 1in thick for every 7ft in length. That means that a keel which is 100ft in length (30.5m) should be 14.2in (0.36m) in breadth. For depth, a false keel was attached below.

Transom

The transom has been drawn straight, for the sake of simplicity, as is specified in the *Treatise*. It is, however, conceivable that it was curved in three dimensions, with a gentle rise in the direction of the deck beams and towards the bow. In the *Treatise* it is also listed amongst the curving timbers.

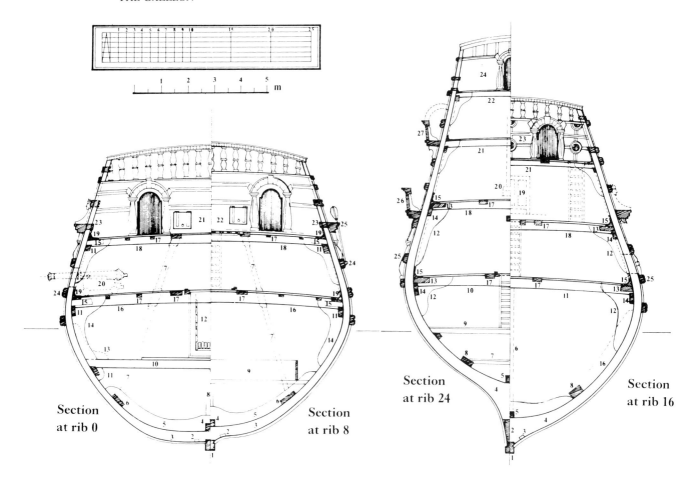

Figs 86a, 86b: Sections of the hull of the reconstruction of a galleon from 1610. We can see the powerful hanging knees which joined the deck beams to the ribs and the wales. Strong riders, vertical and diagonal pillars steadied the floor of the hull if it came aground.

Interior

The division of space within the the ship is, as far as possible, in keeping with the instructions given in the *Treatise*. There is no mention of a cable-tier, but there must have been one (Fig 84, no 25). It would be possible to divide the hold and the decks into additional rooms, but to portray them here would be venturing too far into the realms of fantasy. The false orlop deck constructed inside with the galley (Fig 84, no 24) may also not have existed, in which case the galley would have been in the forecastle. This is where some contemporaneous authors specified it should be.[4] Conventionally-minded shipbuilders at the beginning of the seventeenth century positioned the kettle on the false orlop deck, as exemplified in the *Wasa*. They considered it would be too dangerous in the forecastle, fearing fire, the proximity of the gunpowder, hindrance to the guns, and danger from splintering bricks in the fireplace surround if the ship came under fire.

The mainmasts on galleons (Fig 85, no 29) were still positioned very far forward. This method of construction caused problems of space: firstly, the bowsprit had to be continued past the side of the mainmast; secondly, the space on the lower deck between the mainmast and the false stem (Fig 85, no 31) was very narrow, as the manger (Fig 85, no 36) had to be brought down there to catch water which had been washed in by the hawse or had dropped down from the anchor cable. As we can see from the deck plan, there was, in practice, not enough space for a bow chaser at the forward port.

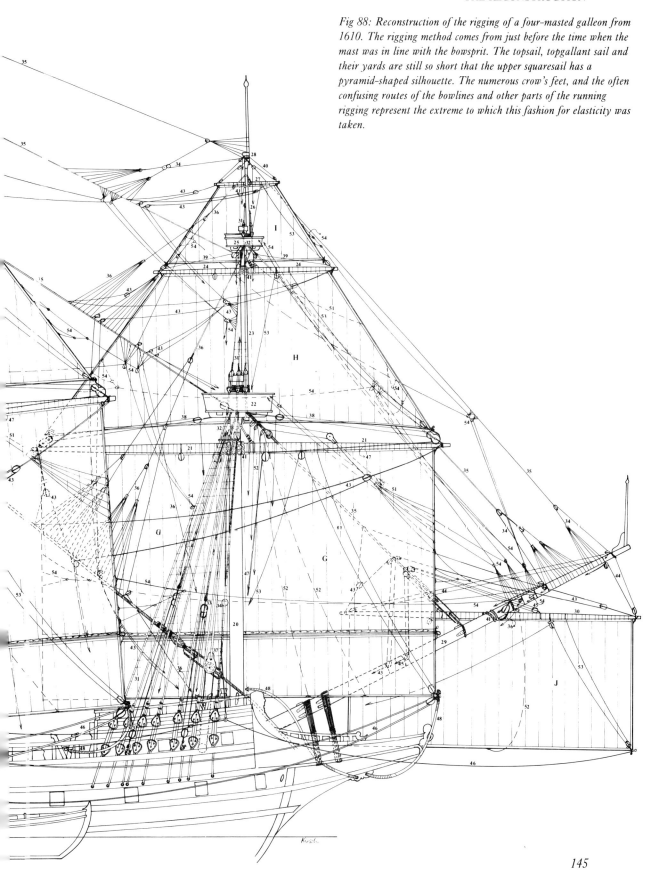

Fig 88: Reconstruction of the rigging of a four-masted galleon from 1610. The rigging method comes from just before the time when the mast was in line with the bowsprit. The topsail, topgallant sail and their yards are still so short that the upper squaresail has a pyramid-shaped silhouette. The numerous crow's feet, and the often confusing routes of the bowlines and other parts of the running rigging represent the extreme to which this fashion for elasticity was taken.

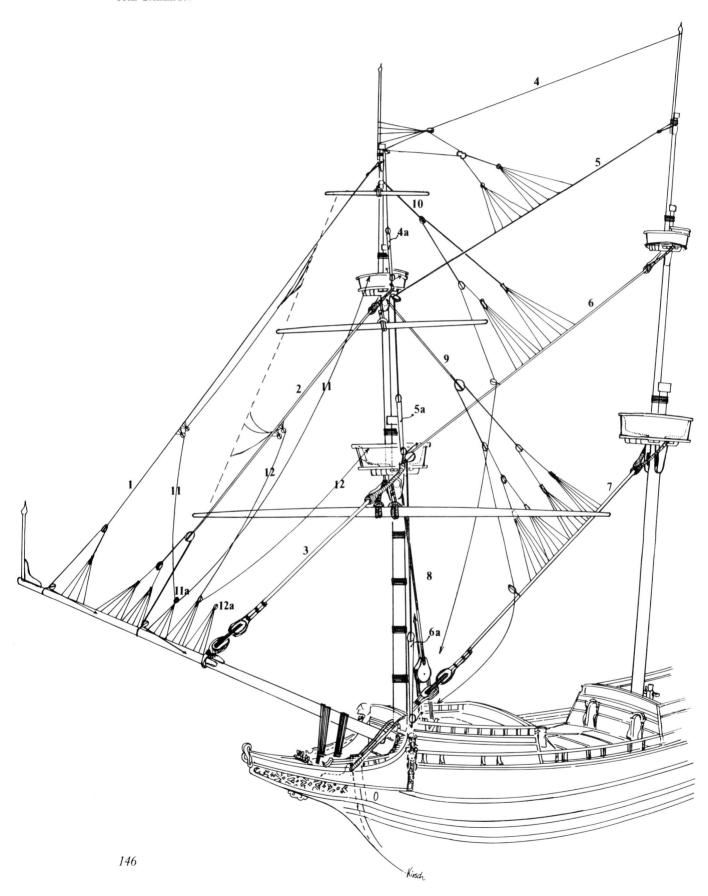

Perhaps this merely served as a reserve port for a further anchor cable, or as an opening through which long goods could be loaded.

Rudder

The arrangement and dimensions of the rudder equipment is pure supposition. Smaller ships had a low companion on the half-deck, from which the helmsman had a view to the front. On larger ships, like the reconstructed galleon, the helmsman stood at his whipstaff on the upper deck (Fig 85). In front of him was the binnacle with lights and compass, as specified in the *Treatise* (see p 172, Fig 83, nos 62, 63 and 'Cross-section at rib 16', Fig 83, no 19). There was a hole above the whipstaff on the halfdeck (Fig 86[B], no 93), and a grating in the quarter-deck above (Fig 83, no 66). The quartermaster or pilot could shout the necessary orders down to the helmsman below. Contemporaneous sources, for example Mainwaring, do of course mention that the helmsman had to watch the lower edge of the mainsail to see whether it was catching the wind; however this was not practicable on large ships. Mainwaring also states that on ships of over 500 tons the men's strength was not sufficient to hold the whipstaff in bad weather. So it was no longer used, and we have to imagine a tackle system in the gun room (Fig 83, no 51) which moved the tiller.[5]

Decks

Gratings, hatchways and scuttles are shown without high coamings, though it is conceivable that high coamings would have been used. The deck beams tapered by approximately one-third of their depth towards the ends. Hanging and lodging knees, which joined the deck beams to the sides of the ship (Figs 86a, 86b) are shown in the reconstruction drawing. It is possible that some deck beams had standards. Additional standing and other knees might be inserted between the deck beams and the side of a ship after many years, to prolong its useful life. That was necessary if, for example, some of the bracing no longer held fast, or if heavy guns were being added.[6]

The arrangement and dimensions of the deck structure rests on supposition. Apart from the fact that the individual elements (ledges, carlings, mast partners, pillars, etc) existed around 1600, we have no precise description of their configuration at this time. The appearance of the reconstruction results from trusting to the shipbuilders' conservatism and looking at similar structures on the Dutch-built *Wasa* and later English ships (Fig 87). Wedges to hold the masts securely in the partners are not shown.

Pumps

The reconstructed ship has only two brake pumps (Fig 84, no 46) with pump handles in the vicinity of the mainmast. Mainwaring mentions other brake or suction pumps on the sides of vessels with a broad base. This meant that the

---

Fig 89: Sketch of some of the stays, halyards and bowlines of the fore and mainmasts of a galleon (not drawn to scale). The practice of distributing the forces over as many parts of the running rigging as possible here reached its zenith.

1 *Fore topgallant mast stay, with lanyard and crow's feet*	7 *Mainstay*
2 *Fore topmast stay, with lanyard, bridles and crow's feet*	8 *Foreyard halyard*
3 *Forestay*	9 *Fore topsail halyard, with lanyard, bridle and crow's feet*
4 *Flagstaff stay with lanyard, bridles and crow's feet*	10 *Fore topgallant sail halyard, with lanyard, bridle and*
4a *Flagstaff stay tackle, belayed to the top*	*crow's feet*
5 *Main topgallant stay*	11 *Fore topgallant bowline, belayed to the top*
5a *Main topgallant stay tackle, belayed to the top*	11a *Double block for starboard and larboard bowlines*
6 *Main topmast stay*	12 *Fore top bowline (starboard), belayed to the top*
6a *Main topmast stay tackle, belayed to the foremast pinrail*	12a *Block for fore top bowline (port)*

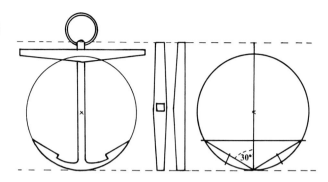

Fig 90: Proportions of an anchor. According to a rule of thumb from around 1600, an anchor of 1 ton in weight had a shaft length of about 12½ ft (3.8m). (Drawing after Tinniswood, 'Anchors and Accesories' Mariners Mirror, vol 31, 1945)

pump staff could be moved by means of a rope held by six or eight men (see Röding's description). The water ran along a channel, a pump dale, across the deck to the scuppers. Chain pumps may well have been installed on English galleons of this period.

Beakhead

Estimating the positions of the two firing positions presents no great problem; we can determine their length and the angle at which they were raked from the Stockholm galleon model (Fig 77). Reconstructing the beakhead is more difficult, as all traces of it have disappeared. The *Treatise* gives its length as being one-fifth of the keel length. The angle of projection should be 12°–13° to the horizontal (Fig 78). This may mean the beakhead deck or the angle of the large beakhead knee. Beakheads rearing sharply upwards seem to have been a feature of Venetian and Spanish galleons. Mainwaring says that they could be recognised in this way from early times.[7]

Deck planking

The deck planking is only partially shown in the reconstruction (Fig 87). From archaeological finds we can assume that the planks, in particular the waterways, were wider around 1600 than in later centuries. Deck planks did not always have parallel edges. Depending on the materials available, they were made in varying widths to save wood.

Decoration

We cannot establish the extent to which a real ship would have been decorated like the Stockholm galleon model. From old pictures we can assume that the hull below the third wale would probably have kept the brown colouring. Monson wrote on this subject: 'The pitch of the Canaries melts not with the sun; therefore good for the upper works in ships'.[8] Many experiments were performed on the coating of the underwater area, but no method was found which could counteract the dreaded *Teredo navalis* (ship worm). 'The worm begins with a hole no bigger than a needle's head, and by degrees becomes as great as a man's finger. The thicker the plank is, the greater it grows,' wrote Monson. He considered the best protection to be sheathing the hull with double planks:

> The best [method] is with thin boards, half inch thick, the thinner the better, and elm better than oak for it does not split, it endures better under water and yields better to the ship's side. The manner is thus: before the sheathing-board be nailed on, upon the inner side of it they smear it over with tar, half a finger thick, and upon the tar another half finger thick with hair, such as the white limers use, and so nail it on, the nails not above a span distant one from another. Some impute the killing of the worm to the tar, others to the hair that involves and chokes it.[9]

Unfortunately Monson does not mention what colour this outer skin was. It may well have been the dull white that we know from old pictures.

Ordnance

If we imagine the reconstructed galleon as a heavily armed merchant ship, we can assume that the ordnance on the lower deck broadside consisted of culverins and demi-culverins. The two stern chasers in the gun room were probably normal-length culverins. The broadside guns could have been shortened culverin-type guns. We can assume that there would have been demi-culverins and sakers on the upper deck. The gun on the halfdeck might have been a saker. All were carriage-mounted. There was not necessarily a gun at every gunport: manning so many guns at the same time might have overstretched the capacity of the crew of a merchant ship. As we know from contemporaneous reports, they were often brought from one side of the deck to the other, so they could thus be used in attack or defence. On long journeys they were stowed in the hold, where they supplemented the ballast, or altered the trim. Some reports describe ships being unable to defend themselves from attack because there was insufficient time for the guns to be brought up from the hold. We can assume there were light perrier-type breech-loaders (eg fowlers) on the half- or quarter-deck, at several points along the arming cloths, where there were posts with holes for the brackets. The bulkheads at the forecastle, halfdeck and quarter-deck were armed with breech-loading guns, which were apparently on beds. They were used in repelling enemy boarders.

Rigging

The following details complete the chapter on rigging. Apart from the stumps of four masts and the bowsprit, only miniscule traces of the rigging have survived on the Stockholm galleon model. We can find the knighthead for the mizzen yard halyard, the nails for the chain plates or chains, and a hole in the stem for the forestay eye. We do not know if the model was fully rigged in its original state. There are no indications of the places where the running rigging was belayed, like cleats, belaying pins, or, at the very least, holes in the arming cloths. Ships of 1600 already had blocks for the sheets of the foresail and cleats for the tacks of the mainsail near the arming cloths in the waist area. There may also have been a block or a pulley in the arming cloths at the waist for the sheets of the mainsail, through which ran the running part of the sheet and from where it could be brought forward.

The suggested reconstruction of the rigging for a ship of the same type as the Stockholm galleon is based on the specifications for the length of the round timbers given by various contemporaneous authors (Fig 88). Different dimensions and ratios are mentioned in the various sources; they have to be harmonised for a reconstruction. I have turned to English sources from the beginning of the seventeenth century: the anonymous manuscript *A Treatise on Rigging* (1620–25), edited by W Salisbury, and the very important work, *The Seaman's Dictionary*, by Sir Henry Mainwaring (1587–1653), an English seaman and adventurer, who made a name for himself as a pirate in the Mediterranean, raiding Spanish treasure ships. On his return to England in 1618 he was pardoned (no doubt for a handsome sum of money) by King James I. That was the usual practice. Mainwaring began a career in public service, and became vice-admiral. He was in command of the fortress at Dover during the years 1620–23, and there wrote the first important English book on seamanship for the gentleman captains of his day, who were often put in command of a ship for all sorts of reasons other than their technical expertise. *A Sea Grammar* by Captain John Smith, first published in 1627, and instructions from a manuscript (dated 1608–10) by Thomas Harriot, served as further sources for the reconstruction of the rigging.

As with the specifications for ship construction, we can also assume that the instructions and seamanship details in these source documents on rigging would have been valid ten years earlier – in the years around 1610. It was a period of change in the area of ships' rigging. All these sources refer to the sprit topmast, which was officially introduced to the Royal Navy in 1618, but appears in pictures from 1600 onwards. The old bonaventure mast has not disappeared completely from the sources (see p 37 ff). All the sources give a very short length for the topmasts and yards, and a substantial length for the lower yards – including the square spritsail yard. That causes the pyramid-shaped outline of the top and top gallant sail in the reconstruction. There are no contemporaneous drawings for the dimensions and appearance of the blocks; we have to search for information in pictures and original models from around the same period (for example, the Peller model). We cannot even be sure of the strength of the standing and running rigging. Basically, we assume that blocks and dead eyes of around 1600 were approximately twice as large as those from the beginning of the nineteenth century.

Fig 89 shows some halyards, stays and bowlines. This should go some way towards clarifying the confusing scheme of rigging. We can see from the course of the bowlines that the sails were not trimmed from the deck or the beakhead, but from the associated tops. The doubled tie of the fore and mainmast led from the squaresail over a wooden block to the port and starboard sides of the mast, which was suspended from the hounds. They led from this block to the halyard (8). The foremast halyard (9) was a single one and simply led over a block in the hounds to the mainstay. The single halyard for the topgallant sail (10) distributed its force on the forestay of the main topmast (6), which led back to the foretop through a block which was stropped on a running basis to the eye of the forestay. The falls of the mainmast stay (6a) went down to the deck at the foot of the foremast. Even the flagstaff stay (4) coming from the top of the mainmast, the significance of which is not clear, distributed its force over very many points in the rigging; amongst them the main topgallant stay (5), which ran through a block below the tops of the foremast, and was stretched by a tackle, the fixed part of which was stropped to the forestay.

Many details cannot be included in a sketch showing an overview of the rigging. I would like to list here some of the missing parts:

Jeers for the fore and mainyard (see Fig 28)

Rings on the lower yards for the gaskets

Top-ropes; which were not always cut short and sometimes led over a block on the deck, or through a knighthead on to the capstan

Backstays for the tops; which were not always fitted

Breast backstays and tackle

Woldings on assembled masts

Catharpins on the fore and main shrouds (see Fig 28)

Netting in the waist area as protection against boarders

Flags and pennants

Arming-cloths in the form of canvas hangings on the rails and tops

Knight blocks: main and fore knights had four blocks – one for the top-rope or the jeer; three for the halyard

Differences in the ropework; mostly it was three-strand rope, but the yard halyards were made from four-strand rope, as this ran better over the blocks in the hounds

Method of securing the blocks – most blocks were stropped; brass blocks were spliced

Knots, only two of which are mentioned in the sources – the bowline knot, by which the bridles of the bowline were tied to the cringles; and a wallknot, a round stop knot made out of the three strands which was used on, for example, the tacks or topsail sheets

Fenders, which played an important part in the appearance of ships of old; they were to be found on the halyards to prevent the yards and their rigging from chafing against the mast; they lay on the forward rail of the forecastle, and, as the foresail tacks passed over this, the bowsprit was also equipped with fenders in the slings area.

Belaying

We now have some contemporaneous hints for some of the places where the running rigging was belayed. The numbers in brackets refer to the numbers in the longitudinal section shown in Figs 83, 84 and 85. In general we can say that the smaller ropes sprouted from the ship's side, especially at night. Sheets and tacks of the lower sails led to staghorns and bevels on the sides. There were racks of belaying pins on the beakhead in front of the bowsprit gammoning and aft of the foremast (no 81) and the mainmast (no 69).

Square spritsail yard

The halyard and lifts were belayed on the bowsprit gammoning. The braces were belayed on the forecastle.

Spritsail

The sheet led through a 'block facing the mainmast' to a staghorn (no 87). The buntline was belayed on the forecastle.

Foresail

The tacks led through the beakhead via the forecastle rail, where there were fenders for them, and were belayed to bitts or staghorns at the height of the foremast (nos 81, 85). The bowlines were belayed to belaying pins on the forecastle. The buntlines went to cleats on either side of the mast. The clew lines were belayed to the rail, at the height of the fore shrouds.

Fore topsail

The sheets ran through blocks to the fore bitt (no 81). The clew lines ran through the top and along the yard (through bullseyes) on the parrel.

Fore topyard

The lifts were belayed on the fore top.

Fore topgallant yard

The lifts were belayed to the fore topmast head.

Mainsail

The tacks and sheets ran through staghorns (nos 74 and 88 repectively); the buntlines went to cleats on either side of the mast. The clewlines were belayed to sides of the ship at the height of the forward yards.

Main topsail

The sheets went through blocks on the bitts of the mainmast (no 69). The clewlines ran through the top and along the yard (through bullseyes) to the rail.

Main topyard

The lifts were belayed in the main top.

Main topgallant yard

The lifts were belayed in the main topmost head. The braces were belayed on the halfdeck rail.

Main topgallant sail

The bowlines were belayed on the foremast.

Top-rope for main and foretops

This was coiled up and stored or secured to the yards when not required. If it was cut short, the lanyard ran through a block (on the deck near the mast) to the capstan.

Mizzensail

The tacks were belayed to the 'deck below the mainmast'. The catharpins were belayed to the block on the yards.

Forestay of the main topmast

The lanyard of the rigging was belayed on the main top.

Mizzen topmast forestay

The lanyard of the rigging was belayed to the mainyards.

Anchors

A ship of the size of our reconstructed galleon carried six to seven anchors (Fig 89). The *Rainbow*, a similar-sized large English galleon of 1586 had six anchors weighing a total of 6000 pounds (2.7 metric tons). For these, she had six anchor cables (see p 21). Unfortunately there are no firm rules on the size and weight of anchors relative to ship size during this period. Basically, the extent to which ships were fitted with anchors increased over the course of the centuries. There were, however, substantial differences between individual ships.

The largest anchor was the sheet, or best anchor (without a stock), which was kept in the ship's hold, and only used as a last resort. An English document from the 1580s gives a weight of 20 hundredweight (ie, 1 ton) 11lb for a best anchor on a ship 36ft (10.97m) wide at the midship beam, and a cable 18in (45.7cm) in circumference.[10] Mainwaring (1625) gives a weight of 2000 pounds (0.906 metric tons) for the sheet anchor on a 500-ton ship.[11] The circumference of the lighter cables for the smaller anchors diminishes by about 1in. These proportions assume that the cables are of the quality of those which the English obtained from the Baltic or Russia. Next came the first, second and third bow anchors (bowers) for anchorage in channels and harbour areas. The stream anchor was even smaller, and used in deep waters to hold the ship fast against a tide. The kedge anchor was the lightest of all, and could be carried in the boat. It was used to hold the ship against a current.

We know the proportions of anchors from this period from looking at contemporaneous pictures. Formulae which allow the size of the anchor to be calcuated from the weight are rather dubious. One such formula ran: S = cube root of (G.2000); S represents the length of the anchor shaft in feet; G the weight of the anchor in tons; 2000 is a constant.[12] Thus an anchor weighing one ton would have a shaft length of 12.29ft, or 3.83m. We should consider a result like this to be only an approximate value. If we take the Dutch idiom 'Skinny as a Spanish anchor' literally, we can see that opinions on anchors, like views on rigging proportions, seem to have varied from one country to another.

Boats

A galleon carried three boats: a long boat, a pinnace and a skiff. Of course there are no standard sizes here, but in a large, well-equipped ship, the long boat was about half the length of the keel. The *Prince*, an English ship of 1610, had a keel length of 115ft (35m) and a long boat of 52ft (15.8m). Another ship which had a keel length of 95ft (28.9m) had a long boat of 51ft 4in (15.6m); yet another had a keel length of 84ft (25.6m) and a long boat of 40ft 6in (13.7m).[13] It was no wonder that boats like this had to be towed, as there was no room for them on board. They stood up to powerful seas, and men were kept ready to pump their bilges. Boat losses were often reported, though: in 1625, all the ships in the English fleet which sailed to Cadiz via the Bay of Biscay lost their long boats.[14] The boats were often lost in battle, when the tow-ropes would get broken.

It was an important mark of prestige for a master to have a large, impressive long boat and a large skiff. In 1618 the English Naval Reform Commission tried, more or less in vain, to standardise the boats on warships and to reduce their size. The long boats on the largest ships were to be 42ft (12.8m) long; others were to be 31ft (9.4m); yet others 28ft (8.5m). Pinnaces, which had hitherto varied in length from 19ft to 30ft, were now to be from 26ft to 29ft long. Skiffs were to be 20ft (6.1m) long. A length-to-breadth ratio of 3.5–3.8:1 was recommended for long boats, and 3.8–4.0:1 for pinnaces. The skiffs were to have a length of 3.1 x the breadth.[15]

Contemporaneous pictures show that most towed boats had a round stern. Some paintings, however, do show boats with flat sterns: for example, those of Hendrick Cornelisz Vroom (1566–1640). The long boats were working boats equipped with a davit with an iron or bronze pulley, over which ran the buoy rope for the kedge anchor, when the latter was being raised or lowered. Apart from that, it was used for the transport of goods, arms, barrels and so on, and for bringing men on to land. The pinnace was for the use of the highest-ranking ship's officer. The skiff, which was a light, fast boat that could be tied to the ship's side in heavy seas, was for the other officers.[16]

Reconstruction plans

Figs 83, 84, 85: Longitudinal Section

  1 Rudder
  2 Hole for the safety line secured to the rudder
  3 Keel with rabbet
  4 Sternpost
  5 Wing transom
  6 Fashion pieces
  7 Transoms and their knees
  8 Sternpost knee
  9 Rising timber, fore and aft
 10 Rising timbers
 11 Floor timbers for ribs
 12 Bread room and steward's room
 13 Deck beam for gun room
 14 Clamps for deck beams for gun room
 15 Deck beam hanging knee
 16 Mizzenmast with partners
 17 Deck beam for lower deck
 18 Vertical pillar
 19 Diagonal pillar, or cross beam
 20 Rider
 21 Foot wales
 22 Deck beam for orlop deck or false orlop deck with clamps and hanging knees
 23 Mainmast with partners
 24 Galley, with brickwork
 25 Cable-tier
 26 Supports for cable-tier
 27 Boatswain's storeroom
 28 Keelson
 29 Foremast with partners
 30 Breast hooks
 31 False stem
 32 Stem
 33 Hawse timbers with hawse
 34 Knee of the head
 35 Upper beakhead knee
 36 Manger
 37 Guiding rod for viol
 38 Scuttles for the boatswain's room and the carpenter's room
 39 Fore knighthead
 40 Main bitts
 41 Scuttles for cable-tier
 42 Gunport of lower deck
 43 Hatchway for galley
 44 Upper deck beam with hanging knees
 45 Clamps for upper deck beam
 46 Pump
 47 Main knighthead
 48 Main capstan on the lower deck
 49 Aft hatchway for hold
 50 Bulkhead for gun room
 51 Gun room
 52 Gunports of gun room
 53 Sweep for tiller
 54 Tiller
 55 Stern gunport
 56 Hole for rudder
 57 Counter pieces
 58 Lower gallery
 59 Bonaventure mast with partners
 60 Captain's cabin
 61 Bulkhead for captain's cabin
 62 Whipstaff with rowle
 63 Binnacle
 64 Scuttle to orlop deck
 65 Gunports of upper deck
 66 Grating
 67 Halfdeck beam with hanging knees
 68 Clamp for halfdeck beam
 69 Mainmast bitt with sheave for sheets of main topsail
 70 Dining room
 71 Front bulkhead for dining room
 72 Staghorn for fore sheet
 73 Jeer capstan in the waist
 74 Staghorn for main tack
 75 Aft bulkhead for forecastle
 76 Scuttle to lower deck
 77 Forecastle gunports
 78 Chaser deck
 79 Bowsprit with foot and partners
 80 Deck beam of forecastle with hanging knee and clamp
 81 Fore bitt with belaying pin rack and block for sheets of fore topsail
 82 Forward bulkhead of forecastle
 83 Beakhead rail
 84 Beakhead grating
 85 Staghorn for belaying the foresail tacks
 86 Scuttle to the upper deck
 87 Staghorn for the sheet of the spritsail
 88 Staghorn for the tack of the mizzen yard
 89 Knight for the halyard on the mizzen yard
 90 Gunport for halfdeck
 91 Bulkhead for halfdeck
 92 Scuttle to halfdeck
 93 Hole above the whipstaff
 94 Upper gallery
 95 Deck beam of quarter-deck with hanging knees and clamps
 96 Poop
 97 Forward poop bulkhead
 98 Knight for the bonaventure yard halyard
 99 Foot of flagstaff
100 Outlicker
101 Rail for quarter-deck

102 Rail for halfdeck
103 Rail for waist
104 Scuttle to upper deck
105 Aft bulkhead for upper cabin
106 Aft bulkhead for main cabin

Fig 87: Lower deck and upper deck

Lower deck

 1 Sternpost
 2 Stern gunport
 3 Transom
 4 Transom knee
 5 Sternpost knee
 6 Deck beam for gun room
 7 Deck beam for lower deck with lodging knees
 8 Carlings
 9 Ledge
10 Scuttle to the bread room
11 Bulkhead for gun room
12 Mizzenmast
13 Aft hatchway to hold
14 Main capstan
15 Pump
16 Mainmast with partners and their covering
17 Hatchway to galley
18 Hatchway to hold and to lower deck
19 Forward hatchway to hold
20 Hatchway to cable-tier
21 Main bitts
22 Hatchway to boatswain's room
23 Hatch
24 Foremast with partners
25 Manger
26 Breast hook
27 Guiding roller for viol
28 False stem
29 Hawse
30 Stem
31 Knee of the head
32 Scupper
33 Bow port
34 Gunports of lower deck
35 Gunports of gun room
36 Cross pillars
37 Example of deck planking

Upper deck

38 Lower gallery
39 Aft bulkhead for main cabin
40 Bonaventure mast foot
41 Forward bulkhead of captain's cabin
42 Hole for the whipstaff with rowle
43 Binnacle
44 Deck beam for upper deck
45 Scuttle to lower deck

46 Grating
47 Main knighthead
48 Mainmast bitts
49 Forward bulkhead of the dining room
50 Jeer capstan
51 Waterway
52 Clamp
53 Forecastle bulkhead
54 Main knighthead
55 Bowsprit foot
56 Foremast bitts
57 Forward bulkhead of forecastle
58 Latrine in the beakhead
59 Cross beam for beakhead grating
60 Bowsprit
61 Gunports of the upper deck
62 Wale broadened to channel
63 Standard on the rail

Fig 80: Poop deck, quarter-deck, halfdeck, forecastle deck

 1 Upper gallery
 2 Aft bulkhead for upper cabin
 3 Deck beam for halfdeck
 4 Ledge
 5 Bonaventure mast
 6 Forward bulkhead for upper cabin
 7 Hole above the whipstaff
 8 Scuttle to the upper deck
 9 Carlings
10 Mizzenmast with partners
11 Bulkhead
12 Knighthead for mizzenyard halyard
13 Grating
14 Hole for the mainyard rope
15 Mainmast with partners
16 Mainmast bitts
17 Example of deck planking
18 Forward halfdeck rail
19 Ports on the halfdeck and the forecastle deck
20 Aft forecastle rail
21 Scuttle to the upper deck
22 Hole for the foreyard rope
23 Foremast bitts
24 Beakhead rail
25 Anchor davit as a substitute for catheads
26 Foremast with partners
27 Forward forecastle rail
28 Forecastle deck beam
29 Quarter-deck beam
30 Outlicker foot
31 Bulkhead for poop
32 Scuttle to the halfdeck
33 Grating above the steerage
34 Forward quarter-deck rail
35 Flagstaff knee and foot

36 Poop deck beam
37 Knighthead for the bonaventure yard

Fig 86a: Section at ribs 0 and 8

1 Keel
2 Limber holes
3 Floor timbers of ribs with futtocks placed above
4 Keelson
5 Riders
6 Foot wales
7 Cross pillar
8 Vertical pillar
9 Cable-tier
10 Deck beam for false orlop deck
11 Clamp
12 Galley
13 Standing knee for orlop deck
14 Hanging knee for lower deck beam
15 Lodging knee for deck beam
16 Lower deck beam
17 Carlings
18 Upper deck beam
19 Waterways with sprikett wales above
20 Gun carriage
21 Bulkhead for halfdeck
22 Forecastle bulkhead
23 Gunwale of ship's side in waist
24 Wales
25 Wale broadened into fore chain wale

Fig 86b: Section at ribs 16 and 24

1 Keel
2 Rising timber
3 Limber holes
4 Floor timbers of ribs with futtocks above
5 Keelson
6 Vertical pillar for lower deck
7 Deck of steward's room
8 Foot wales
9 Floor of bread room
10 Deck beam for gun room
11 Deck beam for lower deck
12 Hanging deck beam knee
13 Lying deck beam knee
14 Clamps
15 Waterways with sprikett wales above
16 Rider 17 Carlings
18 Upper deck beam
19 Binnacle
20 Bonaventure mast foot
21 Halfdeck beam
22 Quarter-deck beam
23 Bulkhead for quarter-deck with port and gunports
24 Poop bulkhead
25 Wales
26 Lower gallery

27 Upper gallery

Fig 88: Rigging

Sails
A Bonaventure sail
B Mizzen sail with bonnet
C Mizzen topsail
D Mainsail with bonnet
E Main topsail
F Main topgallant
G Foresail with bonnet
H Fore topsail
I Fore topgallant
J Spritsail

Round timbers and tops
1 Outlicker
2 Bonaventure mast
3 Bonaventure yard
4 Bonaventure top
5 Mizzenmast
6 Mizzenyard
7 Mizzen top
8 Mizzen topmast
9 Mizzen topsail yard
10 Mizzenmast top
11 Mainmast
12 Mainyard
13 Main top
14 Main topmast
15 Main topyard
16 Main topmast top
17 Main gallant mast
18 Main topgallant yard
19 Main topgallant mast top
20 Foremast
21 Foreyard
22 Foretop
23 Fore topmast
24 Fore topsail yard
25 Fore topmast top
26 Fore topgallant
27 Fore topgallant yard
28 Fore topmast head
29 Bowsprit
30 Spritsail

Standing rigging (without further description)
31 Shrouds
32 Futtock shrouds
33 Breast backstays
34 Lanyards for stay of fore topmast
35 Forestay

Running rigging (without further description)
36 Halyards for yards with their rigging and crow's feet
37 Tie and halyard system for the halyards for the lower yards

38 Lifts for lower yards
39 Combined lifts and sheets for the topsail and topgallant sail yards
40 Lifts for topsail yards
41 Parrels
42 Lifts of the bonaventure yard, mizzen and mizzen topyards, with tackle and crow's feet
43 Braces and their tackle
44 Lifts for the spritsail
45 Braces for the spritsail

46 Sheets of the lower sail and the lateen sail
47 Sheets of the topsail
48 Tacks of the lower sail
49 Tack for the mizzenyard and the bonaventure yard
50 Tack for the mizzen bonnet
51 Martnets
52 Buntlines (starboard only shown)
53 Clewlines (starboard only shown)
54 Bowlines
55 Burton pendants

Notes for model builders

There are several possibilities for building a model of a galleon, ranging from a fully-rigged model containing the inner structures of a ship to a completed replica of the Stockholm galleon. The author has chosen a purely personal compromise for his own model: he has attempted a reconstruction which gives both the impression of an old votive ships and also has the 'correct' proportions of a galleon.

Figs 91 A–F show a hull model which was built largely in keeping with the dimensions of the reconstruction described previously. The model is to the scale of 1:35, which gives a sufficient size for the miniature paintings. The size of the model means that it creates a similar impression to that made by the Stockholm galleon. The latter is 1.27m long (excluding the beakhead). The model hull is 1.45m long from the stern to the beakhead. A precise rendering of the inner structure of a ship has not been attempted. The internal construction of the ship only serves to produce a framework for the parts visible from the outside.

The 'plank on frame' method was chosen, in order to keep down the weight of the completed model. A specially tailored plan had to be drawn for the type of modelbuilding envisaged here. The model has twenty-one ribs, at various

Figs 91/A–91/F: This model hull was built by the author largely in accordance with the reconstruction plan supplied. The front bulkhead has been set back a little, and is therefore broader. It thus resembles most contemporaneous pictures. The model also has a belfry with a ship's bell, on the halfdeck rail, which was not standard equipment at the time.

Fig 91/B

intervals, and care had to be taken to ensure that no ribs lay where gunports were to be cut. The construction was begun 'keel upwards'. A building board served as the base for the first stage of construction. The ribs were held fast to this with the upper parts facing downwards. The ribs had a notch for the keel and an extension above their toptimbers to make them the right height above the building board. After the ribs were mounted on the building board, the keel, stem and sternpost were fitted. Then the two lower wales (that is, the upper ones in terms of the construction) were attached to the rib frame, which was still pointing with the keel uppermost. The planking of the model was begun, starboard and larboard alternately, up to the second wale. Then the ribs and their extensions were loosened from the base block, and the model turned over so that the remaining wales and planking could be applied.

When the model had been planked up to the third wale, the mast partners, the lower deck and the gun room deck were fitted, while they were still within reach. The lower deck was only planked amidships, where it can be seen through the large hatchway. Guns were fitted there with all their accessories. Slit-type constructions on the non-visible parts of the deck serve to let the guns run in and out. As the visible details on each deck were completed, and the exterior was painted and gilded, the planking was continued up the ship's side.

The ribs were sawn from 10mm birch plywood, which is light and allows easy bevelling. The keel, stem, sternpost

Fig 91/C

and the 2.6mm thick planks for the lower parts of the hull consist of ramin, a light fine-grained wood which is easily worked and can be bent if wet. Pear wood was used for the ornamental carving on the arcades, columns etc. It is easily worked with small carpentry tools and leaves a firm edge. The plastic decorative elements (heads, torsos, fruits etc) were modelled with a plastic modelling compound (Fimo) as this can be worked with a modelling knife after it has hardened; this material is ideal for allaying model shipbuilders' fears of models that require a lot of plastic

Fig 91/D

Fig 91/ E

Fig 91/F

ornamentation, because it can be painted and gilded beautifully. There have never been ships with unpainted wooden carvings, so miniature carvings made from bare wood on ship models show us more about the artist's skill than about historic truths.

All parts of the model were painted or gilded up to the decks. There was, therefore, no need to worry about the appearance of the wood grain or the other materials used for the surface structure. The colour scheme used was taken from the decription of the Stockholm galleon (Chapter 6). Acrylic colours were used in painting the model, as they do not need any particular priming and they dry so quickly that work can be continued after the first coat has been applied. Gold leaf was used for gilding. The surface was primed with shellac and shaded with vermilion. The interior of the wales and rails, and the gunports were painted dark red. The parts added for the sake of completeness – the beakhead and the galleries – were painted in shades found elsewhere on the Stockholm galleon. It was intended that the model should create the same sort of time-honoured impression as its prototype, so the deck planks were stained dark and painted with linseed oil; the paintwork and gilded parts received a coating consisting of linseed oil, Van Dyck brown and green, which was then wiped with a soft cloth, to create a little patina on the otherwise newly worked surfaces.

The inspiration for the reconstruction of the beakhead and the galleries came from contemporaneous pictures, especially those of Hendrik C Vroom (1566–1640). Further details were taken from studies in sculpture on renaissance architecture (for example, from the Weser Renaissance). Although I had originally intended to rig the model, I subsequently abandoned that idea. The view of the hull is not distracted by round timbers and sails. With rigging included, the model would have become so large that it would have been difficult to stand it upright. I must admit, though, that I find the prospect of building the somewhat bizarre rigging rather tantalising.

In painting my model, I attempted to reproduce the rich decoration which the builder of the Stockholm galleon model chose (in keeping with contemporaneous tastes) to make his votive ship seem more sumptuous. The decision as to how much of such decoration to include on a purely technical model is a difficult one, but where do we draw the line? Apart from the gilding and the painting below the first two wales, it is difficult to know where – if at all – the votive ship was actually more colourful than its prototype. Of course, the average merchant ship of around 1610 was decorated and painted only sparingly. The vessel which must have served as the prototype of the Stockholm galleon was, however, a singularly large and imposing ship, whose decoration and rigging far exceeded what was necessary.

Ship   A Ship is a Concave body framed of Timber Plank and Iron work & contrived into Severall Decks & Roomes fitted for ye Use of Men munition and Victualls —

Hull   This Ship may be considered as she is a bare Carcass comonly called the Hull with Masts & Yards belonging to ye Carpenters work only, Or as She is compleatly furnished in Warlike Manner with Sailes Anchors Cordage Munition & ye Like fitt to be Imployed at Sea wch belongeth to ye Mariners art also But Because she must be first built before she can be furnished to Sea order will require that we begin with ye Building which is ye Carpenters part

The first thing that falls into consideration is ye Burthen of the Ship, for according as what is proposed to be greater or Lesser So do ye common Dimensions alter

The Dimensions of a Ship —   The Common Dimentions of every Ship are Three viz Length Bredth & Depth, and as these are varied so doth ye Mould and Burthen alter, The Breadth is Arbitrary ye Depth must never be greater then halfe ye Breadth nor Less one Third and the Length never less than double nor More then Treble ye Breadth

The Length is meant of the Keel excluding ye rake of the Stem & Sternepost The Breadth of the Beam at ye Mids ship bend including ye Timbers, ye Depth of the Hold is Taken from that Midships Beam to ye upper edge of the Keel including the flore Timbers & these Three being Multiplyed Cubically one into another & that product Divided by 100 by the Ordinary Rule of Measuring do give ye Burthen of the Ship. howbeit there is a farr more Rationall and certaine way which shall hereafter be Demonstrated

Materialls   When ye Burthen is concluded the Materialls must be provided & fitted They are Timber Plank Tree Nailes & Iron Work

Sorts of Timber   Timber is of three Sorts Streight Timber Compass or Crooked Timber and Knee Timber —

Sorts of Plank   Plank is also of four sorts vizt 4 inch 3 inch 2 inch & 1½ inch

Tree

Appendix

A TREATISE ON SHIPBUILDING, *c* 1620

From a Manuscript in the Admiralty Library

EDITED BY WILLIAM SALISBURY

Introduction

IN spite of the very general interest shown in the ships of the early Stuarts the document which is here printed for the first time has hitherto attracted little attention. It was first noted in the pages of *The Mariner's Mirror* by Mr L G Carr Laughton in 1927 (p 178), and was quoted by him in his *Old Ship Figureheads and Sterns*. The work forms part of a volume preserved in the Admiralty Library catalogued somewhat inadequately as 'Ms 9; Orders and Instructions of the Duke of York, 1660'. In fact, the volume consists of a collection of late seventeenth-century copies of miscellaneous naval documents dating from 1565 to 1695, of which the present treatise occupies ff 78–97.

The original manuscript appears to be now lost, but this only surviving copy, described by Mr Laughton as 'anonymous, undated, incompleted, and even without a title', is of very considerable importance. The description of the internal arrangements and parts of the frame, whilst being in general agreement with Mainwaring's *Seaman's Dictionary*, contains much additional information as well as amplifying his account in other particulars.

The second part of the treatise, containing detailed instructions for drawing the draught and moulding the timbers, is more complete than any other English account of its date, and can only be compared with Deane's *Doctrine of Naval Architecture* of much later date. As an explanation of the old system of whole-moulding it is far superior to Bushnell's *Compleat Shipwright*, and in date and contents the treatise must rank as complementary to the *Seaman's Dictionary* and to the *Treatise on Rigging* first published by the Society for Nautical Research in 1941, and now reprinted in the present volume.

The treatise does not follow the usual format of a work written for the instruction of shipwrights, principally in the omission of any attempt to give instruction in geometry or mathematics. Although it is possible that such sections were omitted by the copyist as redundant, I feel sure that the style is that of a presentation work, from which the dedication including title and author's name was missing when the copy was made. Perhaps the loss included the final leaves, which would account for the copy ending in mid-page. The present manuscript does not include copies of the diagrams, but this omission is not evidence that the originals had also been lost, although the copyist has obviously not referred to them.

It is probable that the writer will never be positively identified, but the work is certainly very closely related to the later notes in the Pepysian Library MS. 2820, *Fragments of Ancient English Shipwrightry*. In the first place, the proportions for the main dimensions and for the sweeps in the midship bend agree almost word for word with those given on a quarto sheet pasted on the last page of the Pepysian manuscript. Secondly, as mentioned in the footnotes, a diagram and calculations in that work were used in error by the author of the treatise as a basis for the calculation of the 'haling down' of the

---

Fig 92: The anonymous Treatise on Shipbuilding *has been preserved in the neat handwriting (still readable today) of a late seventeenth century copyist. It is a unique document of techno-historical importance regarding the state of the art of English shipbuilding c.1620. (*Photo: Public Record Office, Kew, Richmond, Surrey*)*

frame. In addition, I believe that the reference on page 185 to 'the best artificer that ever was' was meant for Matthew Baker himself, although I can offer no evidence for this.

It may be of some significance that the only ships mentioned by name were built (or rebuilt) by different shipwrights; the *Warspite* by Stevens in 1596, the *Lion* (or *Golden Lion*) by Baker in 1609, and the *Prince* by Pett in 1610. Details of their design would presumably only be known to a Master Shipwright or to a person of authority in the king's service. It is possible that the errors in the rules suggested for the 'dead narrowing line' and for the straightening of the toptimbers may indicate that the author was not a practical shipwright, although he obviously had a very thorough knowledge of the subject whilst being rather old-fashioned in outlook. The three shipwrights mentioned above are of course possible candidates, but I do not think that any of these wrote the present treatise. Baker had died in 1613, and the manuscript was almost certainly written after that date. Stevens was alive until some date in 1626, but one of the notes in the Pepysian manuscript is dated April 1627 and appears to be by the same hand as the earlier notes. Phineas Pett is the most likely, but the style is very different from that of his *Autobiography* and he would certainly have referred more to his own work, if only to mention the possibility of a third deck. My own belief, based solely upon the comparative style and use of logarithms, is that it was the work of John Wells, Store Keeper at Deptford Yard. He was the author of the paper on measurement of tonnage printed by M Oppenheim in his *Administration of the Royal Navy*, p 266, where some of the logarithms are misplaced or misprinted.

As mentioned by Mr Laughton, the manuscript was probably not written earlier than 1618, whilst the narrow transom and the expressed partiality for breaks in the deck can scarcely be later than the early 1620s. The only positive evidence is provided by the use of logarithms in the calculations on page 181, although it would appear from the context that these may have been made after the greater part of the manuscript had been written. The note in the Pepysian manuscript dated April 1627 refers to Briggs' *Arithmetica Logarithmica* of 1624, but it is probable that the tables used by our author were taken from Gunter's *Canon Triangulorum* of 1620.

Although we must be grateful for that part which has survived it is a great pity that the original has disappeared. Apart from the loss of means of identification, the missing portion certainly included rules for measuring tonnage as well as the tables referred to in the text, and may also have given directions for rigging and fitting out. In addition, the original had apparently been read over by some person who had added many, if not all, of the marginal notes. There is little doubt that the copyist has embodied some of these in his transcript, and that they cannot now be distinguished, unless by the context, from the original text.

As the manuscript is only a late copy it was felt that there was little point in printing it exactly as written. Apart from a few technical terms whose variations may be of interest, the spelling has therefore been modernised, contractions expanded, and the lack of punctuation remedied as far as practicable. Definite errors in arithmetic and in references to the diagrams have been noted in the text by enclosing the correction within square brackets immediately following the error, and similar brackets have been used to indicate words or phrases inserted to preserve the sense. Additional sidenotes have also been added, as they provide a very useful means of reference. It is hoped that the many points of interest will be discussed at length in future issues of *The Mariner's Mirror*, and no attempt has therefore been made to comment on these at the moment. A certain number of notes have, however, been found to be necessary, as they relate to difficulties encountered either in the transcription or in the reconstruction of the diagrams. Minor points of this nature have been dealt with by footnotes; longer notes appear as an appendix following the treatise.

In conclusion, I must express my indebtedness for assistance received from many quarters. My thanks are due to Lieut-Cdr P K Kemp and Dr R W Ladborough for their invaluable help at the Admiralty and Pepysian Libraries, and to Mr M S Robinson for the use of his transcript of *Fragments of Ancient English Shipwrighty*. Mr J Ehrman and Miss E M Glanville have taken great pains to check references in early books on mathematics at the British Museum, whilst the help and comments by Dr R C Anderson have, as always, been indispensable in matters concerning the period. Above all, the Society for Nautical Research is indebted to the Admiralty for their permision to publish the manuscript in their possession.

Admiralty Library, MS 9

A ship is a concave body framed of timber, plank, and ironwork, and contrived into several decks and rooms fitted for the use of men, munition, and victuals.

Hull

This ship may be considered as she is a bare carcass commonly called the hull with masts and yards belonging to the carpenter's work only, or as she is completely furnished in warlike manner with sails, anchors, cordage, munition and the like fit to be employed at sea, which belongeth to the mariner's art also. But because she must be first built before she can be furnished to sea, order will require that we begin with the building which is the carpenter's part.

The first thing that falls into consideration is the burthen of the ship, for according as that is proposed to be greater or lesser so do the common dimensions alter.

The Dimensions of a Ship

The common dimensions of every ship are three: Viz^t. length, breadth and depth; and as these are varied so doth the mould and burthen alter. The breadth is arbitrary, the depth must never be greater than half the breadth nor less [than] one third and the length never less than double nor more than treble the breadth.

The length is meant of the keel, excluding the rake of the stem and sternpost; the breadth, of the beam at the midship bend including the timbers; the depth of the hold is taken from that midship beam to the upper edge of the keel including the floor timbers; and these three being multiplied cubically one into another and that product divided by 100 by the ordinary rule of measuring do give the burthen of the ship. Howbeit there is a far more rational and certain way which shall hereafter be demonstrated.

Materials

When the burthen is concluded the materials must be provided and fitted. They are timber, plank, tree nails and ironwork.

Sorts of timber

Timber is of three sorts: straight timber, compass or crooked timber, and knee timber.

Sorts of plank

Plank is also of four sorts, Viz.^{t} 4 inch, 3 inch, 2 inch, and ½inch.*

Tree Nails

Tree nails are [of] five sorts distinguished by their lengths; Viz^t. 3 ft., 2½ ft., 2 ft., 1½ ft., and one foot long. They bear their nature in their names, which is a small piece of wood in the form of a cylinder and nail, made of a tree.

Iron Work

Iron work is chiefly bolts, which serve to fasten all together for the better strengthening of the work.

Now seeing that the body of the ship is composed of these few sorts of materials, which according to the nature and use of them in the several parts of the ship receive particular denominations differing from these in general, it will be necessary to know first the several names and uses of every piece of timber and plank, that the Artificer may provide a quantity of each sort proportionable to the greatness of his building.

Names of the Timber

The keel, the keelson, the sternpost, the rudder,† the tiller, the whip-staff, the pillars, the bitts, the carlings and ledges, the knights, the capstan, are all made of straight timber & c.

Names of the Crooked Timber

The stem, the false stem, the hawsepieces,ᵃ the floor timbers, the futtocks, the navall timbers [and] toptimbers, the transom, the fashion pieces, the counters and the foot wales, the riders and the clamps, the risings, the beams, the waterways, the sprickett wales,§ the wales, the chain wales, the harpings, the rails and ribbands, the gun wales and the playners‖ are all of compass timber, or for want of the stuff grown to the purpose wrought out of plank and straight timber to the mould desired.

There are no particular parts of a ship made of knee timbers, but all the several parts are bound and fastened

---

* Probably a mistake for '1½ inch'.
† 'Rother'; in this instance only.
ᵃ 'Halsepieces.'
§ The spirketting, or spirkit rising.
‖ The planksheers.

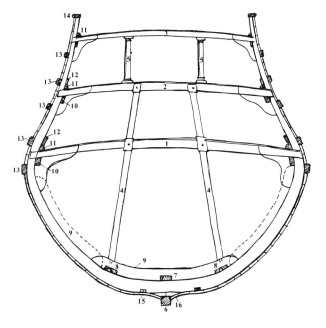

Fig 93: Section at rib 12 aft. The sketch is not drawn to scale, and shows some of the construction elements mentioned in the text of the Treatise on Shipbuilding *(c.1620).*

1 Lower deck beam	9 Riders
2 Upper deck beam	10 Clamps
3 Halfdeck beam	11 Waterways
4 Pillars for lower deck	12 Sprikett wales
and main deck	13 Wales
5 Pillars for halfdeck	14 Gunwale
6 Keel	15 Limber holes
7 Keelson	16 Garboard strake
8 Foot wales	

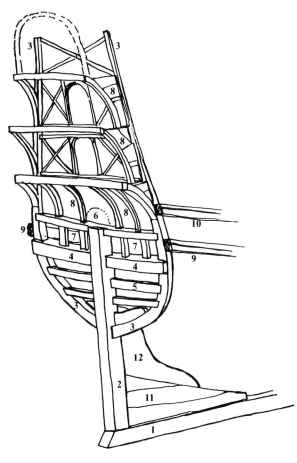

Fig 94: Sketch (not drawn to scale) of the stern construction showing some of the elements of construction mentioned in the text. According to the text, the stern transom should be at the height of the breadth line, indicating the widest part of the stern. However the midpoint of the stern gunports is also supposed to be at the height of the breadth line. As it is not physically possible to meet both of these specifications, the stern transom has been positioned a little lower, at the lower edge of the gunports.

1 Keel
2 Sternpost
3 Fashion pieces
4 Stern transom
5 Transoms
6 Hole for rudder
7 Aft gunports for gun room
8 Counter pieces and filler pieces for the fashion pieces
9 First wale
10 Second wale
11 Dead wood
12 Sternpost knee

with knees. Only the cat heads are two raking knees, the one arm bolted to the ship's side, the other hanging over the bow of the ship with a shiver in the head thereof to trice up the anchor to the bow.

The Keel and Limber Holes

The keel, which is the basis or foundation upon which all the rest of the structure is raised, is one or more straight pieces of timber (Elm) scared and bolted together of the length breadth and depth required, in which are fastened all the floor timbers and rising timbers [which are] fitted with square holes called limber holes, cut out in the bottom of them to convey the water upon the top of the keel in the well where the pump stands.

Keelson

The keelson is one or more pieces of oak timber like unto the keel, which is laid upon the floor timbers and is fast bolted through them to the keel for more strength to the work, placing it straight on it. The rest roundeth according to the rising line and [it] hath a further use also; by leaving the more substance in the middle part thereof, it serves to make a step for the heel of the main mast to stand in.

The Sternpost and Rake

The sternpost is a great straight piece of timber let into the after end of the keel with a strong mortise [and] reclining to the angle of raking into [which] the transoms and fashion pieces are framed which gives the proportion of the stern. The raking both of the stem and stern, by a circle forward on, by a right line afterward on, is the overhanging of the work afore and abaft the keel.

Rudder

The rudder is a great piece of straight timber something longer than the post to receive the tiller at the head thereof, which is hung at liberty upon the post with rudder irons to wind the ship to and fro at pleasure.

Tiller, Whipstaff and Rowl

The tiller is part straight and part compass as the work requireth within board, the one end fastened in the head of the rudder the other playing at liberty at the gun room from side to side of the ship. [It is] put down and hald up by the help of the whipstaff, which is a piece [of] light fir or ash fastened with an iron ring to the fore end of the tiller, moving in a rowl whose iron ax[le] is let in between two beams of the deck, that the rudder might command to and fro with the more facility.

Pillars

The pillars are straight pieces of timber that reach from the wrong heads to the beams of the upper deck, some crossing anglewise bolted in the bilge of the ship to the riders [and] at the orlop and at the deck to the beams, for ease and strength to the ship when she lyeth aground.

Bitts

The bitts are two great pieces of straight timber with a cross piece bolted to them, placed about the loof of the ship upon the orlop [and] fastened to the riders below and kneed to the beams of the orlop aloft, about which the cables are belayed when the ship rides at an anchor.

Carlings & Ledges.

The carlings are short pieces of straight timber let between every pair of beams alongst ships to support the ledges, which are small* pieces of timber laid athwartships from the clamps to the carlings for the more strength to the decks whereup[on] the ordnance are placed.

Knights

The main knights and fore knights, so called because they are commonly carved with a head and a helmet, are two short pieces of straight timber bolted to the beams of the upper deck, with several shivers in them for the halyards and top ropes to hoist and lower the main yard and fore yard with their topmasts.

Main Capstan

The main capstan is a great straight piece of timber which is wrought round to the fashion of a spindle [and] placed abaft the main mast upon the orlop: the foot set into a step under the deck [and] the body of it above fitted with four long bars to go through the head thereof, which with the strength of men is forced about to weigh the anchors [and] hoist the yards, topmasts and things of great weight.

Jeer Capstan

There is a lesser capstan called the jeer capstan commonly placed in the waist of the ship, of like use for lesser weights and to help the other in case of great stress, and in each of these close to deck there are four or five short pieces of timber, according to the squares of the spindle, bolted into it like cleats which are called whelps. The heads thereof [are] rounded off and have a deep score let into them for the surge of the cable in the winding up. They are strengthened with chocks for starting, both below and above to the lower part of the capstan. Upon the decks are fastened two pieces of iron called pawls which serve to stop against the whelps for [the] safety of the men as they purchase the cables.

* MS. 'which are in all pieces. . . .'.

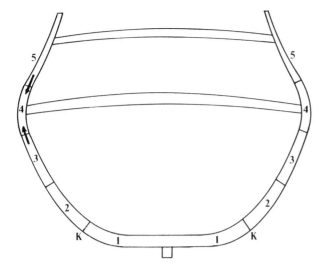

Fig 95: Rib, showing the individual sections, named for clarification. In practice the sections would have been scarfed together, and sometimes even overlapped each other.

1 *Floor timbers with floorhead*
2 *First futtock*
3 *Second futtock*
4 *Third futtock*
5 *Toptimber*

The third futtock (4) might not be required if the second futtock was of sufficient length

Stem and False Stem

The stem is one or more pieces of large compass timber scarfed and bolted together, swept out by a circle whose radius is the rake forward on. It is fastened to the fore top of the keel with a strong scarf and hath two large rabbets on each side thereof one, to receive the butt ends of the planks forward and called the hoodings. In the inside thereof is brought on a large flitch of compass timber bolted to it called the false stem, for strengthening the scarf of the stem pieces and holdings [*sic*].

Hawsepieces

The hawse pieces† are two great flitches of compass timber, placed on each side of the stem one, through the upper part whereof are made two or four circular holes for the cables to pass in and out at as[a] they are strengthened both aloft and below with breast hooks and the step of the fore mast.

† 'Horse pieces'.
[a] Unless 'as' is superfluous, it appears that some words have been omitted.

Floor Timbers

The floor timbers are properly a certain number of timbers both afore and abaft the midship bend, flat the whole breadth of the floor and from thence rounding up to the wronghead which is as high as the first sweep.

Rising Timbers

After those flats, when they rise and narrow more sensibly they are called rising timbers, the narrowing and rising whereof do make the grip forward on and the run aftward on which is the life of the ship's way, and where the line directing these timbers intersect is called the tuck.

[Futtocks]

The futtocks or ribs of the ship are certain round pieces of compass timber swept out according to the mould of every bend, scarfed to the wronghead below and to the navall timbers aloft. In great ships they are framed into parts called the upper and lower futtocks.

Navall Timbers

The navall timbers is properly that part of the bend which belongeth to the upper sweep, which is seldom framed apart but moulded into the upper part of the futtock and into the lower part of the top timbers.

Top Timbers

The top timbers are sometimes straight sometimes circular. They reach from the breadth to the gun wale in every bend, and if it be a hollowing post which is most graceful and wholesome to the ship it rounds both ways, the lower part inwards the upper part outwards: and of these parts consists every bend of timber in the ship.

Transoms

The transoms are divers pieces of compass timber framed to the inside of the sternpost and fasion pieces, the uppermost whereof directeth the height of the lowermost wale and confineth the breadth of the ship after on.

Fashion pieces

The fashion pieces are two great pieces of compass timber, so called because they give the fashion and frame of the stern; they are made with part of the upper sweep and part of the futtock sweep. They serve also in some kinds of buildings with two great rabbets to receive the butt ends of the plank aftward on, as the stem doth forward on.

Counter

The counter pieces are certain small pieces of compass timber, swept out by a circle and placed in the stern between the transom and gallery to support it in the overhanging of the stern, which is done by the help of the bracket in the side thereof.

[Foot wales]

The foot wales are long pieces of compass timber fastened to the floor timbers within board, and wrought up a strake or two from the keelson on each side of the hold in the wrong heads to keep down the lower end of the futtocks, and to bind them and the floor timbers for more strength together, and may be termed a kind of planking the ship with timber. In merchants' ships they shut up all above the foot wales with plank to the clamps, for the due stowage of goods. In the King's ships they use several strakes of timber and plank and leave it open between, the better to discover any leak that may happen.

Riders

The riders are great pieces of compass timber much like the floor timbers, which lie cross the keelson up to the wrong head [and are] fastened to the timbers only for strengths sake. And sometimes there are futtock riders used which launch up to the orlop to strengthen a weak built ship.

[Clamps]

The clamps are long pieces of timber either so grown or hewed compass to the side of the ship, and are fastened with treenails longst ships for the beams of the lower and upper decks to lie upon.

Beams

The beams are likewise long pieces of timber, either grown to the purpose or hewed to the mould, which are laid thwart ships cambering or rounding by a circle and resting at each end upon the clamps. They are bolted to the ship's side with knees and standards to bind all together. Upon them the plank of the decks is laid and fastened with treenails.

Waterways

The waterways are long thick pieces of timber hewed half through the angle of the beam and the ship's side,* the standing part treenailed to the timbers the lower part to the beams of the deck. Into which the plank being close fayed the water which by cambering of the beams settles to the ship's sides is kept from running down into the hold or between timbers to rot them.

Sprikett Wales

Sprikett wales above these are brought on being short pieces of timber (so called) which serve to strengthen those parts of the ship's side where the timbers are cut asunder for port holes.

Wales

The wales are long pieces of timber scarfed together in divers places and made one entire piece reaching from stem to stern, which are used not only to grace the ship's side without board but for strength also by bolting the knees of the decks unto them and for keeping fast the upper ends of the futtocks and navall timbers.

Chain wales

The chain wales are two broad pieces of timber bolted upon one of the wales to the ship's side, reaching from the loof forward and from the main mast aftward according to the spreading of the shrouds. There are certain scores made in them for the chain plates to rest in, into which the ends of the shrouds are fastened, and they are set off on purpose to keep the shrouds from wearing against the ship's sides and to strengthen the masts.

Harping

The harping is the fore part of the wale from the luff to the stem, which because it roundeth more than the rest of the wale must be a special piece of compass timber and is distinguished by a peculiar name.

Rails & Ribbands

The rails and ribbands are next above the chain wales. As they rise higher on the ship's [side] so they are made less for ease to the side, and commonly of plank instead

* This probably means that the lower and outer sides of the timber were bevelled.

of timber. Some of them are imbowed or wrought with a plane for more grace sake which is the chiefest use of them, and are all of them guided by the sweep of the first wale.

[Gun Wales]

The gun wales are pieces of timber or plank scored through in divers places to receive or steady the heads of the top timbers, and the plainsers* are planks that are brought upon them to cover the heads of the top timbers and the closing of the rails and gun wales.

These be all principal timbers belonging to a ship which being artificially framed and set together do make up the naked carcass thereof, which must afterwards be planked both within board and without and bound together with knees as the several parts require. The sorts of planks and treenails are named before, the uses are according to the parts of the ship. From the keel to the breadth without board are commonly used 4 inch and three inch plank, from the breadth upwards 2 inch and inch & half.

Garboard Strake

The first strake above the keel hath a peculiar name and is called the garboard or keelstrake. This and 7 or 8 more in the bilge are brought up of elm or beech plank, which lasteth best under water or where it is always wet; the rest are of oak. The ends of the planks are called the butts, which are commonly bolted to the timbers with iron bolts for fear of starting, and the other part of the plank is fastened with treenails fore and aft, and in many works the butt ends also.

[Planking]

These planks are most over launch each other for strength sake, which is the same in planking that scarfing is in timbering.†

The ends of those planks that are bolted into the rabbet of the stem are called the hoodings, which are more dangerous to spring than the rest of the rounding of the bow, to which circle they grow not but are forced by burning to hollow somewhat near the matter.

In the stern to the sternpost, above that into the

rabbet of the fashion pieces. Within board the use of the plank is chiefly for laying of decks and [in] some places is used also for seeling.*

The orlop deck which are for use of ordnance are planked with 4 inch and three inch plank,† the upper deck with 2 inch plank and inch and half plank and sometimes with Prussia deals for lightness sake, and these are all fastened to the beams of every deck with treenails fitted for them.

[Knees]

After the plank is laid the knees are brought on to bind all together, which are called so from the likeness they have to a man's knee being bent. They are of three sorts: vizt. square knees, in square knees, out square or raking knees.

There are few square knees used in a ship save only about the midships, because the circle[s] therein do seldom cut [one] another at right angles. Every beam of the orlop must have four side knees and two standards, the beams of the other decks fewer as cause shall require.

In square and raking knees are of most ordinary use in every part of the ship. The principalest of them are: one in the beak head to bind the head and stem together; 4 or more sometimes within board called breast hooks which fasten the stem and timber together afore; one at the stern bolted into the keel and stern post to bind them together; 4 and more sometimes in the bread room and gun room to fasten the timber and fashion pieces together abaft. Hitherto of the names and uses of the several sorts of timber, plank, knees &c.

Parts of a Ship

Now of the parts and rooms of the ship, and they are principally 7: the hold; the orlop; the deck; the forecastle; the half deck; the quarter deck; the round house.

Hold [and] False Orlop

The hold is the chiefest part of the ship and is all that concave part of the hull which lies under the orlop down to the floor timbers; it is als[o] for several uses

---

* The planksheers.
† The meaning is that the butts in adjoining strakes were kept as far apart as possible.

* Ceiling. The planking in the hold.
† This should probably read: 'The orlop *and* decks . . . the upper decks.'
^{a} 'Butts.'

subdivided by bulk head[s] or partitions into 5 parts. In the fore part thereof a little abaft the foot of the bitts are made three partitions: one for the powder room; one for the boatswain's store room; and one for the carpenter's store room. Abaft the mast down under the steerage are two other partitions, the one for the bread room, the other for the steward room. All the rest of the hold serves for stowage of victuals, only in some of the King's ships the cook room is also contrived upon the false orlop in the hold (as the safest place in the ship to use firing) which is nothing else but a tier* of beams un-planked† laid about the middle of the futtock for strength sake.

[Orlop]

The orlop, which is the first deck above the hold, is chiefly for the use of ordnance; upon which there are divers port holes cut through the ship's sides to place them in. The fore part thereof is called the fore peak, and in ships that have low hawses a part thereof is called the manger, which is a circle of plank upon the deck between the stem and foremast to receive the water that washes in at the hawse holes and to vent it out again at the scupper holes. The after part divided from the rest with a bulk head is called the gunroom. In the middle of this deck before the main mast there are hatchways cut out to let down provisions into the hold; and the hatches are covers for the hatchways, to be taken off and laid on at pleasure by the help of iron rings fastened to them. They are supported with timber and plank a little above the rest of the work, called the co[a]mings of the hatches. Close by the deck through the water ways and timbers are bored with great pump auger certain holes called scupper holes, which have either pipes of lead [or] of leather nailed to them called scuppers, to convey the water out of the ship's sides.

Near the gunroom abaft and about the bitts before are 2 square hole[s] cut through the deck called scuttles, fitted with covers to them, for such capacity that a man may easily pass down into the hold to the breadroom and stewardroom abaft and to the powder room and other store rooms afore.

* 'Tyre.'
† 'inplanked.'
ᵃ 'fore pyeke.'

[Deck]

The deck differs but in name from the orlop, and reacheth from stem to stern as the orlop doth; where-upon there are likewise port holes cut through the ship's sides for the use of ordnance. This deck is commonly divided by three bulk head[s] in four parts; the fore part from the stem to the first bulk head is called the chase. In this part of late they make the cook rooms, which in merchant ships is used to gain the more room in hold; but in a man of war it hindreth the use of ordnance in a fight, it is more dangerous for fire, and somewhat too near the powder room. That part of the deck between the bulk head and the next abaft the main mast is called the waist of the ship; wherein there are also hatchways cut out to let down provisions into the hold and covered with hatches as in the orlop, and the fore part of the waist and in the chase a scuttle or stairs to go down into the orlop. In this part by the main mast stands the pump, to free the ship from water. Between this and the third bulkhead is the dining room and steerage room, where they stand to steer the ship by the help of the whipstaff moving to and fro at liberty in the rowls. Before this whipstaff stands the bittacle, which is a square frame of deal board fixed to the deck to place the compass in which they sail by. Upon the larboard side of this room and right before the bittacle are two pair of stairs or scuttles for men to pass into the half deck and upon the orlop.

Abaft this bulkhead is nothing but the captain's ca-bin and part of the galleries. In divers ships upon this deck are used gratings between the ordnance, which is nothing else but the cutting of square holes through the plank near the ship's side that the smoke of the ordnance below may have the more vent upwards. Upon this deck there are divers scupper holes cut through the ship's side for conveyance of water, fitted as upon the orlop.

Forecastle

The forecastle is the uppermost part of the foreships directly over the chase and contained between the bulkhead thereof and the stem.

Half Deck

The half deck is over the dining room contained between the bulkheads at the main mast and the steerage.

Fig 96/A

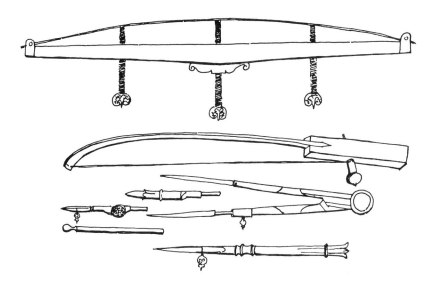

Fig 96/B

Figs 96/A and 96/B: Shipbuilders' drawing instruments in the Elizabethan era consisted of a large pair of compasses, wooden or ivory rules, and drawing pens. Large curves were drawn with bows with adjustable chords. Parchment, ink and some watercolour was used. Drawings were usually made to the scale of ¼in:1ft. Anthony Deane, the shipwright, recommended to apprentices that they should first mark out the drawing in pencil, and then draw over it in ink. He recommended that they used crumbs of white bread for removing pencil lines. (By permission of the Master and fellows, Magdalene College, Cambridge)

Upon these two in great ships there are some small ordnance often planted.

Quarter Deck [and] Round House

The quarter deck is abaft that over the steerage room and captain's cabin & and* the round house abaft that again over the master's cabin. Upon these decks but the forecastle there are several cabins contained for the use and succour of men, chiefly upon the upper decks where there is least use of ordnance.

[Spar Deck]

In deep waisted ships there is often used another slight kind of deck called a spar deck reaching from the forecastle to the half deck, made of long pieces of fir timber called raftrees and supported by the way with stan[t]ion and small turned pillars. Between them is a slight grating of deal for men to walk upon, and from the raftrees to the ship's sides [are] nettings, which are small ropes wrought together like a net that may be furled up and set loose at pleasure; the one part is fastened to the raftrees and the other part to the chain of the iron stantion alongst the waist. The use of them is to keep an enemy from entering when ships lie board and board.

A ship is further distinguished into two general parts longst ships called starboard and larboard: that whole half of the ship which lieth on the right hand of a straight line drawn from stem to stern is called the starboard side, the other whole half the larboard side.

And lastly, she is distinguished into three other general parts thwart ships, which are the bow, the quarter, and the midships. The bow is from the after part of the harping forward on; the quarter from the fore part of the steerage afterward on; between these two parts the rest is called the midships.

[Drawing the Plot]

These things being known and the several parts rightly comprehended we may now proceed to the drawing of the plot, which is nothing else but an optical projection of the body of a ship in 3 several planes, each plane consisting of 2 of the 3 common dimensional belonging to a ship. For if you suppose a ship to be cut three

---

* The repetition '& and' may indicate that some words have been omitted.

several ways, the first thwart ships at the midships bend, this section shall represent unto you the vertical plane of the depth and breadth, which is the plane of the bends.

The second longst ships by a middle line from stem to stern. This section shall represent the perpendicular plane of depth and length, which is the plane of risings.

The third also longst ships from stem to stern by the breadth line. This section shall represent the horizontal plane of breadth and length, which is the plane of narrowings.

Out of these 3 planes and the lines properly belonging to them may every part of the ship be artificially deduced both geometrically and arithmetically by the directions following.

Ship to be 550 Tons

Now because the variety of moulds and buildings are infinite we will propose in our example to make a plot for a ship of 550 Tunns or thereabouts, which will be of most ordinary use and near a mean proportion between the greatest and the least, the rather because by an increasingly or diminishing [of] the scale we may keep the same mould and build [any] other ship of more or less burthen at pleasure.

The common dimensions are all three usually given. If only the breadth be given the rest may be drawn out of that by the rules aforegoing, for the depth must never be more than half nor less [than] ⅓ thereof and the length never less than double nor more than treble the breadth.

Proportion of Breadth to Depth

Suppose that the breadth were 36 foot: the ½ is 18 and the third is 12 which added together makes 30; the half thereof is 15, which is [a] mean between both and were a good proportion for the depth, and of this depth to the breadth is the *Lyon's* mould. The breadth 36 foot: the doubling is 72, the treble is 108, which added together makes 180; the half thereof is 90 foot, a mean between both, of which proportion of breadth to the length is the *Warspight's* mould.

But the best proportion of the breadth to the depth is as 7 to 3, and of the breadth to the length as 9 to 25, and 36 foot of breadth will have 15½ [foot] of depth and 100 foot of length.

[The chief Properties of a good Ship]

When these terms are agreed upon we must next take into consideration the chief properties of a good ship that we may continue the plot accordingly, and they are 3: to go well; to steer well; and to bear a good sail. All [of] which depends upon the choice of lines proper to each several plane, for the rising lines must neither be too high nor too low, nor the narrowing lines too lank nor too full, nor the s[weeps]* of the bend too round or too straight. And the chiefest cause of going and steering well ariseth from the way of the ship fore and aft, which depends upon the narrowing and rising aloft; and for the bearing of the sail from the narrowing and rising alow, that the luff and quarter be kept full and in such proportion one to the other and both to the midships that all parts may bear together. The best lines for all these purposes have by many trials been found amongst the *Potestates ab unitates.*

[Rising alow]

The third power maketh a line which runneth along by the touch and by that means keepeth the water under the bilge of the ship, yet tucks up severally both afore and abaft which gives life and quickness to the ship's way, and this is fittest for the lower rising.

[Narrowing aloft, aft]

The same line also in respect that is runneth along by the touch keeps the side straight and quarter full to the bearing part, and therefore the fittest for the narrowing aloft, afterward on.

Narrowing alow, aft

The narrowing alow aftward on must be by a lank line to the end [that] the water being past the broadest part of the bilge at the midship bend may hang but a while there, but may have a passage aftward without cod or cling to dead[en] the way, and such is the conic section called an ellipse.

Narrowing aloft

The narrowing aloft forward on must be a fuller line than the narrowing aft, that it may run the longer in the touch to keep out the bow to bear with the quarter and that it may round home suddenly to the stem, and such a line doth the fourth power make.

* Part of this word has been erased.

[Narrowing alow]

The narrowing alow forward on must also be a fuller [line] than the same is aft, that the gripe may be more bluff and stout, which conveys the water with more ease under the bilge and from thence to the run without further resistance, and such a line doth the second power make.

Rising aloft rad 4ft 7d a 5ft 8inches F*

Only the rising aloft is part straight and part circular; from the midship bend both ways straight near ¼ of the keel [and] from each extreme of the straight line [rising] by an arch of a great circle that the ship may have play to scend† both fore and aft.

Midship bend

The several lines being concluded we must begin with the midship bend, which lies in the first plane of breadth and depth, out of which all the rest are drawn and into which all the rest may by a kind of perspective be projected.

Therein we are to consider 4 things: first the flat of the floor. Second the proportion of the sweeps. Third the depth of the timbers. Fourth the planning and height of the decks with the rounding of the beams. Fifth the substance of the arch in every sweep, proper to the haling down and putting up of the mould in each bend.

[The Floor]

Merchants covet to have great floors in their ships for gaining of stowage, but thereby they spoil the ship's bearing for most of them grow tender sided and after they are built come to be furred. In a good man of war the floor must never be more than ⅓ nor less than ¼ of the breadth, and of this proportion was the *Prince* built, but more particularly ½ the half the difference between the breadth and depth will be considered for all kinds of shipping.ª

(The Sweeps)

Every bend consists of 3 sweeps, and if you use a hollowing post, of 4. The first sweep is called the sweep of the

* These figures do not appear to have any connexion with the upper rising line.
†'send.'
ª The last part of the passage shows signs of alterations. Cf. Pepysian MS. 2820: '. . . ½ the difference of breadth and depth will be convenient for the floor of all kinds.'

wrong head: the centre thereof must always be upon a perpendicular raised to the extreme of the floor line, and the radius of that sweep must always be less than the depth and less than the difference [between] half the breadth and half the floor, for with this difference are all the sweeps contained. The best proportion will be one third of the depth and difference added together; so the depth 15 foot 6 inches and the difference 13 foot 6 inches both together is 29 foot 0 inches, the ⅓ thereof is 9 foot 8 inches for the semidiameter or radius of the first sweep.

The third sweep is the sweep of the breadth or navall timbers, whose centre must always be upon the breadth line of the floor.§ The radius of this arc may be less or equal to the radius of the lower sweep but never more, and is commonly called one fourth of [the breadth];* but the best proportion is as 15 to 19 of the lower sweep, and then the radius is near 7 foot 8 inches for the upper sweep.

The middle sweep, called the futtock sweep, doth only touch and include the other two and so makes one entire circular line of all three. The radius thereof must

§ The words 'of the floor' are obviously a mistake, and should be ignored.
* The catchword proves that some words have been omitted by the copyist. Those inserted have been taken from Pepysian MS. 2820.

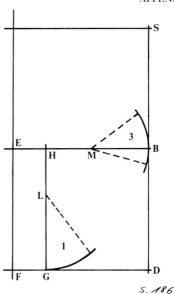

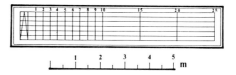

Fig 97/ B: Construction of the midship frame, 2nd step: The full rib is composed of four arcs. The position of two of these arcs (1 and 3) can be seen in the drawing.
Curve 1 is the floorhead sweep: its midpoint (L) lies on one of the vertical lines which delimits the floor. We can determine its radius thus:

$$\frac{\dfrac{Height\ GH}{3} \times \frac{1}{2}(Breadth\ EB) \times \frac{1}{2}(Floor\ EH)}{3}$$

This gives a result of 9ft 8in.
Curve 3 is the breadth sweep. Its midpoint (M) is on the line of maximum breadth (EB). Its radius is 7ft 8in, that is, 15/19 of the radius of curve 1.

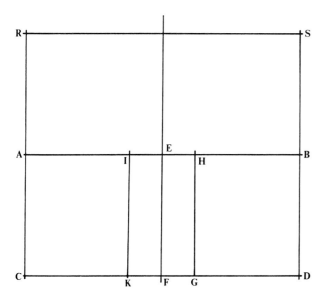

Fig 97/ A: Construction of the midship frame, 1st step: The drawing shows the rectangle in which the midship frame was constructed, in accordance wih the instructions from the Treatise. *The base line (CD) shows the height of the floor. Two vertical lines (KI and GH), on either side of the centre line (FE), mark out the width of the floor. At 9ft this is in keeping with the rule that the floor on a good warship should never be more than one-third or less than ¼, of the width, which in this case is 36ft. The line AB is at the height of the midship frame, giving the greatest breadth of the ship as 36ft (10.9m). Its distance from the base line makes the depth of the rib 15½ft, which is in keeping with the optimal breadth to height ratio of 7:3. The line RS is at twice the depth of the rib.*

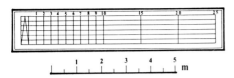

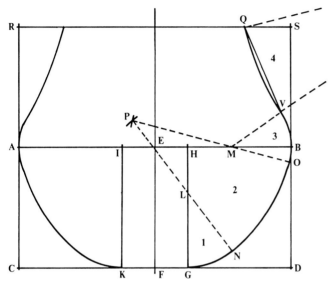

Fig 97/C: Construction of the midship frame, 3rd step: The completed rib shows the remaining arcs, 2 and 4. Curve 2 is the reconciling sweep, which joins its neighbouring curves 1 and 3 to form a single, curving line. The best measurement for its radius is 6/10 of the breadth: that is, 21ft 6in. We can find its midpoint if we do the following: first, subtract the radius of curve 1 from the radius of curve 2, and, using the remainder as the radius and L as the base point, draw an arc at P. Second, subtract the radius of curve 3 from the radius of curve 2, and, using the remainder as the radius and M as the base point, draw an arc at P. The point P, the intersection of these two arcs, is the mid-point of curve 2. Curve 4 is the toptimber sweep. Its radius corresponds to the breadth of the ship, 36ft. It continues from curve 3, and runs to the point Q, which lies one-third of the way along the line RS. We can find its midpoint by using this radius to project an arc outwards from Q, then adding the radius of curve 3 to this radius, and projecting an arc outwards from M which cuts the first arc. The point of intersection is the midpoint of Curve 4. With the compasses open we draw in the curve from V to Q. Note that a straight toptimber line has also been drawn in, as a possible alternative to Curve 4. (After Salisbury)

ever be greater than half the breadth and less than the whole breadth, and may be longer or shorter as you desire to have the futtock righter or rounder. The best proportion will be as 6 to 10 of the breadth and so the radius of this sweep will be 21 foot 8 inches long. The breadth of the ship is the best proportion for the sweep of the hollowing post, which you may make more or less with a longer or shorter radius, and so the radius of that sweep is 36 foot.

The floor and semidiameter of the sweep[s] being determined, now draw the bends; but first you must make the scale according to which the bend and every part of the parts will be greater or less.

First therefore make a parallelogram of the breadth and depth, A. B. C. D. Divide A, B and C, D into halves at E and F; from each side thereof set the half of the floor to G and K; let fall perpendiculars to them from I and H. Take the length of the first sweep 9 foot 8 inches of[f] a scale of equal parts, and setting [one] foot of the compass in G extend the other to *C* [L] and draw the arch G, N for the wrong head (Fig 97C). Next take the length of the 3rd sweep of[f] the same scale, 7 foot 8 inches, and setting one foot of the compasses in *h* [B]

extend [the] other to M and draw the arch 6th [O, B, V] for the breadth sweep.

Thirdly out of the futtock sweep 21 foot 8 inches take the length of the first sweep [and] with the remainder of 12 [foot] 0 [inches] from *b* [L] make an arch of a circle at P. Also take the length o the third sweep 7 foot 8 inches out of the futtock sweep 21⅔ [feet], [and with] the remainder 14 foot 0 inches from M cross the former arch at P. That intersection is the centre of the futtock sweep, therefore set one foot of the compasses in P, extend the other to N and with that extent make the futtock sweep N, O which shall only touch and include the other two. This done, continue the 2 perpendiculars A, C and B, D upwards to double the depth at R and S, and draw the line R, S parallel to A, B. Take ¼ at the least or ⅓ at the most of the ½ breadth and set it upon this parallel for the head of the post from S to *G* [Q], and with the radius of 36 foot the whole breadth seek out the whole centre to draw the circle from *g* [Q] to touch the upper sweep at V thus: from *g* [Q] with the length of 36 feet make an arch of a circle at random; unto 36 feet add the radius *V*, O [M, O] 7 foot 8 inches, the whole line will be 43 foot 8 inches [and] from the centre M with the length of 43 foot 8 inches [and] from the centre M with the length of 43 foot 8 inches cross the former arch; the intersection shall be the centre. Shorten the compasses from that centre to *g* [Q] and at that index draw the circle *g*, v [Q, V]; so have you drawn the whole bend consisting of [the] four several sweeps aforesaid.

Instead of [a] hollowing post you may have it straight. Draw a straight line from *g* [Q] to touch the upper sweep at V, and you have your desire. And though this be the ordinary yet I rather commend the hollowing post, which is more comely to the eye and more ease to the ship's side; seeing by tumbling thereof the weight of

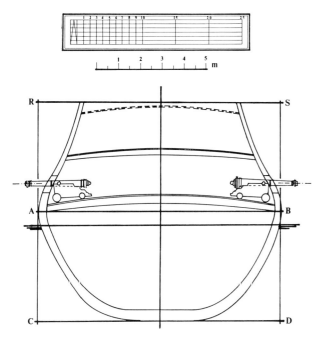

Fig 98: This section of the midship area, from the instructions in the Treatise on Shipbuilding *(c.1620) shows the thickness of the ribs without internal or external planking. From 17in (43.18cm) at the floor timbers, the thickness decreases to 5in (12.7cm) at the line RS, which is at twice the depth of the rib. The lower edge of the lower deck beam is at the height of the greatest breadth, AB. All the deck beams taper towards the sides of the ships by one-third of their thickness. Together with the 14in (35.5cm) curve of the beam, that results in a noticeable curvature of the decks. The decks have been positioned so that the gun muzzles are approximately 6ft (1.82m) above the waterline. The upper deck beam is positioned 6ft 3in (1.91m) above the lower deck, which results in a comfortable amount of standing room. The dotted line shows the position of the halfdeck above the upper deck, allowing 6ft of standing room. The halfdeck would not, of course be in the midship area, but aft of it. The forecastle deck could have been at the same height. (After Salisbury)*

the ordnance and of the upper work is brought so far into the body of the ship that it is supported without stress, whereas in a straight post they both over hang the side, which is a great burden to it.

[The Timbers]

The sweeps being drawn which represent the outside of the timbers you must draw the like for the inside also, but first the depth of the timbers must be proportioned. The floor timbers must be 12 or 13 inches deep above the limber holes, the navall timbers 9 or 8 inches at least, and the top timbers at double the depth 5 inches, and so decreasing these places by degrees. Which being set off by a scale, shorten the sweeps to these proportions and upon the same centres draw the inside of the timbers as aforesaid.*

[The beams]

The next thing is the laying of the beams for placing of the decks. Therein we are to consider the distance of the ordnance to pass. 5 foot is a good proportion for the lower edge of the midship ports to carry out the ordnance all weathers. Let the lower edge of the beam for the orlop [be] pitched at the breadth; so shall it be 2 foot above the water line. The deck will be 14 inches, the lower edge of the port 1 foot 8 inches above the deck, and the mouth or muzzle† of the pieces near a foot. In all, from the ordnance to the water will be 6 foot or thereabouts. Let the beam camber 14 inches in the middle above the straight line; so have you 3 pricks to draw the lower edge of the beams by. And let it be 16 or 18 inches deep in the middle and two thirds each end, and so have you 3 other pricks to draw the upper edge of the beam by.

The next deck may be 7 foot 3 inches from plank to plank, which will be 6 foot 3 inches under the beam. The beam [is] 12 or 14 inches deep in the middle and ⅔ at each end; it may round 9 inches; and by these things given draw the beam of this deck as you did the former.

The half deck may be 6 foot above the other; the beam 9 or 10 inches deep in the middle [and] ⅔ at the end; it may round 6 inches from the straight line; and by these you may also draw the beam of the half deck.

---

* The sweeps of the inside and outside of the timbers are not, of course, concentric.
† 'mussell.'

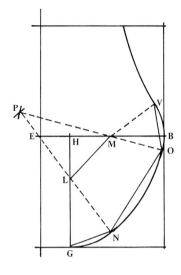

Fig 99: The chords of the various rib curves. The anonymous author of the manuscript on shipbuilding c.1620 is attempting to determine the exact length of the various curves by calculating the length of the chords of the three lower curves (GN, NO, OV), and the angle at L, P, and M. This is because too much error would occur in transferring the measurements from the little drawing to the full-size ship. Unfortunately some erroneous figures have been used in the manuscript, which makes the technique unusable.

[The Substance of the Sweeps]

Lastly we consider in this plane the substance of the three sweeps which make the bends, for out of them the rest are deducted both forward and aftward on. The first is G, N from the floor to the wrong head, which taken off with the compasses is found to be 6 foot 8 inches. The second is N, O from the wrong head to the touch of the upper sweep, and is found to be 14 [foot]. The third is V, O from the touch of the futtock sweep to the touch of the top timbers, and is found to be 4 foot. But because a little mistake of the compasses upon the scale may breed a great error in moulding of the rest of the bends upon the ship, it will be requisite to find these substances for more surety's sake arithmetically after this manner.

[Calculation of the Substances]

The substances are found by the angles; we must therefore first find the three angles of the sweeps, L, P, & M. Draw the line L, M from the centre of the first sweep to the centre [of the] third sweep; you have then the triangle L H M right angled at H, whereof the 2 sides M, H and L, H are given, to find L, M the third side by the fourth case of right angled plane triangles. *L*, H [G, H] the depth is 15 foot 6 inches and L, G the radius for the lower sweep is 9 foot 8 inches, therefore L, H [is] 5 foot 10 [inches]; E, B the half breadth is 18 foot out of which take E, H the half floor 4 foot 6 inches, there rests H, B 13 foot 6 inches; again take M, B the radius of the upper sweep 7 foot 8 inches out of H, B 13 foot 6 inches, you

have H, M 5 foot 10 inches. Now because this triangle falls out to be equicrural the angles at the base are equal, and because the three angles of every plane triangle are equal to two right angles, and the angle at H is 90^d, therefore the angles at L and M are 45^d apiece. You may therefore find the side L, M two ways, by the square root or by proportion: for the square of M, H and the square of L, H added together do make the square of L, M whose square root is the side L, M desired. Or by proportion [by] the fifth case of right angled plane triangles: for as H M L 45^d 0′ is unto H, L 50.9* (70 inches) so is M H L 90^d 0′ to *b*, m [L, M] 101.8 inches. Next you have the oblique triangle L P M of three known sides, to find the angles; for L, *M* [L, N] is [equal] to L, G, which taken out of P, N 21 foot 9 inches leaves P, L 12 foot 3 inches. Also M, O is equal [to] M, B which taken out of P, O, equal to P, N, leaves P, M 14 foot 3 inches. Wherefore you may find any of the angles without respect to the perpendicular after this manner, and with greater ease by help of logarithms.

* This length should be 49.5 inches, and that of L, M 99 inches. The angle L P M should be 36°, as stated later, and the remaining calculations on this page are faulty. The errors seem to have been noted by an earlier reader, and there is a marginal note which appears to read: 'Questioned by M^d Cooper'.

The solution is without doubt to be found in Pepysian MS. 2820. On p 91 of that work is a very similar diagram and solution of the same problem, but based on sweeps of 9 feet 6 inches, 21 feet 9 inches, and 7 feet 6 inches respectively.

L, M is	101.8	inches
M, P is	171	
L, P is	147	

The sum	419.8	
The ½ sum	209.9	- - -	7677:9875
The 1st difference	108.1	- - -	7966:1743
The 2d diff.	38.9	- - -	1589:9496
The 3d diff.	62.9	- - -	1798:6506

19032:7620

The ½ the logar. - - - - - - 9516.3810 of half the angle P, 18ᵈ 11′, therefore the whole angle is 36ᵈ 22′.

Substance of the wrong head

Out of the half sum of the three sides subtract each side, you have the difference. Unto the arithmetical complement of the half sum [is] added the arithmetical complement of the difference of the side opposite to the angle desired, and unto them the logarithms of the other two differences. The half of the sum is the logarithm of the tangent of half the angle desired.

You may find the other two angles at L and M after the same manner, but it will be as easy by the ordinary proportion; for as L, M 101.8 is [to] L P M 36ᵈ 0′, so is M, P 168 inches to M L P 85ᵈ 20′ and L, P 14 inches to L M P 58ᵈ 40′. Take H L M 45ᵈ 0′ out of P L M 85ᵈ 20′ there remains P L H 40ᵈ 20′, equal to G L N is equicrural the angles at the base are equal, wherefore take G L N 40ᵈ 20′ out of 180ᵈ the remains 139ᵈ 40′ for the other two angles, and each of them 69ᵈ 50′. Wherefore as L G N 69ᵈ 50′ is to L, N 116 inches so [is] G L N 40ᵈ 20′ to G, N 79.98 inches, the substance of G, N 6 foot 8 inches.

Substance of the futtock sweep

Again, because the triangle P N O is equicrural the two angles at N and O are equal; the angle at P is found to be 36ᵈ 0′, therefore the other two angles 144ᵈ 0′ and each of them 72ᵈ 0′. Now as P N O 72ᵈ 0′ is to P, O 260 inches, so is N P O 36ᵈ 0′ to N, O 160.6 inches, or 13 foot 5 inches almost for the substance of N, O the futtock sweep.

Substance of the upper sweep

Lastly, for the upper sweep take the angle L M H 45ᵈ out of the whole angle L M P 58ᵈ 40′, there resteth the angle P M E equal to the angle O M B 13ᵈ 40′, which

reserve. Make S, T equal to M, B and draw M, T parallel to B, S and another line from [M] to Q, the head of the post, So have [you] a new triangle M T Q right angled at T, whose sides M, T and T, Q are given; for M, T is 15 foot 6 inches equal to the depth and T, Q is 1 foot 4 [8] inches (the differnce between ⅓ of the half breadth and the radius of the upper sweep). Wherefore as M, T 186 inches is to M, T 100000 so is T, Q 28 [20] inches to the tangent of T M Q 6ᵈ 8′, therefore [is] M, Q the secant* thereof. Multiply this secant by 186 for the length of Q, M and cut off from the total 5 figures; so have you 186.5 [inches]† for the length of Q, M. Then in the triangle Q V M right angled at V seek the angle Q V M: as Q, M 187.08 is to Q V M 90ᵈ so is M, V 92 inches to M Q V 29ᵈ 33′; therefore Q M V 61ᵈ 29′, which added to T M Q 6ᵈ 8′ makes the whole angle T M V 67ᵈ 35′. Out of the right angle T M B take the angle Q M V, there resteth V M B 22ᵈ 25′. Lastly add the angle O M B (formerly found to [be] 13ᵈ 40′) to the angle V M B 22ᵈ 25′ so have you the angle V M O 36ᵈ 5′ by which to find the substance V, O desired; for the triangle V M O being also equicrural the angles at V and O are equal. Subtract 36ᵈ 5′ out of 180ᵈ there resteth 143ᵈ 55′, the half whereof 71ᵈ 58′ is the angle at V or O. Then as M V O 71ᵈ 58′ is to M, O 92 inches, so is V M O 36ᵈ 5′ to V, O 57 inches (4 foot 88⅘ inches) the substance of the upper sweep V, O.

2nd Plane of Length and Depth

The making of the moulds whereby to frame every other bend out of the midship bend belongeth also to this plane of breadth and depth, which be three: the floor mould; the futtock mould; and the top timber mould. But because they are of no use till the graduation be put upon them, which are to be drawn out of the lines of the other planes, I will leave them to a more proper place and now proceed with the next plane, which is the perpendicular plane of length and depth. Therein we are to consider nine things:

First, the laying of the keel. 2. The rakes of the stem and stern with the length of the post. 3. The grip and tuck. 4. The running lines both alow and aloft. 5. The swimming line. 6. The hanging and drawing of the wales, chain wales, rails, &c. 7. The placing of the decks with their length and partitions. 8. The due cutting out

* MS. 'second.'   † This should be 187.08 inches.

of ports upon every several deck. 9. And lastly, the head, galleries, and counters.

[Stem and] Rake of the Post

First draw an infinite straight line at pleasure which shall represent the lower edge of the keel A, B. (Plan 4) Set of [f] ⅓ of the keel from B to D and draw the line E, D crossing A, B at right angles, which shall represent the place of the midship bend. At 12 or 13 inches distance draw a parallel [line above this for the upper edge of the keel. You may draw another parallel]* at 3 or 4 inches distance for limber holes called a dead rising line; which being taken into the rising for the timbers they shall retain their full depth without any maim† by cutting out those holes to convey the water. Some use an unequal dead rising which will do well also, and they draw a straight line from the pitch of the forefoot to the stern post, allowing one third of the greatest rising upon the ⅓ of the keel, which they make more or less as they will have the ship draw more water abaft than afore. To the fore part of the keel B raise the perpendicular C, B which shall be a parallel to the midship line E, D, upon which line will be the centre of the sweep that draws the stem. The semidiameter thereof must never be more than the whole breadth nor less than ¾ thereof: the best proportion is as 7.125 foot to 9 foot of the breadth. If then the breadth be 36 the semidiameter shall be 28.5 foot, which being taken of[f] the scale with your compasses set one foot in B, extend the other *b c* [to C], and draw the circle B, F up to a quadrant for the rake of the stem in the outside of the timber. Let the depth of the stem be 20 inches at F and equal to the keel at B; shorten the sweep the difference of those two depths and by the points of H G find a new centre to draw the circle H, G for the inside of the stem.§ Let the rake of the stern post I, K never recline from the zenith more than an angle [of] 22 [degrees] no[r] less than 18 [degrees] or the complement thereof to the horizontal line, and at this angle draw the straight line I, K for the post: the length

whereof must never be more than ⅔ of the breadth nor less than ½ of the depth from the skeg to the counter.

Height of the Tuck

The tuck at N may be ⅔ of the depth in a perpendicular [line, or] as 11 to 14 of the depth upon the post; and so it will be 10 foot 4 inches in perpendicular on 11 foot 1.5 inches upon the post.

[Gripe and] Lower Rising Line

The gripe upon the stem at O may be higher or lower as you desire to make the fore foot bluffer or lanker. Some pitch it as it hapneth wheresoever the straight line [which] is drawn from the centre of the rake unto half the substance thereof cutteth the stem, and some allow ⅓ of the perpendicular of the tuck for the rising upon the perpendicular of the stem: but the best proportion is as 8.55 to 10 [there]of. The perpendicular of the gripe will be 8 foot 10 inches from the edge of the keel.† By these three points (at N the tuck, at M the midships, and at O the gripe) the curve line must be drawn for the lower rising, but it will be first convenient to find the extremes and middle of the upper rising line also that the parallel[s] which space out of the bends may be drawn for both at once.

Upper Rising Line [and] Height of the Breadth Line

The upper rising line directeth both the depth of every bend and the laying of every breadth to pass for the bearing of the ship in mid-ships. The height of that breadth line both at S and K, the stem and stern, is most properly drawn out of the depth. Let the perpendicular of the breadth line at K be to the depth at P as 100 to 75, or add ⅓ of the depth unto the depth itself; so have you for the perpendicular of the breadth line at K 20.66 foot. The perpendicular of the breadth line at S will be to the depth at P as 9 to 8; and so have you at S 17.5 foot for the perpendicular of the breadth. These three points being given (at K, P, & S) you may carry this breadth line by a circle from stem to stern, so it be of a large radius to keep down the breadth near to a straight line in the midships, and by such a circle whose radius was

---

* Unfortunately several words have been omitted. Those inserted are suggested as conveying the sense of the passage. See Notes.
† MS. 'maine.'
§ See Notes.

† This is the only instance in which the base or ground line used is specifically named. See Notes.

365* parts hereof *X* to an inch was the breadth of the *Lyon* carried. But because every circle doth raise the breadth in the quarters somewhat too high where it should be kept down to bear with the luff, the best way to help this defect will be to carry the breadth from the midships by a straight line near ¼ of the keel each way to Q and *v* [R]; always ending upon the same even space for the more easy fnding the centres of those arcs which must be joined to this straight line and continued to make up the upper rising line both to stem and stern.

A stempiece of 30 foot rake, 2 foot† of 25 foot apiece, to be 16: 18: or 20 inches square. Beams of 30 foot long to be 18 inches square, or 18 inches broad [and] 20 inches deep, ⅔ always at the end; of 4 foot long, two foot deep in the middle. Floor timbers 17 inches broad at the top 18 inches at the fashion piece or 18 inches square [*sic*].

The spacing of the Bends

The lower rising line giveth the length of the ship at the narrowing alow, and the upper rising line at the narrowing aloft; wherefore having the extremes of these lines you may now draw the parallels by which to distinguish the spaces and number of bends. Unto ⅔ of the keel 66 foot 8 inches add the rake of the post 8 foot 4 inches; so have you the length aftward on containing 75 foot. Divide that by 2 foot 6 inches, which is a fit proportion for timber and space to a ship of this burthen; so have you 30, the number of bends aftward on. Unto ⅓ of the keel 33 foot 4 inches add the inward rake of the stem 26 foot 8 inches;‡ so have you 69 foot, which divided by 2 foot 6 inches as afore gives 24, the number of bends forward. Or if you list to have fewer bends increase the timber and space; which being 3 foot instead of 2½ foot will divide 60 [foot] into 20 equal parts, and then there shall be but 20 bends forward. Neither is it material to make the bends fore and aft of equal distances, but you may vary and alter them as other circumstances shall induce you. The timber and spaces being thus found out, let fall 2 perpendiculars: the one from K [to] A

* This figure is certainly too small. It should probably be 565, or even 865.
† This should probably have read '2 pieces'. The whole of this list of scantlings seems to have been inserted out of its context.
‡ This is 2 inches short of the correct rake, but was probably adopted in order to obtain an even number of stations.

abaft, the other from S to U afore. Divide the whole length K, S and A, U into *45* [54] equal spaces, each space containing 2½ foot. Or if you make but 50 bend[s], from the midship P, D to A 30 and from thence to S, U 20. Unto each dimensions draw parallel lines to the perpendicular[s] K, A and S, U. So may you upon these lines prick out the circles, both for the rising alow and aloft, after this manner.

[The pricking of the Lower Rising Line]

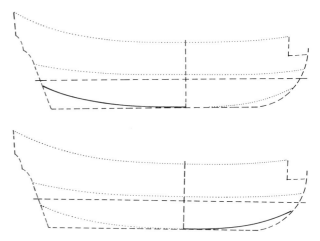

Because the tuck is one half of the post from the skeg to the breadth line, therefore the perpendicular of the tuck is half the perpendicular of the post from the breadth line and consequently divides the distance between the skeg and the outmost perpendicular into halves, each part containing 4 foot 2 inches rake. [Take] 4 foot 2 inches out of 5 foot, the distance of the two aftermost bends, there remains 28 bends and 10 inches for the greatest rising abaft at the perpendicular of the tuck; but because it falls on no even bend multiply it cubically. 10 inches is equal to ³³⁄₁₀₀ of 100, therefore 28.33 bend[s] will make a ③ of 22737.9. Wherefore as 22737.9 the ③ of the greatest rising is to 10.33 [foot] or 124 inches (the length of that line), so is the ③ of 24 to 6 foot 3.38 inches; of 20 to 3 foot 7.6 inches; of 16 to 1 foot 10.43 inches; of 12 to 0 foot 9.45 inches; of 8 to 0 foot 2.79 inches; of 4 to 0 foot 0.35 inches; and thus you may set out the risings of every other bend also. For the risings forward on you must likewise seek the perpendicular of the gripe, which falls 2 foot 3 inches from the 17 bend and 9 inches from the 18. Multiply 17.75 bend[s] cubically; you have 5592 for the cube of the greatest rising. Wherefore as 5592 the ③ of the greatest rising is to 8 foot 10 inches (the length of that line), so is the ③ of 17 to 7 foot 9 inches; and of 14 to 4 foot 4.5 inches; and of 11 to 2 foot 1.4 inches; and of 8 to 9.7 inches; and of 5 to 2.37 inches; and so of the rest. Having set of [f] the lengths of these lines, draw them all into one circular line from the tuck to the gripe and you have the lower rising line desired.

The pricking of the Upper Rising Line

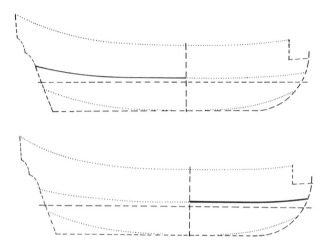

The parts of the upper rising line made by a circle may be set out in like manner; but because there are two points given you shall need but a third point to draw any circle truly by. Take 15 foot 6 inches the depth out of 20.66 [foot] the greatest rising, there remains 5 [foot] 2 [inches] or 62 inches for T, K, equal to the versed sine of that arc; and T, Q is 21 bends, every bend containing 30 inches, the whole line 630 inches equal to the right sine of that arc.

By which two numbers reduce the inches into sines. The square of 630 inches divided by 62 inches giveth 6401.6, unto which add 62 so have you 6463.6 the diameter, therefore the radius of that circle [is] 3231.8. By which divide 630 increased with ciphers so have you 19493, the right sine of that [arc]; whose complement taken out of the radius leaveth *716* [.01918] for the versed sine, answerable to 62 inches. To find the versed sine of the 24 bend, [say] as 630 the 30 bend is to 19493 so [is] 450 (the number of the 24 bend) to 13923 the right sine thereof; whose complement [taken] out of the radius giveth 973, the versed sine of the 24 bend. [Wherefore as 12918 (the versed sine of the 30th bend) is to 62 inches so is 973 (the versed sine of the 24th bend)]

to [31.46 inches], the length of that line.* By these three points draw the circle from Q to K. Again take 15.5 the depth out of S, U 17.5, there remains S, X 24 inches equal to the versed sine of that arc; and *S*, X [R, X] is 12 bends, each bend containing 36 inches, therefore the whole line 432 inches equal to the right sine of that arc. By these two numbers reduce the inches into sines. The square of 432 divided by 24 giveth 7776, unto which add 24; the whole diameter is 7800 and the radius of that circle 3900. By which divide 432 inches increased with ciphers so have you 11077, the right sine of that arc; those complement taken out of the radius leaveth 617 [.00615] the versed sine, answerable to 24 inches. To find the versed sine of the 15 bend, say as 432 [is] to 11077 so is 252 to 64610 [.06462], whose complement taken [out] of the radius leaveth [.00213] the versed sine of the 15 bend. Wherefore as 617 [615] the versed sine of the 20 bend is to 24 inches so is *208* [213] the versed sine of the 15 bend to 8.2 inches, the length of that line. By these points draw the circle from *u* [R] to S: so have you done with the narrowing line.

S, U double the rising of the Gripe.

[Rising of the Top Timbers]

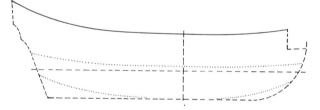

I might here add a third rising line for carrying the top timbers, but because the proportion of double the depth set off from the breadth line upon every bend doth very well direct the same, it shall not be needful to draw any other line.

The Swimming line

The next thing to be drawn in this plane of length and depth is the swimming line, which is a principal thing to be regarded for the good qualities of the ship. From that line are set off the decks and ports for the

---

* At this point the manuscript does not make sense. The words inserted are suggested as having probably been omitted by the copyist.

ordnance, higher or lower as we will have them lie to pass; therefore of right there should be marks made on the ship's side to direct the mariner to keep her always in that trim, neither to sink her deeper nor let her swim shoaler. The depth of this line is taken off the midship bend, for where the two upper sweeps intersect each other with respect to the thickness of the plank (which intersection is easily found by drawing a straight line through the centres of the upper sweep and futtock sweep), from thence to the ground line is the true depth of the swimming line. Which depth being marked upon the midship line and upon each perpendicular of the upper rising, draw a straight line from stem to stern. So have you the swimming line desired.

The Wales

The next thing to be drawn is the lower wale, by which all the rest are guided. Because the wales are all drawn by a circle there will need no more to be found but three points; the one at the stem; the other at the stern; the third about the midship. The top of the post whereon the transom is framed giveth the point in the stern for the lower edge of the wale, and let the depth of it upon the perpendicular afore be as 8 to 7 of the perpendicular of the breadth. So shall the point be 15 foot *4* [5] inches from the found line. By these two points draw a circle that may touch the swimming line a little before the midships whose radius will be *834* [534] parts whereof ten to an inch, and unto that another concentric at a foot distance for the upper edge of the wale; so have you done with the first wale. At 2 foot 8 inches distance from that draw the second wale; and at 3 foot the third wale upon which place the chain wale; and [at] 2 foot the fourth; and at 2 foot 4 inches the fifth wale; all concentric each to [the] other. So have you done with the wales and rails up to the gunwale; in like manner proceed with the ribbands above these.*

The Decks [and] Orlop

The next thing to be set out in this plane of length and depth is the decks with their lengths and partitions. The decks in the midships are formerly set out upon the [midship] bend from whence we may take their propor-

---

* For remarks on this section, see the Notes.

tions. Let the lower edge of the beam for the orlop be pitched at the breadth line, which will lie 2 foot *8* [0] inches above the swimming line. To lay this deck flush fore and aft cannot be done without cutting the wales, which is both disgraceful and weakening to the ship. The best artificer that ever was used a fall for the gun room abaft and a rise for the chase afore, and these bring all things well to pass and a greater strength to the ship than the flush deck, but every man may please his fancy. If you will have it flush fore and aft let it rise 2 foot more above the swimming line both afore and abaft than it [lies] in the midships, and so it will lie well to pass. But if you will have a rise before and a fall abaft, let the rise in the luff and the fall in the quarters be 20 inches apiece. So shall the gun room (divided with a bulkhead from the rest) and fore peak lie upon a level, and the deck between camber conveniently to keep the wales whole and to place ports at an equal height above the deck. The level of the fore peak is always from the pitch of the fore foot forwards; the length of the gun room may be ³/₁₀ of of [sic] the keel from the perpendicular of the breadth or as 9 to 19 of the whole length which will be 30 foot from the aftermost perpendicular and falls about the 20th bend aft.§

[The Deck]

The next deck may run flush at the height it hath in the midships from the [fore] foot afterwards; from thence forwards it may rise as the orlop did to give the more room for the use of the ordnance, and cook room if it be contrived there.† This deck hath 3 bulkheads or partitions: the first at the pitch of the fore foot which gives the length of the chase forward on; the 2nd abaft the main mast and gives the length of the waist; the 3rd at the captain's cabin a little abaft the steerage.

[The Forecastle]

Above this deck is the fore castle. The deck thereof may lie at the height of the half deck set out in the midship bend; the length may be ²/₃ of the inward rake and must be cut off at the 3rd timber forward on, for more conveniency in placing the bowsprit and fashioning the head.

---

§ See Notes.
† If the cookroom was in the Chase, i.e. on the upper deck, it is difficult to see how a rise here could give more room.

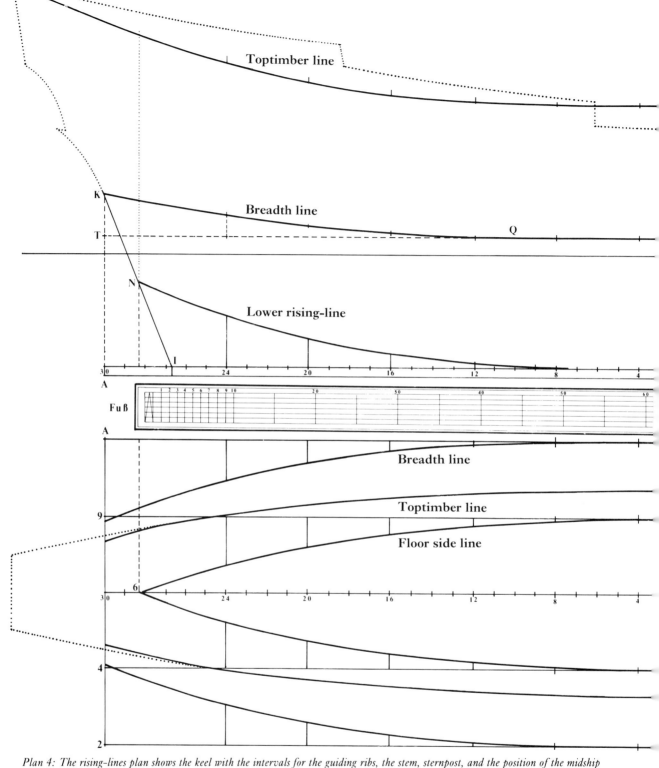

Plan 4: The rising-lines plan shows the keel with the intervals for the guiding ribs, the stem, sternpost, and the position of the midship frame (ME). There are thirty rib markings aft of the midship frame; twenty forward of it. Fore and aft, they are at different intervals to each other. They are guiding ribs, which define the final shape of the vessel. The remaining ribs would be added between the guiding ribs during the construction of the ship. The midpoint of the curve of the stem is on the vertical line HC.

The lower rising-line, the breadth line and the toptimber line are important lines which shipbuilders used in constructing their moulds. These were the curved templates from which the shape of the ribs was worked. Note the clear separation of the curves of the lower rising-line and the breadth line fore and aft of the midship frame. Various arithmetic and geometric methods were used to derive these curves. That explains why different terms were sometimes used for these parts.

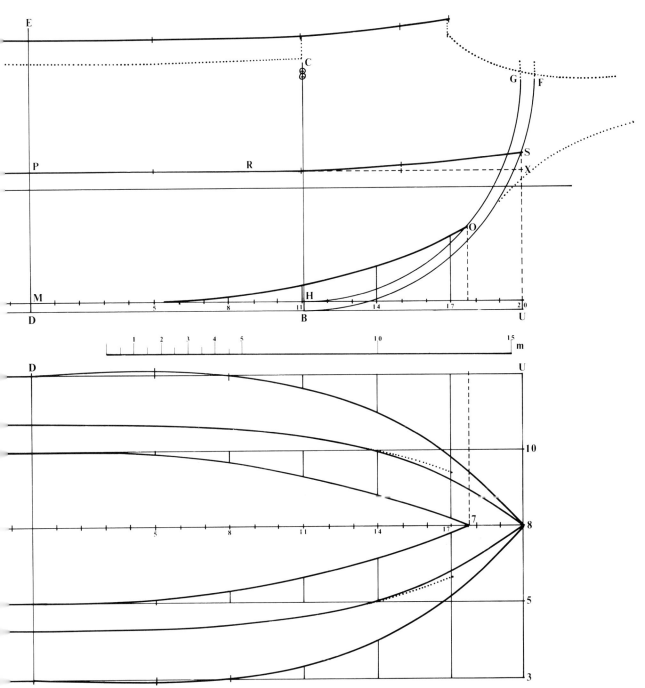

The broken line is pure guesswork, and only shown to indicate the position of the various elements in the construction of the ship's hull. The broken vertical line at N is an auxiliary line, which I have added for the reconstruction of the hull; see also the manner in which hulls are portrayed today.

We can see the lateral boundaries of the floor, the toptimber line and the breadth line in the plan view. If, as is specified, we use the toptimber line for the construction of the rib futtocks, we find that the stern and the forecastle are too narrow. I have therefore shown, by the dotted line at the bow and the stern, a suggested curve of the toptimber line which keeps a harmonious run of the lines.

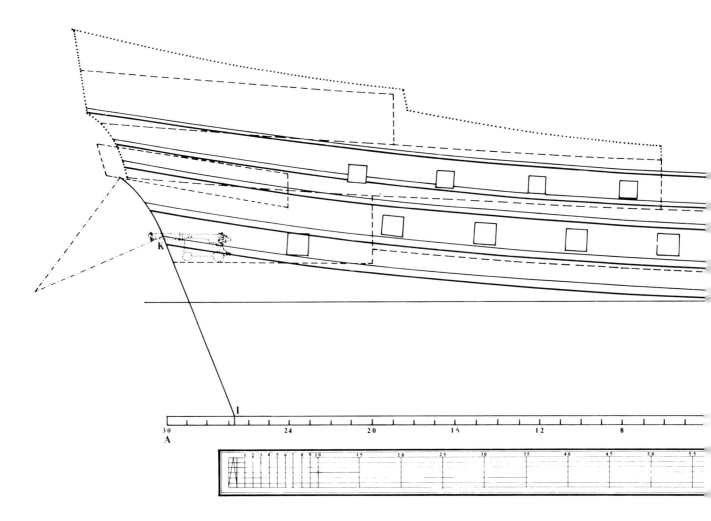

Plan 5: The rising-lines have been omitted from this side view in the interests of clarity. The wales run at the corrected intervals suggested by Salisbury. The breadth of the wales also corresponds to his suggestions.

The broken lines running lengthwise show the upper edge of the deck planking on the ship's side. The aft portion of the lower deck has been set back, and continues as the gun room deck. In some ships its great height was reduced by an intermediate deck. Next comes the upper deck, the halfdeck and quarter deck, at the heights suggested.

The position of the bulkheads, apart from the forecastle bulkhead, is not clear, and has to be guessed at. They are therefore shown by broken lines. A poop has been omitted.

From the position of the decks we can, at the least, derive the height of the lower edge of the gunports. The length of 2½ft (specified in

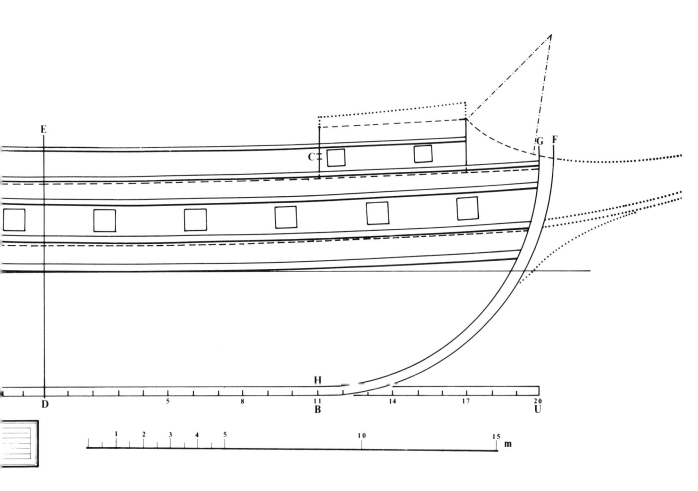

the text) for the sides of the gunports on the lower deck is reduced to 2ft on the upper deck. The distance between the lower edge of the gunport and the deck has also been reduced, as the ship carries lighter guns on the upper deck. The text merely gives the distance between the gunports, so we have to guess their number and position.

It is not clear whether the ship had a complete arming cloth in the waist area. The evidence from the Stockholm galleon model and contemporaneous illustrations would suggest that this was unlikely. Consequently no gunports have been drawn in the waist area, although there would certainly have been guns on this part of the deck.

The dotted line of the arming cloths on the beakhead and forecastle is pure supposition. (After Salisbury)

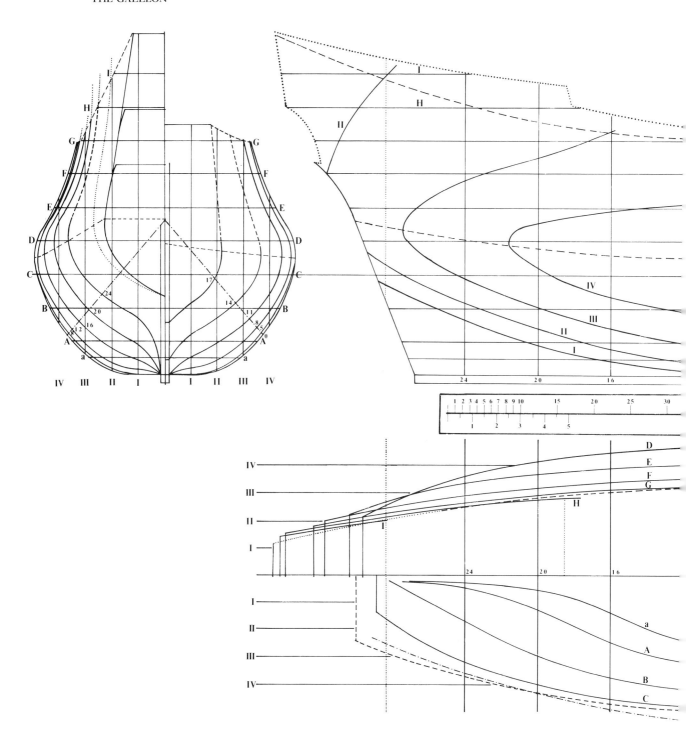

Plan 6: Rib plan, waterlines and longitudinal sections: Here the author has attempted to compare the construction drawing techniques of the seventeenth century with those of today. Astonishingly, it seems that (apart from a few questions of interpretation) the complex, three-dimensional hull of a ship from this period can be reconstructed from a few pages of text. It is true that we no longer have the original drawings. The relative simplicity of the 300-year-old method of designing ships allows us today virtually to complete the various steps. We owe this to the method of whole-moulding, in which several arcs were placed together and positioned according to the rising-lines.

190

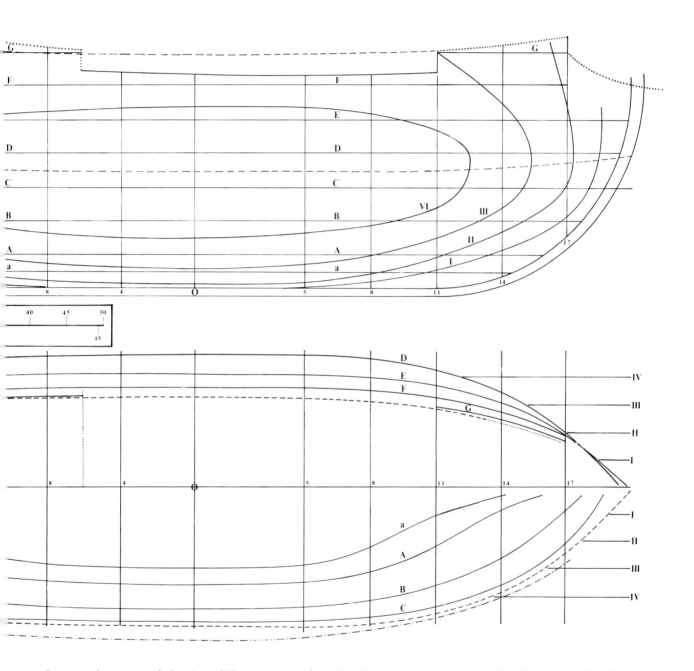

Later on, when curves with changing radii became increasingly used in ship construction, so simple a method of portraying a ship's hull lost its feasibilty.

The longitudinal section clearly shows how the sharpest curve of the ship's side, and consequently the maximum breadth of the hull, lies in the area of the breadth line (shown by a broken line).

The Half Deck

The height of the half deck is given afore and may run flush to the stern. It may be in length as the dining [room] which is as 30 to 100 of the keel abaft. In this are contrived several cabins for the master and his mates and the quarter masters, the necessary ministers for sailing the ship at sea.

Quarter Deck

The deck may lie 6 foot above the half deck, and is of length from the aftermost bulkhead to the stern; whereupon if the height of the work will give leave there may be also cabins contrived for the succour of men. But these things belonging to the finishing part may be altered as pleaseth the workman.

Port Holes [and] Distance and Square of the Ports

The next thing to be considered when the decks are laid, is the due placing [of] the ordnance and cutting out of the port holes for them. Let the lower edge of the two midship ports lie two foot 4* inches above the breadth and then will the muzzle of the piece lie 6 foot at least from the water, which is enough to bear them out all weather. All the rest will lie higher according to the hanging of the decks. Let every port be 8½ foot asunder, or where you are straitened by reason of the bulkheads &c., 7 foot at least. Let the middle part of the two sternports in the gun room lie even with the breadth. Let every port be 2½ foot square, and all the ports upon the upper placed between the ports of the lower deck; and this will be directions sufficient for them.

Counter, Galleries, and Head.

The last thing is but [a] matter of ornament, yet if proportion be not observed the whole work will be much disgraced by the uncomely winning of the ship. Let the sweep of the counter be as 11 to 10 of the depth, which will be 77 [17] foot; and let the substance of that arc from the head of the post to the bottom of the galleries be one half of the sweep, which will be 8½ foot. The length of the galleries may be ⅙ of the whole length, and the depth in the steeving line ⅕ thereof. So will the length be 22 [foot] and the depth 4 foot 4 inches. The head without the stem to the forepart of the beast may

* This height is given on p 179 as 2 feet 10 inches, which is probably correct.

be ⅕ of the keel or as 10 to 11 of the galleries, and may steeve an angle of 130ᵈ or between that and 120ᵈ.† The rounding of the hawse piece‡ up to the fore castle may be with a sweep whose radius is in proportion to the depth as 29 to 31, and so it will be 14 foot and a half; and thus we have done with the second plane of length and depth.

The third Plane of Length and Breadth

The third plane of length and breadth suppose[s] the ship to be cut in pieces somewhat near horizontally at the orlop lies, and representeth unto us the flat frame of the ship and breadth between every timber according to the narrowing both aloft and alow; and therein we may consider 4 things. First, the length of the ship both alow and aloft; secondly, the breadth of the stern in proportion to the midships; thirdly, the narrowing of the ship both alow at the wrong head and aloft at the breadth line; fourthly, the bevelling of every bend of timber in the several places of the sine marks.§

The Length Alow and Aloft

The length of the ship both alow and aloft is confined by the rising lines; wherefore continue the two perpendiculars of the breadth line K, A and S, U unto 3 and 2 of the whole breadth of the ship, and at [that] distance [draw] the line 2, 3 parallel to A, U, the lower edge of the keel. So shall 2, 3 be equal to K, S and give the length of the ship at the breadth aloft. Divide the space A, 2 and U, 3 the whole breadth, into four equal parts and draw parallels to 2, 3 at every fourth part; as are the lines 4, 5 and 6, 7 &c. Next continue the perpendicular N of the tuck and O of the grip unto the middle line of this plane, and where they intersect it at 6 [and] 7 shall be the length of the ship at the breadth alow.

[Breadth of the Transom]

The greatest Narrowing Aloft & Alow

In the next place proportion the breadth of the transom, for according to that must be the greatest narrowing

† These angles are impossible, and should doubtless read 13° and 12°.
‡ The half rail, above the main rail of the head.
§ Later, on f. 95v [p 197], the manuscript reverts to the more usual form, 'surmarks'. In the old system of whole moulding these points are *sine* marks in the proper sense. It is tempting to assume that *sur*mark is a corrupted form of the word.

aloft aftward on. Some make it ½ of the breadth and so the greatest narrowing is one fourth thereof. The best proportion is as 10 to 19 of the whole breadth, and then the greatest narrowing aloft will be 9½ foot of a side. The greatest narrowing alow is according to the flat of the floor, ¼ of the breadth. Those two extremes in narrowing being given, the one upon the perpendicular of the breadth of [the transom] the other [upon that] of the tuck, we may now proceed to set off the rest of the narrowing upon every several bend.

[The Upper Narrowing Line aft]

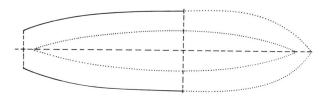

First therefore continue the parallel of each bend, according to the spaces formerly set out, from one side of this plane to the other. Then because the greatest narrowing aloft doth fall upon the 30th bend, and that have [we] formerly determined to narrow by the ③ power line, I say: as the ③ of 30, (27000), is to the length of that line 9 foot 6 inches or 114 inches, so is the ③ of 24; of 20; of 16; of 12; of 8; of 4; &c; unto 4 foot 10.36 inches; to 2 foot 9.77 inches; to 1 foot 5.3 [inches; to 7.29; 2.15; and 0.27 inches] as on the other side.* Which lengths taken off the scale and set upon the several parallels to which they belong shall give pricks by which [to] draw one entire circular line without angles from *c b* to *g* [D to 9]; so have you the upper narrowing line aftward on.

[The Lower Narrowing Line aft]

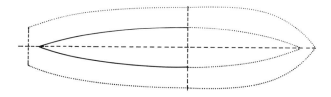

The lower narrowing line aft is made of one of the conic sections called the ellipses, which must be

* This direction appears to refer to the dimensions within the brackets, which in the copy were placed in the margin.

continued beyond the perpendicular to the intersection of the shortest diameter which in this case is always the ½ breadth.† Wherefore set off the ½ breadth from the skeg outwards; so shall you make up 34 bends. The ellipse may be calculated many ways, the easiest of all by the table of natural sines after this manner. Divide the radius 100000 by 34, the number of bends. There will come forth 2941, the 4th number proportionable, being a natural sine which doubled, tripled, quadrupled, &c., gives the rest. Suppose I would seek the lines of the 24; 20; 16; 12; 8; and 4 bends, &C. Multiply each number increased a unity by 2941: so have you for 24, 73525–6773$^\sigma$–12.20$^\rho$; for 20, 61761–78640$^\sigma$–14.16$^\rho$; for 16,49997–86603$^\sigma$–15.59$^\rho$; for 12,38233–92399$^\sigma$–16.63$^\rho$; for 8,26469–96433$^\sigma$–17.36$^\rho$; for 4, 14705–98914$^\sigma$–17.80$^\rho$; all of them natural sines whose complement (marked $^\sigma$) multiplied by 18, the half breadth, shall give those numbers (marked $^\rho$) within; and deducting them out of 18, the half breadth, shall give [for] 24, 5.80; 20, 3.84; 16, 2.41; 12, 1.37; 8, 0.64; 4, 0.20. Which lengths of each line being pricked down upon the parallels answering thereto, by those points draw one entire circular line without angles from the midships to the intersection of this perpendicular with the middle line. So have you an ellipse line for the narrowing alow aftward on.

[The Upper Narrowing Line forward on]

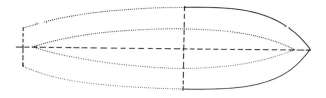

The upper narrowing line from the midships forward on is by the 4th power; wherefore take off the greatest narrowing which for the most part is just the half breadth because the narrowing of both sides forward on meets upon the stem, and should be 18 foot. But because a full bow aloft will bear the better, increase that line with a dead narrowing of 12 inches on a side to come off at nothing in the mid-ships, and then the extreme narrowing afore is 19 foot or 228 inches. Now whether you use 20 bends of 3 foot apiece, or 24 of 2 foot & a half, it

† See Notes.

produces the same line: for as the ④ power of 20 (160000) is to 228, so is the ④ power of 17; 14; 11; 8; and 5; unto 19 foot 11¼ inches; 4 foot 6.74 inches; 1 foot 8.86 [inches; 5.83 inches; and 0.89 inches;]* for the length of the lines proper to those bends. Or again, as the ④ power of 24 (331776) is to 228, so is the ④ power of 21; 18; 15; 12; 10; &c., unto 72.14; 14.25; &c., as afore. Which numbers [being] taken of the scale and pricked down from the dead narrowing line upon each bend belonging to them, draw one entire circular line without any angles from the midships to the middle line of this plane at 8; and so you have the upper narrowing line forward on as was desired.†

The Lower Narrowing Line forward on

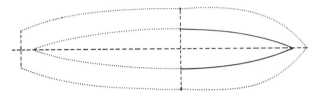

The lower narrowing line forward on is an artifical line made by the triple of every bend increased by the ② power, because the ② power is found to be a little too lank a line to join with the ④ power. The manner is thus: Let the first bend be one; the second 3 times one; the third 3 times 2; the fourth 3 times 3; &c. &c. So the 18 [bend] shall be 3 times 17 which is 51; and that increased by the ② power shall give 2601; the 17 shall be 3 times 16; the 14,3 times 13; the 11, 3 times 10 the 8, 3 times 7; &c. These numbers increased by the ② power shall give 2304; 1521; 900; 441; [and] 144 for the 5 [bend] & c. Then seek the greatest narrowing, which is [the] same either upon the perpendicular or the 18th bend and is found to be 9 foot 2 inches, or 100 [110] inches. Wherefore as 2601 the number of the 18 bend [is to] 110 inches, the line thereof, so is 2304 the number of the 17th bend, and 121 & 900 & 441 &c., unto 97.44 [inches] the line of the 17th bend, and 64.32 of the 14th, and 38.00 of the 11th, and 18.65 the length of the line for the 8th bend. Which being pricked down upon the parallels wherunto they are proper, draw one

---

entire circular line without angles in those pricks from the midship to the intersection of the middle line and perpendicular of the gripe. So have you the lower narrowing desired.

[The Narrowing of the Top Timbers]

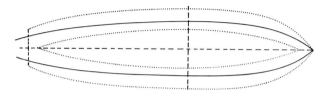

I might here also add another narrowing line for the guiding the top timbers, according as we will have the ship broader or narrower aloft. Some use to narrow by ⅛ by ⅐ of the whole breadth; but the best proportion is ⅙. Which being constantly kept at double the depth of every bend doth give a very good narrowing line for that purpose, which may be given in numbers and drawn as the former lines are.

The Reason of spoiling Many Ships

These lines being all drawn the plot is finished, which ought to be the true model§ of the ship proposed to be built. But there are many good artificers that can draw a plot well and build a ship also, that if their work be compared with their plot you will find them very little to agree; and so many times good ships are spoiled in the building whose principal lines were well contrived in the plotting. The chiefest reason is want of skill in Arithmetic and Geometry to take all things truly of [f] the plot. For if they trust to a small scale, which many times is not above the 10th part of an inch for a foot, divided into 12 parts for every inch, and if they mistake but the 100th part of an inch upon the scale it must needs produce an error of an inch in the ship, though it be but 100 times greater than the plot.

[To draw the Bends fore and aft.]

To draw therefore out [of] the midship bend all the rest according to the true draught of the plot, you must find the measures of every part arithmetically. Let us make an instance of some bends, for according to them all the rest may be drawn; so that forward on you may mould

---

* In the manuscript the figures within the brackets were placed in the margin.
† See Notes

§ MS. 'midle.'

Forward on

Bends.	Rising Alow		Rising Aloft*		Narr. Alow.		Narr. Aloft	
	Ft.	Ins.	Ft.	Ins.	Ft.	Ins.	Ft.	Ins.
5.	0	2.37	0	0	0	6.09	0	0.89
8.	0	9.70	0	0	1	6.66	0	5.83
11.	2	1.4	0	1.47	3	2.06	1	8.86
14.	4	4.5	0	5.95	5	4.32	4	6.34
17.	7	9.00	1	1.44	8	1.44	9	11
Greatest	8	10	2	0	9	2	19	0

Aftward on

Bends.	Rising Alow.		Rising Aloft*		Narr. Alow.		Narr. Aloft.			
	Ft.	Ins.	Ft.	Ins.	Ft.	Ins.	Ft.	Ins.	Ft.	Ins.
4.	0	0.35	0	0	17	9.60	0	2.40	0	0.27
8.	0	2.80	0	0	17	4.32	0	7.68	0	2.16
12.	0	9.42	0	1.26	16	7.96	1	4.44	0	7.29
16.	1	10.33	0	6.5	15	7.08	2	4.92	1	5.30
20.	3	7.6	1	4.95	14	1.86	3	10.24	2	9.77
24.	6	3.38	2	7.45	12	2.52	5	9.48	4	10.36
Greatest	10	4	5	2.00			9	2	18	0

* MS. 'abaft'. This error led the copyist to repeat several figures, which have not been reproduced.

5 bends, Viz[t]. the 5th; the 8th; the 11th; the 14th; and the 17th; and afterwards [on] 6 bends, Viz[t]. the 4th; the 8th; the 12th; the 16th; the 20th; and the 24th. The first thing to be done is to calculate and set down in a table the rising[s] and narrowings of all the bends that they may be in areadiness for the same: [See table above].

[To make the 20th Bend aft.] [Fig 100]

This table and the like being prepared you may make every other bend out of the midship bend; as for example the 20th bend aft:

1st. Make a parallelogram of the breadth and depth of the bend, after this manner; upon the ground line B, C raise the middle line E, F perpendicular thereto.

2nd. Out of the table take the narrowing aloft, 2 foot 9.77 inches, which subtracted out of the ½ breadth 18 foot leaveth 15 foot 2.23 inches, the half breadth of that bend. Take that of[f] the scale and set it from E to C and from E to B, and [at] that distance draw two parallels to the middle line, A, C and D, B.

3rd. Out of the table take the narrowing alow, 3 foot 10.24 inches, which subtracted out of 4 foot 6 inches, the ½ floor, leaveth 7.76 [inches] which take of

the scale and set from E to G and from E to H, and draw the two parallels H, I and G, K from the breadth of the floor in that bend.

4th. Take the rising alow of that bend, found in the table to be 3 foot 7.6 inches; which taken off the scale set from H to L and from G to M and draw the line L, M parallel to B, C.

5th. Subtract this rising alow out of the whole depth 15 foot 6 inches, and to the remainder 11 foot 10.4 [inches] add the rising aloft, 1 foot 4.95 inches. The depth of that bend above the rising shall be 13 foot 3.35 inches, which set from L and M upwards to I and K [and] draw the line D, K[D, A] parallel to the breadth line. Let A, O be equal to M, K* and draw another obscure line P, O at double the depth to B, C, upon which line set off ⅓ of the half breadth B, C [B, E] from 0 to 4. Take the height of that bend of[f] the plot from the breadth line to the top of the post, which set from A to 3 and from D to 2, [and] draw another parallel to B, C as is 3,2.

* Although this statement is quite definite, M, K should probably read, G,K. See Notes.

3 Parts of the Midship Mould

6th. Take G, L the radius of the first sweep of the Midship bend, which set from M to Q and from *B* [L] to R [and] draw the arcs M, N and *B* S [L, S]. Next take the radius of the 3rd sweep M, O of the midship bend, and set that from A to T and from D to *R* [V] and draw the arcs A, X and D, Z. Thirdly, take the radius of the 2nd sweep, P, N of the midship† bend, and setting one foot in W (which centre is framed as afore) with the other draw the arcs N, *X* [N, Z] and S, *Z* [S,X]. Then take the sweep of the top timbers Q, *R*[Q, V] and with it draw the arc from 5, through the prick at 4, up to the parallel 3,2. Lastly, set off from E the middle of the bend the half breadth of the keel each way to 6 and 7, and with the arc of the lower sweep draw the circles *b*, N [6, N] and 7,5 [7, S] for the hollowing of the timbers up to the sweep above the rising. So have you as you desired, and thus must all the rest of the bends be also drawn. But because this would be very tedious to draw every bend severally we may by a speedier way, making the midship bend into three several parts or moulds and setting upon them the several risings &c. of every bend, mould all the rest by them.

Floor Timber Mould

The first is called the floor timber mould, which containeth all the flat of the floor and all the arc of the wrong head, and parts of the arc of the futtock 2 or 3 foot above the sine mark made at the wrong head for scarf.

Futtock Timber Mould

The second is the futtock timber mould, which containeth all the arc of the futtock and the arc of the breadth and part of the arc of the wrong head, and hath 2 sine marks to bring this and the floor mould right together; the one at the wrong head and the other at the intersection of the 2nd and 3rd sweeps. And if it be too long to manage [it] must be cut asunder in the middle and have another sine mark there.

Top Timber Mould

The third is the top timber mould, which containeth all the length of the longest post and all the arc of the breadth, and some part of the futtock mould also: and

† MS. 'middle bend.'

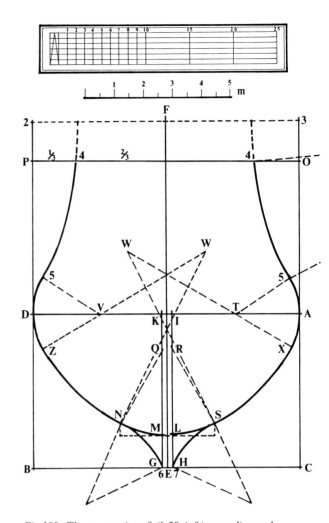

Fig 100: The construction of rib 20 (aft), according to the instructions in the Treatise on Shipbuilding *(c.1620). This drawing shows how the curves (1-4) derived for the midship frame are used to create a new rib. The rising-lines are used to determine the distribution of space and the general direction of the curves. The lower rising-line is in the region of ML, and gives the height of the floor. The breadth line goes through points D and A at the broadest point. The toptimber line lies at the height of line PO, and goes through point 4.*

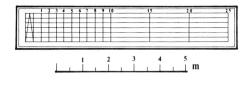

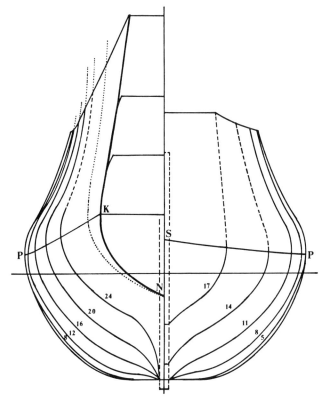

Fig 101: Rib plan from the instructions in the Treatise on Shipbuilding *(c.1620). The midship frame is identical to rib 4, aft. As the curve of the toptimbers gradually becomes straight towards the bow and the stern, the parts of those ribs which no longer comply with rib 4 are shown as broken lines. The stern and the dotted guiding rib, shown there, are derived from the course of the waterlines and the rising-line plan. The upper end of the ribs is defined by the toptimbers. In the middle part the breadth line marks the point of maximum breadth (P–K) and (P–S). The lower rising-line and the floor are not shown, as its side edge does not lie on the outer edge of the rib. The thickness of the keel is based on supposition. according to Witsen (1671), the thickness of the keel should be 1/25 of the maximum breadth.*

hath two sine marks to bring this and the futtock mould right together; the one at the intersection of the 2nd and 4th sweeps and the other at double the depth of the midship bend to guide the top timbers by.

To graduate the Floor Mould

The floor mould hath three perpendiculars; the one for the middle line of the depth the other two for the extremes of the flats. From the outward flat draw a straight line upon which you may put the risings aftwards on. From the middle line draw two other straight lines and upon them set the narrowing both aloft and alow as they are calculated in the table. Let the perpendiculars be drawn on the other side also; from the outward perpendicular set the risings forward on, from the middle line [set] the narrowings forward both aloft and alow as you did aftward on.

To graduate the Wrong Head

Upon the arc of the wrong head draw a straight line for the substance thereof, upon which set out the haleing down of the lower part of the futtock upon the wrong head.

To graduate the Futtock

Upon the lower part of the futtock, from the middle section to the sine mark at the wrong head, draw a straight line whereupon set the haleing down of the futtock. Upon another straight line draw[n] from thence to the upper sine mark, set ou[t] the putting up of the futtock.

Graduating the Top Timbers

Upon the top timber mould draw two straight lines from the lower sine mark upwards and downwards. Set the haleing down thereof from the sine mark upwards, and the putting [up] from the sine mark downwards; and so have you done graduating the moulds.

The use of these graduations is by applying all the parts together to mark out upon the timber the frame and shape of any bend you desire, agreeable to the several lines upon the plot; as by this example may appear.

[Moulding the 20th Bend aft]

Suppose I would mould out of the 20th bend of timber aft:

1st. I strike a ground line upon the foot of the timber and cross it at right angles with a middle line for the depth.

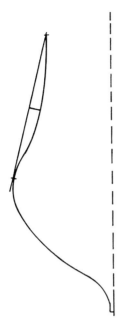

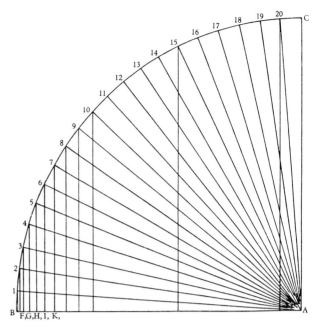

Fig 102: Diagram of a rule of thumb, showing the steps to use in determining the gradations of the toptimbers, according to the text. The ribs amidships curve completely inwards; the curve becomes flatter towards the bow and the stern, eventually becoming a straight line. This rule is not totally satisfactory, as the height of the ribs increases towards the ends of the ship, and the straight line becomes longer and steeper.

*Fig 103: Another method of gradually reducing the curve of the toptimbers, as described in the text, but it does not give any fair lines for the portion of ribs aft of the midship frame. In practice, shipbuilders almost certainly solved this problem by another method. (*Drawing by Salisbury*)*

2nd. I set off the rising of that bend from the ground line, at the length it is marked upon the floor mould.

3rd. I seek the depth of the bend, which set off the rising line I draw a parallel to the ground line for the breadth.

4th. I take the narrowing aloft out of the greatest breadth and at that breadth draw a parallel to the middle line.

5th. I set the narrowing alow upon the middle line of the timber, and score out by the mould both within and without the frame of the mould.

6th. I bring down the sine mark of the lower part of the futtock to the haleing down thereof upon the wrong head, and score out that part of the futtock.

7th. I bring down the lower end of the upper futtock to the haleing down marked upon the lower part, and score out the upper part of the futtock.

8th. I put up the top timber upon the head of the futtock according to the mark of putting up, that it may fit his breadth at the upper surmark, and score out by it

the top timber mould. And so is the whole bend truly moulded with all his parts.

And this being done on the one side, the moulds must be turned over and the same drawn on the other side of the timber for the other half of the bend. The like must be done for every bend of timber that you will mould.

The timbers being marked out by the moulds, they must be hewed into proportion by those lines; not in a perfect square, but according to the bevel of the bend.

Bevelling, what [it is]

The bevelling of the bend is nothing else but the winding about of the timber, or hewing away that which is superfluous to bring every part thereof to agree with the rising and narrowing lines of the plot. For seeing [that] the whole bulk of the ship doth grow less and less from the midship timber both fore and aft, and also rise by degrees as it lessens, each timber hath his proper bevel or winding to bring all together to agree with the lines drawn upon the plot.

How to find it

From these lines it is therefore most proper to draw the bevel of the timber, which seeing they are all given in numbers may be easily found after this manner.

The bevel for the rising is but the height of the timber abaft more than it is afore. Suppose I would know what it is for the 24 bend aft: the rising of the 24 bend is 6 foot 3.35 [inches] and of the 25 bend is 7 foot 1.45 inches; the difference [is] 0 foot 10.70 inches* for [the] distance of the two bends which are 30 inches asunder, and therefore the half thereof 5.35 inches is the bevel for the rising of the 24 timber. That is, it must be higher in the after part than in the forepart 5 inches and 35 centems of an inch.

The Bevel of the Wrong Head

I[n] like manner the bevel of the narrowing alow is guided by the lower narrowing line. The narrowing alow of the 24 timber is 5 foot 9.48 inches [and of the 25 bend 6 foot 4.8 inches], the difference 7.32 inches at the distance of 2½ foot. Therefore the half thereof 3.66 inches is the bevel at the wrong head, where the after part [of] the 24 timber must wind inwards from the square of the fore side† 3.66 inches, and the fore part of the inside as much.

I[n] like manner the bevel of the narrowing aloft is guided by the upper narrowing line. The narrowing aloft of the 24 timber is 4 foot 10.36 inches, and of the 25 [timber] 5 foot 6 inches; the difference 7.64 inches at the distance of 2 foot 6 inches. Therefore the half thereof, 3.82 inches, is the bevel at the breadth, where the after part of the timber must wind inwards from the square of the foreside 3.82 inches, and the fore part of the inside as much.

The Bevel at the Top Timbers

After the same manner is the bevel of the top timbers found; for seeing the ⅓ of the half breadth set off upon every bend maketh a perfect narrowing line, the top timber must bevel according to that line and may thus be found. The ⅓ of the half breadth set off upon every bend maketh a perfect narrowing line, the top timber must bevel according to that line and may thus be found. The ⅓ of the half breadth of the 24 bend is 52.55 inches. ⅓ of the half breadth of the 25 bend is 50 inches, the difference 2.55 inches; the half is 1.27 [inches] for the bevel of the top timbers in the 24 bend, and thus is the bevelling found in the rest of the bends.

The Hollowing of the Post

There remains how to bring the hollowing of the top timbers to a straight line both forward and aftward on. If you like to use a straight post that labour is saved, but because the hollowing post is both most comely to the eye [and] most easy to the ship that fashion is rather to be followed though it be more troublesome in working.

If the same hollowing be continued fore and aft that is in the midships, the quarter and forecastle will be straitened too much with the tumbling of the post. It will be therefore convenient by degrees to work out the hollowing of the post that at last it might come to a straight line, which may be done after this manner. Continue the top timber of the midship bend to the extreme heights both afore and abaft; from the head of the timbers in those places draw straight lines to touch the upper sweep; upon the middle of each line draw perpendiculars home to the hollowing, the length of which perpendicular measured upon the scale shall give the greatest hollowing both forward and aftward on. Some use to divide these perpendiculars into so many equal parts as there are bends from the midships both ways, and to abate upon every bend one of those parts which will do very well.

But the best and most artificial way of abatement is by sinical parts of the versed line; wherefore let each perpendicular be made the radius of a circle and let a quadrant thereof be divided into as many equal parts of degrees and minutes as there are bends from the midships to the bend that shall have the first straight post. The sine of the complement proper to each degree deducted out of the radius leaveth the versed sines which are the lengths of the lines to be abated upon every bend.

As for example: [Fig 103]

Let A, B the radius be 20 inches, equal to the greatest hollowing aft, which I would bring to a straight line at the 21 bend. Divide the quadrant C, B 90 degrees by 21; so you have 4.285 degrees for each part, which doubled, tripled, quadrupled, &c., gives the degrees and parts

* The error in the difference cannot be explained, and must have occurred in the original.
† MS. 'fore saile.'

proper to each bend. Take the complement of each degree (as 99729 for 4.285 5degrees; and 98883 for 8.57 degrees; and 73313 for 42.855 degrees, the number of the 10 bend) out of the radius; so have you 00279 and 1117 and 26687, the versed sines of those bends. So as if you will use the sector and make the perpendicular A, B the radius, these versed sines taken off the same sector shall give the parts B, D, B, E, and B, F, & C., to be abated out of the greatest hollowing till you come to the 21st bend, which will be a straight line as is A, C.

If you will have the same given in inches and parts that you may work by the scale, multiply each versed sine by 20, because of the 20 included bends, and cut off five figures from the right hand. So have you .05580 for the first bend, and .22340 for the second, and 5.33748 for the tenth bend, and 18.50 inches for the 20th bend. Which parts being decreased upon the perpendiculars proper to each bend will bring the hollowing of the 21st bend to a straight line as was desired, and as you may see in the table hereafter calculated for that purpose.*

* See Notes.

Notes on the Reconstruction of the Diagrams

[The diagrams which fall within the treatise in this edition are after Salisbury's and the references to them here have been amended from the original. The folio numbers relating to the volume in the Admiralty Library have been removed and so Salisbury's notes now refer to the relevant pages of this edition.]

As might be expected in a document of this date, the instructions given are not entirely free from ambiguity. That they can be followed at all easily is a first-class testimonial to the clarity of the unknown author. The following notes refer only to difficulties encountered in redrawing the draught and to points in the reconstruction which are dependent upon an interpretation of doubtful passages.

Tonnage. Page 175

In order to arrive at a burthen of 550 tons it is necessary to assume that the depth used is that from the breadth line, and not the depth in hold as stated on page 000. The ship taken as the example would then measure 558 tons burthen and 744 tons and tonnage, a very respectable size for her time.

Dead Rising. Page 182

It does not appear that any dead rising line was actually drawn in the sheer plan, or allowed for in the body plan. All heights are given from a common base or ground line, which is only defined in the case of the gripe, whose height is given from the edge of the keel. It is clear that some words in the original were omitted by the copyist, and I have read the reference as indicating merely what *might* be done.

Sweep of the Stem. Page 182

Read literally, the inner sweep of the stem would not be a tangent to the keel at the touch, and the stem would narrow rapidly to this point. The author was not too happy when sweeping both sides of a tapering timber, as in the instructions for the body plan, and I think the passage should read either 'shorten the sweep by the *greater*' or '*lower* the *centre* by the difference' of these two depths. The inner sweep would then pass exactly through the point O of the gripe. This looks correct in this case, although in other contemporary draughts the gripe often fell on the fore side of the rabbet of them.

Wales. Page 185

The errors indicated in the figures for the height of the lower wale and the radius of its sweep are self evident and there can be no doubt of the correct lengths. Unfortunately there are no means of checking the figures for the upper wales. As their

widths are not given I have assumed that each would be a little narrower than the one below, the sidings of the second to the fifth wales being 10, 9, 7, and 5 inches respectively. Whatever widths are used, however, there can be no doubt that the distances between the wales are wrong, and would result in a very 'disgraceful' appearance. In the first place, the fifth wale would be cut to pieces by the upper deck ports. Secondly, the third wale would be cut by the ports in the fore peak if there was a rise in the deck as strongly recommended by the author in the text.

Of the four distances given, there is little difficulty in selecting two which are suspicious. The height of the second wale must be correct, as it is confined within narrow limits by the ports of the lower deck and gunroom. There is also no reason to question the distance between the third and fourth wales.

In the case of the third wale, however, there are other grounds in addition to that already mentioned for thinking the distance too little. It happens that the distance from the second wale is expressed in the manuscript as *3 ft.*, an abbreviation usually used when followed by a number of inches. I think it highly probable that these inches have been missed out. Probably '10 inches' was read by the copyist as '0 inches' and omitted as being unnecesary.

Similarly, the distance of 2 feet 4 inches from the fourth to the fifth wales is very unlikely. If these wales are not to be cut the upper deck ports must be placed between them, and even if these ports were a little smaller than those of the lower deck there must be some allowance if they were to follow the sheer of the deck without cutting the wale. The most likely clerical error would be to copy 11 as 4, or 3 as 2, and I think the distance should be 2 feet 11 inches.

This difficulty over the wales has been treated at some length because of their importance as structural members at this date. Their heights in the sheer plan have been drawn both as instructed and also as suggested.

Ports. Page 192

The position of the ports in a fore and aft line may not of course be strictly accurate, but the number shown is probably correct. Although the manuscript states that all the ports were of the same size, 2½ feet square, this is not borne out by pictorial evidence and I think it would be permissible to make the upper ports a little smaller and nearer to the deck than those on the orlop. Alternative heights have been indicated for the ports in the fore peak, as it is not altogether certain that there was a rise in the deck there.

Gunroom. Page 185

Neither of the proportions given works out satisfactorily. The first probably means that the length on the fall was ³⁄₁₀ of the after part of the keel, or 20 feet. The second, that the fall was ⁹⁄₁₉ of the whole keel abaft the midship, actually about 27½ feet from the after perpendicular. Section 20 is approximately midway between these two points.

Half Deck and Quarter Deck. Page 192

The length of the quarter deck is open to doubt. We are first told (page 173) that the half deck is over the dining room, and the quarter deck abaft that over the steerage is left unnamed, but we have to bear in mind that in the steerage is 'a pair of stairs for men to pass into the half deck'.

The confusion between the two names, so often mentioned in *The Mariner's Mirror*, could scarcely be better exemplified. I have however followed the instructions and placed the break of the quarter deck over the aftermost bulkhead, which is in turn placed far enough abaft the fore end of the gun room to allow the whipstaff to pass upwards into the steerage. It is nevertheless quite possible that the quarter deck should extend forward over the steerage.

Head. Page 192

As mentioned in the footnote, the steeve of the head should be 12–13º. This certainly refers to the upper side of the main knee, whose height on the stem is not stated. The position suggested cannot however be far wrong, as any material change from that shown would entail difficulties in placing the hawseholes.

Similarly, no definite height is given for the hance piece, neither are we told if the deck in the beak head is level with the upper deck. All these points are closely related to the height of the decks forward, and the existence or otherwise of a rise. The outline of the head shown in the sheer plan must therefore be regarded as purely conjectural in so far as heights are concerned.

Lower Narrowing Line. Page 192

A puzzling feature of many early draughts is that the half breadth of the floor in the floor plan exceeds that in the body plan. The present treatise provides an explanation for this apparent anomaly. By drawing a curve whose narrowing exceeds the half breadth of the floor in the midships, the centres of the floor-sweep fore and aft cross the middle line, and the sweep then serves only to guide the foot of the futtock-sweep.

This is an ingenious remedy for an inherent defect in 'whole moulding' from the sweeps of the midship bend, and unless the floor is kept narrow, its sweep short, and its rising lifted

sharply at the ends, the lower sweep will prevent the design of a fine run.

It should be noted that the tuck is stated to be the intersection of the lower rising line with the stern post, and that the fashion pieces are framed by the upper futtock sweeps only. This agrees with the present interpretation, as the heels of the fashion pieces are actually let on to the stern post a little above the tuck itself.

Upper Narrowing Line, Forward. Page 194

The description of this line provides another indication that the author may not have been familiar with the practical application of a 'dead' rising or narrowing line. It will be seen that if the dead narrowing line runs off to nothing at the midships, and the narrowing as taken from the tables is marked on each frame, the ship will be actually wider at the first seven frames forward than it is in midships. In practice, the side between these points would probably be kept to a straight line, and I have assumed this to be the case when drawing the complete body plan (Fig 101).

This desire to round out the bow, reflected in the instructions to keep the breadth line low in the quarters and luff, arose from the need to provide adequate displacement to support the heavier armaments then coming into fashion. That it was a time of change from older methods can be seen from the breadth line itself. Although it is only 2 feet higher on the stem than in midships, the stem itself raking forward above this point, the author still runs his half breadth line in the floor plan to the head of the stem, instead of the true point some 1½ feet further aft.

Toptimber Line. Page 194

The rising and narrowing of this line are treated very causally by the author. This is a pity, for in neither case is the question quite as simple as he states.

The rising of the toptimber line is on several occasions stated to be double the depth. The difficulty is that in the specific example given on f. 94v this depth is taken from the main breadth to the lower rising line, and not to the keel. Now this is most unlikely, since on every timber the lower rising is more than double the upper rising, with the result that a top timber line so drawn would be lower fore and aft than in midships. It would also have the effect of increasing the angle of tumblehome towards the ends of the ship. The rule for narrowing the toptimber line is also over-simplified, and ignores the necessity for reducing the amount of tumblehome towards the bow and stern.

It would appear from the remarks in the manuscript that it is most unlikely that a toptimber line was drawn in either the sheer or floor plans of the original draught. As, however, this line is essential for the reconstruction of the frames, I have drawn the narrowing line according to the instructions, while the broken lines in the sheer and floor plans show the line suggested for the reconstruction in Fig. 101. For the same reason the heights of the drifts have been indicated, although the only clue is the amount of hollow in the topside at timber 21, and it must be emphasized that these heights are purely guess-work.

Hollowing of the Post, or Toptimbers. Page 200

As in the case of the dead narrowing line, there is a strong suspicion that the author had never seen his method proved in practice. The calculations for reducing the hollow to a straight line are not good, for two reasons. First, the amount of straightening between adjacent timbers should not exceed the amount by which the ship narrows in the same distance, and the straightening should therefore not commence until about the fourth timber aft and eighth forward. Secondly, the amount by which the hollow is reduced between adjacent timbers should be least at the commencement and finishing, and greatest mid-way between. The method described would leave a very noticeable bump on the first straight timber, and is in fact inferior to the rule of thumb method also mentioned.

The greatest difficulty arises from the rules by which the toptimbers are drawn. If these are straight from stem to stern there is no trouble, as all are drawn through the toptimber line and the topside is automatically faired. When, however, a hollow is used, straightening out towards the ends of the vessel, we are told that the straight toptimbers are drawn to the head of the post, as in Fig 100. Now this does not allow for the abrupt increases in height at the drifts, which would cause the angle of tumblehome to become suddenly more upright. I can suggest no obvious interpretation of the instructions, and therefore in Fig 101 I have drawn the toptimbers of only those frames of which I am fairly confident. We can at least be sure that the toptimber became straight at the 21st timber aft, and also that it straightened out forward. This would rule out any pronounced flare under the cathead, at timber 17.

It will also be noticed that in Fig 101 the forward frames do not produce a fair body underwater. These have been drawn according to the instructions, but it is obvious that the breadth sweep should be reduced in some way. How this was done, I cannot say. Like ourselves, our forbears were very impressed by a formula having the appearance of scientific accuracy, and were probably slightly ashamed of mentioning any point which could not be 'brought to rule'.

A Treatise on Shipbuilding, edited by W Salisbury, was first published by The Society for Nautical Research in 1958, and appeared in No. 6 of their Occasional Publications series.

Notes

Notes on Chapters 1–8
Unless otherwise stated, all translations of quotations, drawings and photographs are by the author. Full bibliographical details of the works referred to can be found in the Bibliography.

Introduction
1. Kemna, *Der Begriff 'Schiff' im Französischen. Eine Lexigraphische Untersuchung*, Diss. Marburg 1901, p123
2. Baldinger, *Dictionnaire Étymologique de l'Ancien Français*, Tübingen, 1974, and von Wartburg, *Französisches etymologisches Wörterbuch*, vol 4, Basel 1952, p27

Chapter 1 *The development of the galleon*
1. Cipolla, *Guns, Sails and Empires*, p82
2. Ibid, p83
3. Usher, *Spanish Ships and Shipping in the Sixteenth and Seventeenth Centuries*, p190
4. Lane, *Venetian Naval Architecture about 1550*, pp24–29, and Lane, *Venetian Ships and Shipbuilders of the Renaissance*, p51.
5. Corbett, *Drake and the Tudor Navy*, vol 1, p29
6. Andrews, *The Spanish Caribbean*, p88
7. Ibid, p68
8. Cipolla, *Guns, Sails and Empires*, p85
9. Oppenheim (ed), *The Naval Tracts of Sir William Monson*, vol 2, p318
10. Corbett, *Drake and the Tudor Navy*, vol 2, p339
11. Pimental-Barata, *The Portuguese Galleon*
12. From a review of Diarios da Navegacão de Carreira da India nos anos de 1595–1597. 1600 e 1603', ed Quirino da Fonseca, Lisbon, 1938, in: *Mariners Mirror*, vol 26, 1940, p318
13. Pimental-Barata, *The Portuguese Galleon*
14. *The Travels of Peter Mundy*, vol 3, Part 1, pp59–60
15. Mandelslo, *Journal and Observation*, p90
16. From: Vincenzo Maria di Santa Caterina, 'Le viaggio all India Orientale, Venice 1678', p458, in: Cipolla, *Guns, Sails and Empires*, p88
17. Boxer, *Admiral João Pereira Corte-Real . . .*, and: *The Tragic History of the Sea 1589–1622*, p2ff
18. Unger, *The Ship in the Medieval Economy*, p260
19. Corbett, *Drake and the Tudor Navy*, p4
20. Russel, *Visions of the Sea*, p43
21. Howard, *Sailing Ships of War 1400–1680*, pp78–9
22. Trevelyan, *Illustrated History of England*, p296
23. Oppenheim, *A History of the Administration of the Royal Navy*, p52
24. Rubin de Cervin, *Bateaux et Batellerie de Venise*, p51
25. Corbett, *Drake and the Tudor Navy*, vol 1, pp27–8
26. Ibid, p37
27. Oppenheim (ed), *The Naval Tracts of Sir William Monson*, vol I, p3
28. Trevelyan, *Illustrated History of England*, p341
29. Oppenheim, *A History of the Administration of the Royal Navy*, p119
30. Hawkins, 'Die dritte beschwerliche Reise, unternommen in den Jahren 1567 und 1568 mit der Jesus von Lübeck, der Minion und vier anderen Schiffen nach Guinea und Westindien', from: Hampton, *Sir Francis Drake*, p190
31. Oppenheim, *A History of the Administration of the Royal Navy*, p124
32. Ibid, p125
33. Ibid, p126
34. Corbett (ed), *Papers Relating to the Navy during the Spanish War 1585–1587*, pp263–4
35. Oppenheim, *A History of the Administration of the Royal Navy*, p132
36. Martin, *Spanish Armada Tonnages*
37. Oppenheim (ed), *The Naval Tracts of Sir William Monson*, vol I, General Introduction
38. Ibid, vol 2, p235
39. Corbett, *The Successors of Drake*, p417
40. Oppenheim (ed), *The Naval Tracts of Sir William Monson*, vol 2, pp91–2
41. Ibid, pp94–5
42. Ibid, vol 2, p243
43. Corbett, *Drake and the Tudor Navy*, vol 1, p357
44. Oppenheim, *A History of the Administration of the Royal Navy*, p205
45. Ibid, p257
46. Unger, *Dutch Shipbuilding before 1800*, p25
47. Crone, *Onze Schepen in de Gouden Eeuw*, p27
48. van Beylen, in: *Maritieme Geschiedenis der Nederlanden*, vol 2, p61
49. Hagedorn, *Die Entwicklung der wichtigsten Schiffstypen bis ins 19 Jh*, p77
50. Howard, *Sailing Ships of War 1400-1800*, p89

51 Usher, *Spanish Ships and Shipping in the Sixteenth and Seventeenth Centuries*, p190
52 Unger, *Dutch Shipbuilding before 1800*, p112
53 Corbett (ed), *Papers Relating to the Navy during the Spanish War 1585–1587*, Appendix B, p337
54 Scammell, *The World Encompassed*, p328, and Boxer, *The Portuguese Seaborne Empire, 1415–1825*, p210

Chapter 2 *Rigging*
 1 Baker, *The New Mayflower*, p38
 2 Anderson, *The Rigging of Ships*, and *Seventeenth Century Rigging*
 3 Lees, *The Masting and Rigging . . .*
 4 Howard, *Sailing Ships of War 1400–1860*
 5 Hoeckel, *Modellbau von Schiffen*
 6 Mondfeld, *Wasa*
 7 Clowes, *Sailing Ships*, pp60–61
 8 Sandahl, *Middle English Sea Terms*, pp18–19
 9 Clowes, *Sailing Ships*, p71
10 Ibid, p70
11 From: Jane, *The British Battle Fleet*, p40
12 Moore, *Rigging in the Seventeenth Century*
13 Oppenheim, *A History of the Administration of the Royal Navy*, p124
14 Moore, *Rigging in the Seventeenth Century*
15 Pepper, *Harriots Manuscript*
16 Anonymous, *A Treatise on Shipbuilding*, p47
17 Manwaring, *The Life and Works of Sir Henry Mainwaring*, vol 2, p157
18 Ibid, p188
19 Ibid, p235
20 Ibid, p249
21 Ibid, p106
22 Ibid, p186
23 Ibid, p186
24 Howard, *Sailing Ships of War*, p125
25 Howard, *Sailing Ships of War*, p63
26 Albion, *Forests and Sea Power*, pvii
27 Howard, *Sailing Ships of War*, p130
28 Smith, *A Sea Grammar*, p20
29 Manwaring, *The Life and Works of Sir Henry Mainwaring*, vol 2, p226
30 Moore, *Rigging in the Seventeenth Century*
31 Anonymous, *A Treatise on Shipbuilding*, p52
32 Baker, *The New Mayflower*
33 Villiers, *Ein Königreich für ein Schiff*

Chapter 3 *Ordnance*
 1 Corbett (ed), *Papers Relating to the Navy during the Spanish War*, Appendix A, p335
 2 Oppenheim (ed), *The Naval Tracts of Sir William Monson*, vol 1, p6
 3 Rule, *The Mary Rose*, p13
 4 Cipolla, *Guns, Sails and Empires*, p30
 5 Padfield, *Waffen auf See*, p52

 6 Ehrenberg, *Hamburg und England im Zeitalter der Königin Elisabeth*, p296
 7 Corbett (ed), Papers Relating to the Navy during the Spanish War, pp27–29
 8 Oppenheim, *A History of the Administration of the Royal Navy*, p124
 9 Cipolla, *Guns, Sails and Empires*, p36
10 Corbett (ed), *Papers Relating to the Navy during the Spanish War*, Appendix A, p316
11 Guilmartin, *Gunpowder and Galleys*, p173, and Lewis, *Armada Guns*, p48
12 Lucar (1588), 'Three Books of Colloquies', in Corbett (ed), *Papers Relating to the Navy during the Spanish War*, p320
13 Bourne, 'Art of Shooting', and Norton, 'The Gunner', in Corbett (ed), *Papers Relating to the Navy during the Spanish War*, p320
14 See note 12, p320
15 See note 13, pp318, 321
16 Ibid
17 Ibid
18 Corbett (ed), *Papers Relating to the Navy during the Spanish War*, p318
19 Lewis, *Armada Guns*, p52
20 See note 12
21 Guilmartin, *Gunpowder and Galleys*, p170
22 Corbett (ed), *Papers Relating to the Navy during the Spanish War*, pp331–2
23 Ibid, and Norton, *The Gunner (1628)*, p58
24 See note 12, p333
25 Oppenheim, *A History of the Administration*, pp124, 156
26 Furttenbach, *Architectura Navalis* (1629), p91
27 Corbett, *The Successors of Drake*, p432
28 Oppenheim (ed), *The Naval Tracts of Sir William Monson*, vol 4, p43
29 Guilmartin, *Gunpowder and Galleys*, p291. This claim has recently been questioned by Richard Barker, 'Bronze Cannon Founders: Comments upon Guilmartin, 1974, 1982', in *International Journal of Nautical Archaeology and Underwater Exploration*, 1983, vol. 12,1, pp67–74
30 Corbett (ed), *Papers Relating to the Navy during the Spanish War*, p327
31 Wignall, *The Armada Shot Controversy*, p467
32 Cipolla, *Guns, Sails and Empires*, p65
33 Guilmartin, *Gunpowder and Galleys*, p173
34 Saar, *Reise nach Java*, p153
35 Oppenheim (ed), *The Naval Tracts of Sir William Monson*, vol 4, pp34, 44
36 Guilmartin, *Gunpowder and Galleys*, p60
37 Anderson, *A Sixteenth-Century Ship of Lübeck*, p152
38 Speckle, Daniel, 'Architectura', from Essenwein, p96
39 From Essenwein, p98
40 Ibid
41 From Essenwein, p77
42 Müller, *Deutsche Bronzegeschützrohre*, p184

43 Moody, *Old Naval Gun-Carriages*, p301

Chapter 4 *In Battle*
1 Anderson, *Naval Wars in the Levant*, p73
2 Oppenheim (ed), *The Naval Tracts of Sir William Monson*, vol 4, pp99–100
3 Gray, *Spinola's Galleys in the Narrow Seas*, p71
4 Corbett, *The Successors of Drake*, pp369–3
5 Ibid, p393
6 Gray, *Spinola's Galleys in the Narrow Seas*, p76
7 Oppenheim (ed), *The Naval Tracts of Sir William Monson*, vol 4, p102
8 Ibid, p103
9 Strachan, *Sampson's Fight with the Maltese Galleys*, p282
10 Ibid, p282
11 Ibid, p283
12 Ibid, p287
13 Ibid, p288
14 Laughton (ed), *State Papers Relating to the Defeat of the Spanish Armada*, vol 1, pxlix
15 Contreras, *Das Leben des Capitan Alonso de Contreras*, trans: Arnald Steiger, pp84–86
16 Wignall, *The Armada Shot Controversy*, p487
17 Laughton (ed), *State Papers Relating to the Defeat of the Spanish Armada*, vol 2, p11
18 Cipolla, *Guns, Sails and Empires*, p86
19 Corbett, *Drake and the Tudor Navy*, vol 1, Preface to 2nd edn, 1899
20 Manwaring, *The Life and Works of Sir Henry Mainwaring*, vol 2, p102
21 Oppenheim (ed), *The Naval Tracts of Sir William Monson*, vol 4, p98
22 Corbett (ed), *Fighting Instructions 1530–1816*, p42
23 Oppenheim, *A History of the Administration of the Royal Navy*, p241
24 Corbett, *Drake and the Tudor Navy*, p388
25 Trevelyan, *Illustrated History of England*, vol 1, p344
26 Corbett, *Drake and the Tudor Navy*, p388
27 Ibid, p389
28 Ibid, p390
29 Oppenheim (ed), *The Naval Tracts of Sir William Monson*, vol 4, p90
30 Ibid, p215
31 Ibid, p104
32 Corbett (ed), *Fighting Instructions 1530-1816*, p41
33 Oppenheim (ed), *The Naval Tracts of Sir William Monson*, vol 4, p95
34 Manwaring, *The Life and Works of Sir Henry Mainwaring*, vol 2, p144
35 Boteler, *Boteler's Dialogues*, p301

Chapter 5 *The Men*
1 Scammell, *Manning the English Merchant Service*, p131
2 Andrews, *The Elizabethan Seaman*, p246
3 Oppenheim, *A History of the Administration of the Royal Navy*, pp127–8
4 Scammell, *Manning the English Merchant Service*
5 Corbett (ed), *Papers Relating to the Navy during the Spanish War*, p265
6 Andrews, *The Elizabethan Seaman*
7 Oppenheim, *A History of the Administration of the Royal Navy*, p135
8 Laughton (ed), *State Papers Relating to the Defeat of the Spanish Armada*, vol 2, p96
9 Ibid, vol 1, p53
10 Kemp, *The British Sailor*, p4
11 Ibid, p6
12 Corbett, *Fighting Instructions*, p37
13 Scammell, *Manning the English Merchant Service* p1
14 Oppenheim, *A History of the Administration of the Royal Navy*, p384
15 Ibid, p135, and Kemp, *The British Sailor* p9
16 Smith, *A Sea Grammar*, pp48–9
17 Corbett, *Fighting Instructions*, pp37, 40
18 Slyngisbie, *Relation of the Voyage to Cadiz*, p52
19 Corbett, *Fighting Instructions*, pp40, 44
20 Oppenheim (ed), *The Naval Tracts of Sir William Monson*, vol 2, p436
21 Slyngisbie, *Relation of the Voyage to Cadiz*, p57
22 Corbett, *Fighting Instructions*, p40
23 Boteler, *Boteler's Dialogues*, p18
24 Corbett, *Fighting Instructions*, p40
25 Boteler, *Boteler's Dialogues*, p18
26 Ibid, p19, and James Humphreys (1568), 'Orders to be used in Kings or Queens Majesties Ships', from Kemp, *The British Sailor*, p13
27 Corbett, *Fighting Instructions*, p44
28 Boteler, *Boteler's Dialogues*, p19
29 Corbett (ed), *Papers Relating to the Navy during the Spanish War*, pp259–60
30 Corbett, *Drake and the Tudor Navy*, p386
31 Boteler, *Boteler's Dialogues*, p29
32 Röding, *Allgemeines Wörterbuch der Marine*, p818
33 Boteler, *Boteler's Dialogues*, p29
34 Olechnowitz, *Der Schiffbau der Hansischen Spätzeit*, pp42–43
35 Oppenheim (ed), *The Naval Tracts of Sir William Monson*, vol 4, p31
36 Ibid, pp32-3, and Corbett, *Drake and the Tudor Navy*, vol 1, p387, and Masefield, *On the Spanish Main*, p313
37 Ibid, pp33–5
38 Boteler, *Boteler's Dialogues*, p24
39 Oppenheim (ed), *The Naval Tracts of Sir William Monson*, vol 4, pp45–6
40 Boteler, *Boteler's Dialogues*, p22
41 Röding, *Allgemeines Wörterbuch der Marine*, vol 2, p302
42 Boteler, *Boteler's Dialogues*, p20
43 Scammell, *Manning the English Merchant Service*

44 Oppenheim (ed), *The Naval Tracts of Sir William Monson*, vol 4, p55
45 Boteler, *Boteler's Dialogues*, p13
46 Ibid, p15
47 Oppenheim (ed), *The Naval Tracts of Sir William Monson*, vol 4, p61
48 Ibid, p57
49 Ibid, p57
50 Ibid, p59
51 Ibid, p59, and Boteler, *Boteler's Dialogues*, p15
52 Ibid, p60, and Boteler, *Boteler's Dialogues*, pp11–12
53 Boxer, *The Tragic History of the Sea, 1589–1622*
54 Schurhammer, *Franz Xaver*
55 Pyrard, *The Voyage of François Pyrard*
56 Linschoten, *Itinerarium ofte Schip-vaert naer Oost ofte Portugaels Indien*
57 Pimentel-Barata, *The Portuguese Galleon*
58 Boxer, *The Tragic History of the Sea, 1589–1622*, p11
59 Ibid, 'The Naval and Colonial Papers of Dom António de Ataíde', in Boxer, *From Lisbon to Goa, 1500–1750*
60 Ibid, 'The Sailing Orders for the Portuguese East-Indiamen of 1640 and 1646', in Boxer, *From Lisbon to Goa, 1500–1750*
61 Mundy, *The Travels of Peter Mundy*, vol 4, p35
62 Schurhammer, *Franz Xaver*, p21, and Pyrard, *The Voyage of François Pyrard*, vol 2, part 1, p197
63 Schurhammer, *Franz Xaver*, p17
64 Boxer, 'Moçambique Island and the "Carreira da India"', in Boxer, *From Lisbon to Goa, 1500–1750*
65 Ibid,
66 Valignano, *Historia del principio . . . de la Compania de Jésus*
67 Pyrard, *The Voyages of François Pyrard*, vol 1, p11
68 Ibid, vol 2, part 1, p199
69 Ibid, vol 2, part 1, p185
70 Linschoten, *Itinerarium ofte Schip-vaert naer Oost ofte Portugaels Indien*, p136

Chapter 6 *The Stockholm galleon model*
1 Jaeger, *Das Peller-Modell von 1603*
2 Bobrik, *Handbuch der praktischen Seefahrstkunde*, p115
3 Laughton, *Gunnery, Frigates and the Line of Battle*
4 Clowes, *Sailing Ships, Their History and Development*, p71
5 Landstöm, *Das Schiff*, p358
6 Baker, *Fragments of Ancient English Shipwrightry*
7 Soop, *Kriegsschiff Wasa: Skulpturen*, and Callender, *The Portrait of Peter Pett and the Sovereign of the Seas*
8 Göttlicher, *Materialen für ein Korpus der Schiffsmodelle im Altertum*
9 Interpretation of the symbols and mythical creatures comes from Lipfert, *Symbolfibel; Mode, Fabeltiere und Dämonen*, and Molsdorf, *Christliche Symbolik der mittelalterlichen Kunst*

Chapter 7 *Early depictions of ship construction*
1 Lane, *Venetian Naval Architecture about 1550*, and Anderson, *Italian Naval Architecture about 1445*
2 Lane, *Venetian Ships and Shipbuilders of the Renaissance*, p63
3 Lane, *Venetian Naval Architecture about 1550*
4 Anderson, *Italian Naval Architecture about 1445*
5 Furttenbach, *Architectura Navalis*, p33
6 Witsen, *Aaloude en Hedendaagsche Scheeps-Bouw en Bestier*, p88ff
7 Timmermann, *Die Suche nach der günstigsten Schiffsform*, p32
8 Bobrik, *Handbuch der praktischen Seefahrstkunde*, p168ff
9 Baker, *The New Mayflower*, p32
10 Corbett, *The Successors of Drake*, p417
11 Anonymous, *A Treatise on Shipbuilding*
12 Corbett, *The Successors of Drake*, p417
13 Abell, *The Shipwright's Trade*, p30
14 Lavery, *Deane's Doctrine of Naval Architecture*, p26
15 Oppenheim, *A History of the Administration of the Royal Navy*, p127
16 Ibid, p129
17 Pett, *The Autobiography of Phineas Pett*, Introduction, pp75–6
18 Ibid, p58ff
19 Pepper, *Harriot's Manuscript on Shipbuilding and Rigging* (c.1608–10)
20 Chapelle, *The Search for Speed under Sail*, p16
21 From Oppenheim, *A History of the Administration of the Royal Navy*, p186
22 Kirsch, *Traditionelle Schiffbautechniken in der Ägäis*

Chapter 8 *The Reconstruction*
1 Furttenbach, *Architectura Navalis*, facing p88
2 Jaeger, *Das Peller-Modell von 1603*
3 Laughton, *State Papers Relating to the Defeat of the Spanish Armada*, vol. 2, p250
4 Manwaring (ed), *The Life and Works of Sir Henry Mainwaring*, vol 2, p131
5 Ibid, p255
6 Laughton, *State Papers Relating to the Defeat of the Spanish Armada*, vol 2, p250
7 Manwaring (ed), *The Life and Works of Sir Henry Mainwaring*, vol 2, p94
8 Oppenheim (ed), *Naval Tracts of Sir William Monson*, vol 4, p54
9 Ibid, p53
11 Corbett (ed), *Papers Relating to the Navy during the Spanish War 1585–1587*, p268
10 Manwaring (ed), *The Life and Works of Sir Henry Mainwaring*, vol 2, p88
12 Tinniswood, *Anchors and Accessories*
13 May, *The Boats of Men of War*, p.2
14 Oppenheim, *A History of the Administration of the Royal Navy*, p339
15 May, *The Boats of Men of War*, p2
16 Boteler, *Boteler's Dialogues*, p195

Bibliography

Abell, Sir Westcott,
  The Shipwright's Trade, Conway Maritime Press, London, 1981
Albion, Robert Greenhalgh,
  Forests and Sea Power: The Timber Problem of the Royal Navy 1652–1862, Harvard University Press, Cambridge 1926
Anderson, R C,
  "Italian Naval Architecture about 1445", *Mariners Mirror,* vol 11, 1925, p135
  – *Naval Wars in the Levant,* The University Press, Liverpool, 1952
  – *The Rigging of Ships in the Days of the Spritsail Topmast 1600–1720,* Conway Maritime Press, London, 1982
  – *Seventeenth Century Rigging: A Handbook for Modelmakers,* Model and Allied Publications Ltd, Hemel Hempstead, 1974
  – et al. "A Sixteenth-Century Ship of Lübeck", *Mariners Mirror,* vol 2, 1912, p152
Andrews, Kenneth R,
  The Spanish Caribbean: Trade and Plunder 1530–1630, Yale University Press, New Haven and London, 1978
  – "The Elizabethan Seaman", *Mariners Mirror,* vol. 68, 1982, p245
Anonymous,
  A Treatise on Shipbuilding, c.1620 and *A Treatise on Rigging,* c.1625, (eds) W Salisbury and R C Anderson, The Society for Nautical Research, Occasional Publications, no 6, London, 1958
Baker, Matthew,
  Fragments of Ancient English Shipwrightry, (MS), Cambridge, England, Magdalene College Library, Magdalene College, Pepys 2820
Baker, William A,
  The New Mayflower: Her design and Construction, Barre Gazette, Barre, Massachussetts 1958
Beylen, J van,
  "Scheepstypen", in *Maritime Geschiedenis der Nederlanden,* vol 2, De Boer Maritiem, Bussum 1977
Bobrik, Eduard,
  Handbuch der praktischen Seefahrtskunde, 1848; (repr) Horst Hamecher, Kassel, 1978
Boteler, Nathaniel (Nathaniel Butler),
  Boteler's Dialogues, (ed W G Perrin) Navy Records Society, vol 65, 1929
Bourne, William,
  Art of Shooting in Great Ordnance, 1587
Boxer, C R,
  "Admiral João Pereira Corte-Real and the construction of Portuguese East Indiamen in the early seventeenth century", *Mariners Mirror,* vol 26, 1940, pp 388–406
  – *The Portuguese Seaborne Empire,* 1415–1825, Hutchinson, London, 1969
  – *The Tragic History of the Sea,* 1589–1622, The Hakluyt Society, Second Series, no CXII, The University Press, Cambridge, 1959
  – *From Lisbon to Goa, 1500–1750.* Studies in Portuguese Maritime Enterprise, Variorum Reprints, London 1984 (contains ten essays by Boxer published elsewhere)
Brackenbury, Sir Henry,
  Ancient Cannon in Europe, Part II, Proceedings of the Royal Artillery Institute, V, 1865–6
Callender, Geoffrey,
  The Portrait of Peter Pett and the Sovereign of the Seas, Yelf Brothers Ltd, Newport, Isle of Wight, 1930
Chapelle, Howard I,
  The Search for Speed under Sail, 1700–1855, New York 1967, (repr) Conway Maritime Press, London, 1983
Cipolla, Carlo M,
  Guns, Sails and Empires: Technological Innovation and Early Phases of European Expansion, 1400–1700, Pantheon Books, New York, 1965
Clowes, C S Laird,
  Sailing Ships, Their History and Development, Part 1, His Majesty's Stationery Office, London 1932, (repr) 1951
Contreras, Alonso de,
  Das Leben des Capitán Alonso de Contreras – von ihm selbst erzählt, Manesse Bibliothek der Weltliteratur, Zürich, 1961
Corbett, Julian S,
  Drake and the Tudor Navy, 2 vols, London, 1899
  – *The Successors of Drake,* London 1919
  – (ed) *Papers Relating to the Navy during the Spanish War 1585–1587,* Navy Records Society, vol 11, London, 1898
  – (ed) *Fighting Instructions 1530–1816,* Navy Records Society, vol 29, London, 1905
Crone, G C E,
  Onze Schepen in de Gouden Eeuw, Amsterdam, 1943
Ehrenberg, Richard,
  Hamburg und England im Zeitalter der Königin Elisabeth, Jena, 1896
Essenwein, A,
  Quellen zur Geschichte der Feuerwaffen, F A Brockhaus, Leipzig, 1877, (repr) Akademische Druck und Verlagsanstalt, Graz, 1969
Falconer, William,
  An Universal Dictionary of the Marine, London, 1780, (repr) David and Charles Reprints, Newton Abbot 1970
Furttenbach, Joseph,
  Architectura Navalis, 1629, (repr) Georg Olms Verlag, Hildesheim, New York, 1975

Göttlicher, A,
 Materialien für ein Korpus der Schiffsmodelle im Altertum,
 Verlag Philipp von Zabern, Mainz 1978

Gray, Randal,
 "Spinola's Galleys in the Narrow Seas 1599-1603", *Mariners Mirror*, vol 64, 1978, pp71-83

Guilmartin, John Francis, Jr,
 Gunpowder and Galleys, Changing Technology and Mediterranean Warfare at Sea in the Sixteenth Century, Cambridge University Press, London, 1974

Hagedorn, Bernhard,
 Die Entwicklung der wichtigsten Schiffstypen bis ins 19. Jahrhundert, Verlag von Karl Curtius, Berlin 1914

Hampden, John (ed),
 'Sir Francis Drake', *Piratum Dienst der Queen*, Droemar Knaur, Munich & Berlin, 1981

Hoeckel, Rolf,
 Modellbau von Schiffen des 16 und 17 Jahrhunderts, (ed) Lothar Eich, Verlag Delius Klasing, Bielefeld and Berlin 1966

Howard, Frank,
 Sailing Ships of War 1400–1860, Conway Maritime Press, London 1979, (German ed) *Segel-Kriegsschiffe 1400–1860*, Bernard & Graefe Verlag, Koblenz 1983

Jaeger, Werner,
 Das Peller-Modell von 1603, Verlag Delius Klasing, Bielefeld and Berlin, 1973

Jane, Fred T,
 The British Battle Fleet, S W Partridge, London, 1912

Kemp, Peter,
 The British Sailor: A Social History of the Lower Deck, J M Dent & Sons, London, 1970

Kirsch, Peter,
 Traditionelle Schiffbautechniken in der Ägäis, Das Logbuch 1, 1985, p29

Landström, Björn,
 Das Schiff, C Bertelsmann, Bielefeld

Lane, Frederic Chapin,
 Venetian Ships and Shipbuilders of the Renaissance, The John Hopkins Press, Baltimore, 1934
 – "Venetian Naval Architecture about 1550", *Mariners Mirror*, vol 20, 1934, p24
 – "Tonnages, Medieval and Modern", in *Venice and History*, The John Hopkins Press, Baltimore, 1966

Laughton, John Knox (ed),
 State Papers relating to the Defeat of the Spanish Armada, Navy Records Society, 1895, Reprint 1981 (2 vols)

Laughton, L G Carr,
 "Gunnery, Frigates and the Line of Battle", *Mariners Mirror*, vol 14, 1928, pp341-63

Lavery, Brian (ed),
 Deane's Doctrine of Naval Architecture, 1670, Conway Maritime Press, London, 1981

Lees, James,
 The Masting and Rigging of English Ships of War 1625–1860, Conway Maritime Press, London, 1979

Lewis, Michael,
 "Armada Guns: A Comparative Study of English and Spanish Armaments", *Mariners Mirror*, vol 28, 1942, pp41–72, 104–107

Linschoten, Jan Huyghen van,
 Itinerarium ofte Schip-vaert naer Oost ofte Portugaels Indien, Amsterdam, 1623

Lipfert, Klementine,
 Symbol-Fibel: Eine Hilfe zum Betrachten und Deuten mittelalterlicher Bildwerke, Johannes Stauda-Verlag, Kassel, 1964

Lucar, Cyprian (trans),
 Tartaglia, Niccols: Three Bookes of Colloquies Concerning the Arte of Shooting in Great and Small Peeces of Artillery, London, 1588

von Mandelslo, Johan Albrecht,
 Journal und Observation (1637–40), (ed) Margarete Refslund-Kleman, Copenhagen, 1942

Manwaring, G E (ed),
 The Life and Works of Sir Henry Mainwaring, vol 2, Navy Records Society vol 56, 1922 (contains *The Seaman's Dictionary*, c.1625)

Martin, Colin J M,
 "Spanish Armada Tonnages", *Mariners Mirror*, vol 63, p365

Masefield, John,
 On the Spanish Main, Conway Maritime Press, London, 1972

May, W E,
 The Boats of Men of War, Maritime Monographs and Reports, no 15, National Maritime Museum, Greenwich, London, 1974

Mode, Heinz,
 Fabeltiere und Dämonen, Leipzig, 1977

Molsdorf, Wilhelm,
 Christliche Symbolik der mittelalterlichen Kunst, Akademische Druck- und Verlagsanstalt, Graz, 1968

Mondfeld, Wolfram zu,
 Wasa: Schwedisches Regalschiff von 1628, Mosaik Verlag, Munich, 1981

Moody, J D,
 "Old Naval Gun-Carriages", *Mariners Mirror*, vol 38, 1952, p301

Moore, Alan,
 "Rigging in the Seventeenth Century", *Mariners Mirror*, vol 2, 1912, pp267–74; vol 3, 1913, pp7–13; vol 4, 1914, pp260–5

Mundy, Peter,
 The Travels of Peter Mundy, in Europe and Asia, 1608–1667, (ed) Richard Carnac Temple, vol 3, part 1: Hakluyt Society, Second Series, no XLV, London 1919; vol. IV: Hakluyt Society, Second Series, no LV, London, 1924

Norton, Robert,
 The Gunner, shewing the whole Practise of Artillerie . . . , London, 1628; (repr) Da Capo Press Theatrum Orbis Terrarum Ltd, Amsterdam, New York, 1973

Olechnowitz, Karl Friedrich,
 Der Schiffbau der Hansischen Spätzeit: Eine Untersuchung zur Sozial- und Wirtschaftsgeschichte der Hanse, Weimar, 1960

Oppenheim, M A,
A History of the Administration of the Royal Navy and of Merchant Shipping 1509–1660, London, 1896
— (ed) *The Naval Tracts of Sir William Monson*, vols 1 and 2: Navy Records Society, vol 22, 1902, vol 4: Navy Records Society, vol 45, 1913

Paasch, H,
Vom Kiel zum Flaggenknopf, 1091; (repr) Hamburg/Norderstedt, 1978

Padfield, Peter,
Waffen auf See Delius Klasing, Bielefeld and Berlin

Pemsel, Helmut,
Seeherrschaft. Eine maritime Weltgeschichte von den Anfängen der Seefahrt bis zur Gegenwart, 2 vols, Bernard & Graefe Verlag, Koblenz, 1985

Pepper, Jon V,
"Harriot's Manuscript on Shipbuilding and Rigging, c.1608–1610", in *Five Hundred Years of Nautical Science 1400-1900*, Proceedings of the Third International Reunion for the History of Nautical Science and Hydrography, 1979, National Maritime Museum, Greenwich, London, 1981, pp204–16

Pett, Phineas,
The Autobiography of Phineas Pett, (ed) W G Perrin, Navy Records Society, vol 51, 1918

Pimentel-Barata, Joao da Gama,
"The Portuguese Galleon 1595–1625", in *Five Hundred Years . . .* (see Pepper), pp181–191

Pyrard, François,
The Voyage of François Pyrard of Laval to the East Indies, the Maldives, the Moluccas and Brazil, (ed) Albert Gray, 2 vols, Burt Franklin Publisher, New York (repr) 1964, Hakluyt Society, First Series, no 76, London, 1887

Röding, J H,
Allgemeines Wörterbuch der Marine, 1794 (repr) 1969

Rubin de Cervin, G B,
Bateaux et Batellerie de Venise, Edita Lausanne-Vilo, Paris, 1978

Rule, Margaret,
The Mary Rose, Conway Maritime Press, London, 1982

Russel, M,
Visions of the Sea. Hendrik C Vroom and the Origin of Dutch Marine Painting, published for the Sir Thomas Browne Institute by E J Brill, Leiden University Press, 1983

Saar, Johann Jakob,
"Reise nach Java, Banda, Ceylon und Persien 1644–1660", in Naber, L'Honoré S P (ed) *Reisebeschreibungen von Deutschen Beamten und Kriegsleuten im Dienst der Niederländischen West- und Ost-Indischen Kompagnien 1602–1797*, vol 6, Haag, 1930

Sandahl, Bertil,
Middle English Sea Terms: (vol 2) *Masts, Spars and Sails*, Uppsala, 1958

Scammel, G V,
"Manning the English Merchant Service in the Sixteenth Century", *Mariners Mirror*, vol 56, 1970, p131

– *The World Encompassed. The First European Maritime Empires, c.800–1650*, Methuen, London, New York, 1981

Schurhammer S J, Georg,
Franz Xaver, sein Leben und seine Zeit: Asien (1541–1552), vol 2 and *Indien und Indonesien (1541–1547)*, vol 1, part 1, Herder, Freiburg, Basle, Vienna, 1963

Slyngisbie, Sir William,
"Relation of the Voyage to Cadiz, 1596" (ed) Julian S Corbett, in *The Naval Miscellany*, vol 1, (ed) John Knox Laughton, Navy Records Society, vol 20, 1902

Smith, John,
A Sea Grammar: with the plaine exposition of Smiths accidence for young sea-men, enlarged, London, 1627; (repr) (ed) Kermit Goell, London, 1970

Soop, Hans,
Kriegsschiff Wasa: Skulpturen, Stalling Verlag, Oldenburg, 1979

Speckle, Daniel,
Architectura. Von Vestungen. Wie die zu unsern zeiten mögen erbawn werden . . . , Strasburg 1589; (repr) Unterscheidheim, 1971

Steel, David,
The Elements and Practice of Naval Architecture, London 1805; (repr) Sim Comfort Associates, London, 1977

Strachan, Michael,
"Sampson's Fight with Maltese Galleys", 1628, *Mariners Mirror*, vol 55, 1969, pp281–9

Timmermann, Gerhard,
Die Suche nach der günstigsten Schiffsform, Schriften des Deutschen Schiffahrtsmuseums, 11, Oldenburg, 1979

Tinniswood, J T,
"Anchors and Accessories, 1340–1640", *Mariners Mirror*, vol 31, 1945, pp84–105

Trevelyan, George Macauley,
Illustrated History of England, Longmans, London, 1956

Unger, Richard W,
Dutch Shipbuilding Before 1800, Van Gorcum, Assen/Amsterdam, 1978
– *The Ship in the Medieval Economy 600–1600*, Croom Helm, London, 1980

Usher, Abbot Payson,
"Spanish Ships and Shipping in the Sixteenth and Seventeenth Centuries", in *Facts and Figures in Economic History*, Cambridge, Mass, 1932

Valignana SJ, Alessandro,
Historia del Principio y Progresso de la Compania de Jesús en las Indias Orientales, 1542–1564, (ed) Josef Wicki SJ, Rome, 1944

Villiers, Alan,
Ein Königreich für ein Schiff, Hans Dulk, Hamburg, 1960

Wignall, Sydney,
"The Armada Shot Controversy", in *Marine Archaeology*, (ed) D J Blackman, Colston Papers, no 23 London, 1973

Witsen, Nicolaes,
Aaloude en Hedendaagsche Scheeps-Bouw en Bestier, Amsterdam, 1671

Index

Page reference in italic denote illustrations or captions to illustrations.